GRAY GHOSTS OF THE CONFEDERACY

GRAY GHOSTS

OF THE
CONFEDERACY

Guerrilla Warfare in the West, 1861-1865

RICHARD S. BROWNLEE

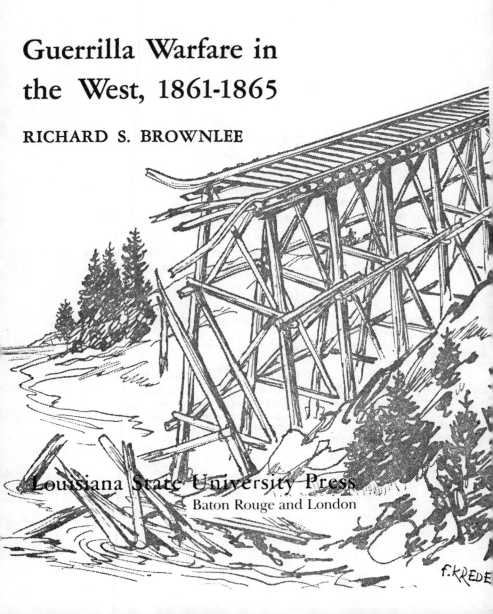

Louisiana State University Press
Baton Rouge and London

F. KREDE

Library of Congress Catalog Card Number 58-14213

Copyright © 1958, 1986 by Richard S. Brownlee

All rights reserved

Manufactured in the United States of America

Louisiana Paperback Edition, 1984

97 96 95 94 93   12 11 10 9 8

Library of Congress Cataloging in Publication Data
Brownlee, Richard S.
   Gray ghosts of the Confederacy.

   Bibliography: p.
   1. United States—History—Civil War, 1861–1865—Underground move-
ments. 2. Guerrillas—West (U.S.)—History—19th century. 3. Missouri—
History—Civil War, 1861–1865—Underground movements. 4. Kansas—
History—Civil War, 1861–1865—Underground movements. I. Title.
E470.45.B76   1984   973.7′09778   83–19634
ISBN 0–8071–0333–0
ISBN 0–8071–1162–7 (pbk.)

TO ALICE

Preface

▋▋

T HIS book is based on historical facts. It is hoped that these facts have been presented in a fashion to interest the general reader of military history. From the rather extensive amount of material available for the period, in addition to the evidence long known to historians, an attempt has been made to utilize sources contemporary to the day which seemed as free as possible from irrational bias concerning the events and conditions of a facet of the Civil War on the western border of the United States. In order to emphasize this new material only a selected bibliography has been included. If certain popular or classic sources have been omitted from the bibliography it is because it was believed other material was more appropriate to the author's intention.

This book attempts to set forth what occurred when the Civil War west of the Mississippi River degenerated into

widespread insurrection and almost complete military ty-
ranny. In dealing with the characters involved the author has
not hesitated to credit each with personal responsibility.
Others, in writing of the time, have chosen to present the
events as inevitable. It is the opinion of the author, after
years of research and study, that the men dealt with here, in
common with men of all other ages, were men of free will.
Because of this there seems to be no reason to withhold from
them the praise or condemnation they deserve as they created
history.

So very many persons have helped in the preparation and
writing of this book it is impossible to express gratitude by
naming them all. Dr. Lewis E. Atherton, Dr. Thomas A.
Brady, Dr. Elmer Ellis, Dr. W. Francis English, and Dr.
Amos J. Snider, of the University of Missouri, have been
friendly task masters. Without their help and encouragement
this work would not have been accomplished. I am especially
indebted to the staffs of the State Historical Society of Missouri and the Missouri Historical Society for cheerful assistance in research. In the reading and preparation of the manuscript I would like to thank Mr. Albert M. Price, Judge Roy
T. Williams, Mr. John Williams, and Dr. Albert Castel who
offered many constructive suggestions. I would also like to
inform my wife here that she was of far greater assistance than
she knows or believes.

RICHARD S. BROWNLEE

Contents

		PAGE
Preface	.. ..	vii
1	The Missouri-Kansas Storm Center	3
2	Sterling Price's Guerrillas	22
3	The Union Military Occupation of Missouri	42
4	William Quantrill's Guerrillas	53
5	Porter Raids in North Missouri	76
6	From Independence to Arkansas	92
7	Lawrence is Destroyed	110
8	Quantrill and the Confederacy	128
9	Martial Law	142
10	Control of the Populace	157
11	"Bloody Bill" Anderson and George Todd	180
12	The Last Campaign	206
13	The Final Struggle	223
14	Surrender	232
	Selected Bibliography	247
	Appendix .. .., ..	253
	Index	263

Maps and Illustrations

PAGE

District of the Northeast 80

Districts of the Frontier and Southwest 96

District of the Border and the Central District 114

The Confederate Guerrilla Theatre of the War 130

District of the Northwest 184

following page

General Henry W. Halleck 52

General Samuel R. Curtis

"Order Number Eleven"

William C. Quantrill

"Bloody Bill" Anderson

Bill Anderson and Two of His Boys

"Little Archie" Clement

Fletcher Taylor, Frank and Jesse James

xi

GRAY GHOSTS OF THE CONFEDERACY

1

The Missouri-Kansas Storm Center

I N the years between 1861 and 1865 when the United
States was tormented by civil war and while massive
armies slowly maneuvered and grappled for control of
the Eastern seaboard and the Mississippi Valley, the vast and
lightly settled country just west of the Mississippi, the western border, was wracked by insurrection and continuous
guerrilla conflict.

The Civil War on the border after 1861 was not the same
as that fought elsewhere in the nation. Born of a turbulent
frontier, fostered and centered in the state of Missouri by a
tragic political and military situation, there emerged with
the duly constituted military forces of the Trans-Mississippi
Department of the Confederacy a number of irregular bands

of pro-Southern fighting men known as guerrillas. Almost unique in the history of the Civil War, acting at wide variance with the conventional military tactics of the period, these colorful and savage partisan cavalrymen ranged the border from Missouri to Texas for four long, terrible years.

Led by desperate men such as William C. Quantrill, Bill Anderson, George Todd, Joseph C. Porter, John Thrailkill, and Upton Hays the guerrillas, most of them only boys, fought a total war. West of the Mississippi they plunged a fairly stable, congenial, and conservative society into intense partisan conflict that was felt by every man, woman and child. This was not a war of great armies and captains, this was bloody local insurrection, a war between friends and neighbors—a civil war in the precise definition of that term. Here organized bands of men killed each other and the civil population hundreds of miles behind the recognized battlefronts. Here there was ambush, arson, execution and murder; warfare without rules, law or quarter. In this area existed harsh military government that suspended civil law and the legal and constitutional rights of the people.

Popular interest in the western Confederate guerrilla organizations is due to several factors. In the first place, their wild cavalry tactics were of such a fabulously dashing, cruel and mysterious nature that they gave rise in later years to a great body of folklore and legend. Secondly, many of their deeds were of such relentless and calculated violence it was not possible for their contemporaries to write of them without indulging in wildly controversial condemnation or praise. To many persons of Southern sentiment, who lacked western idols, they personified the militant Confederacy and were all Robin Hood heroes. To other men, whose sympathies lay to the North, the guerrillas were only unprincipled thieves, "bushwhackers," and pathological criminals. Finally, because of the unique qualities required for leadership, many of the guerrilla officers were strange and fascinating characters, and certain of the men, boys such as Frank and Jesse James and Coleman and James Younger, went on in lawless border history to become legendary figures.

In a strictly military sense the combat utility and effectiveness of the Confederate guerrilla has always been evident, yet there has been hesitation to credit him with it. Hundreds of primary local accounts and literally thousands of official government reports attest to it. The attack threat of the guerrillas, combined with their unorthodox but highly successful tactics, kept the Union military forces of the border, who overwhelmingly outnumbered them, mobilized, harassed and not available for utilization in other theatres where they were needed badly. Vicious guerrilla activity directed against the civil population created such fear and disorganization that in many areas normal society collapsed entirely.

The history of the western Confederate guerrillas began in the state of Missouri several years before 1861, and there the conditions were created and the events came about that gave birth to them. At the advent of the Civil War Missouri was still largely a frontier state—a Southern frontier state. In 1860 some three quarters of the people had their origin in or were descended from parents who were born in other slave states. Thus they were of decided Southern background and many of them had family ties and cultural affiliation with the old border slave states. By 1860 slaves made up only about nine per cent of the population of Missouri, but the institution was still an important factor in the agricultural economy and was increasing in the rich farm areas of the central and western portion of the state. There were few large slaveholders, but a great many men owned one or two Negroes who were valuable personal property, indicative of wealth and in some cases advanced social status. Since Missouri's admission to the Union slavery had been inextricably bound to other social institutions and was taken for granted by most men.

The average settler in Missouri had come from the South in the 1830's and forties, had taken up a small farm on the great rivers of the state, and had gone into general agriculture or the small cultivation of hemp or tobacco. He lived a simple hospitable life based on the more conservative patterns of other Southern communities. However, if the daily life of the individual family of Missouri was pleasant and fairly easygoing, there also lay over the nature of these people a dark patina of border ruthlessness. They were of the great generation of frontier gun-carriers whose fathers had fought the British and Indians east of the great river. The stark and brutal reality of the new western frontier existed just to the west of their state line in the Indian-populated area of the plains. This was the area they crossed and recrossed on their military and commercial marches westward, and many of them believed the plains would control the future of their society.

To most Missourians the Civil War actually began in 1854 with congressional passage of the Kansas-Nebraska Act. By that year there had gathered along the Missouri-Kansas line men with convictions so at variance, so explosively emotional over the expansion of slavery, they dared to express them by illegal force.

The provisions of the Kansas-Nebraska Act which left the legality or prohibition of slavery in the two territories to those men who would settle there in good faith were deemed satisfactory by most Missourians who had reason to be interested. Was it not natural to presume that Kansas would be settled by Missourians and others from the South? Consequently, concern over the settlement of the territory became acute only when it was felt that the peopling of the area was being influenced by Northern abolitionists. Slaveholding Missourians had adequate reason to be aware of the threat to their human property in a third free area on their state's border. Their primary interest in the settlement of Kansas, beyond the normal frontier urge to speculate in new lands, was to insure their property.

It became apparent to Missourians as soon as emigration began that vociferous interests in the North were also interested in the political future of Kansas. The Eastern press, led by Horace Greeley, sent reporters to the border, and a barrage of anti-slavery, anti-Missouri news and editorials soon appeared in its pages. To their surprise Missourians were on almost any occasion able to read of themselves as "slaveocrats," whose only interest in Kansas was based on an unsavory and immoral hunger to expand slavery throughout the entire West. As a result of this inflammatory publicity and the violence it provoked many Northern men came to imagine the whole people of Missouri as "Border Ruffians" and waiting secessionists.[1] This conception, in most instances erroneous, was to lead to tragic consequences when Missouri was occupied by Northern troops during the Civil War. Conversely, many leaders of the Confederacy also gained a false impression of the loyalty of the majority of Missourians once the war came.

Assisting the Eastern free-soil editors, poets and authors were the New England and allied emigrant societies. The purpose of these organizations was to advertise the natural desirability of Kansas and to offer lowered transportation rates to voters who would move there and support free-soil politics. As a result of such vigorous propaganda the people of Missouri by July, 1854, believed they were witnessing a continuous stream of Northern settlers passing through the state toward Kansas. Rumor soon had it that these migratory groups conspicuously lacked agricultural implements and

1 Lloyd D. Lewis, "Propaganda and the Missouri Kansas War," *Missouri Historical Review*, XXXIV (October, 1939), 3-17.

women, and instead carried surplus rifles of the latest model. Many Missourians came to the conclusion that these "pioneers" were traveling on Eastern emigrant society complimentary tickets. One fact was obvious. If the emigrant societies were not actually supplying Kansas with many people those they did send were giving the area a shrill and vital anti-slavery leadership.[2]

The movement into Kansas infuriated numerous Missourians. Under their noses a fanatical hegira seemed to be taking place, one that upset the comfortable assumption that the territory was destined logically to become a friendly slave state. The radical pro-slavery leaders of Missouri declared a border war on Kansas. In 1854 and 1855 several thousand Missourians rode into Kansas and participated illegally in the territorial elections. These men came armed and did not hesitate to use force and intimidation at the polls. They were led by some of Missouri's most prominent political figures. As a result of the elections pro-slavery candidates received handsome fraudulent majorities and a constitution making slavery legal was approved. This unforgivable action by Missourians created hysteria in the North.

Although only a handful of men from Missouri took part in the Kansas elections, their unlawful presence and use of force tended to substantiate the harsh and uncomplimentary light in which the state was already held in the North. And although Kansas voted herself free in honest elections in 1858, the tampering by Missourians was never forgotten.

2 From statistics available it seems that when Kansas voted overwhelmingly against slavery in 1858 it was because of a free-soil population that had come primarily from the middle-Atlantic and newer mid-west states. See William O. Lynch "Population Movements in Relation to the Struggle for Kansas," *Indiana University Studies*, XII (1925), studies 65-68, p. 403; Ralph V. Harlow, "The Rise and Fall of the Kansas Aid Movements," *American Historical Review*, XLI (October, 1925), 25; W. H. Isley, "The Sharps Rifle Episode in Kansas History," *American Historical Review*, XII (April, 1907), 549-50.

From 1855 until 1860 the situation on the border approached anarchy. Missouri gangs invaded Kansas and besieged and occupied Lawrence. To obtain arms they looted the United States Arsenal at Liberty Landing at home. Numerous fights and murders took place over land claims and these embroilments were eagerly identified with the slavery issue. Along the state line men banded together and formed protective and raiding associations, and, as usual in such twilight areas, characters of the most fanatic and vicious temperament were drawn to the scene.

Following the attack on Lawrence murderous old John Brown and his sons hacked to death with broadswords five men and boys entirely innocent of the raid. Free-soil Kansans such as James H. Lane, James Montgomery and Dr. Charles R. Jennison raised companies and attacked pro-slavery men in Missouri and Kansas. In retaliation George W. Clarke and Charles Hambleton preyed on Kansans, and their forays culminated in the massacre of ten free-soil men on the Marias des Cygnes River in 1858. Slave-stealing, arson and looting became commonplace and the term "Bleeding Kansas" gained some reality.[3]

From the excitement, lawlessness and horror of the Missouri-Kansas border warfare of the fifties came one of the most significant causes for the guerrilla conflict, and for its nature, which took place on the western frontier between 1861 and 1865. Although numerically very few Missourians had taken an active part in the Kansas outrages, their state had gained a name in the North as a hotbed of radical, violent, pro-slavery people. The Eastern press, the flaring debates over Kansas at Washington, the intemperate praise of

[3] For the Kansas guerrilla warfare between 1855 and 1860 see: Jay Monaghan, *Civil War on the Western Border* (Boston, Toronto, 1955), 16-116; James C. Malin, *John Brown and the Legend of Fifty-Six* (Philadelphia, 1942), 560-70; Jonas Viles, "Documents Illustrating the Troubles on the Border," *Missouri Historical Review*, I and II (April, October, 1907).

Missouri in the South and condemnation in the North, had created the opinion that Missourians were ardently Southern. The Missouri-Kansas frontier had become aroused, trained and conditioned to ugly irregular warfare. Many border Missourians had developed hatred for "abolitionist Yankee Kansans," and many Kansans considered all Missourians ruffian slaveholders.

These evil seeds of dislike and distrust were to bear shocking fruit on the border once the Civil War began. Then the Kansas raiders of the 1850's found themselves cloaked with the implied or actual authority of the United States. Able to move into Missouri freely, or ordered into the state as forces of occupation, they were prone to consider all Missourians disloyal to the Union. In payment, the Missouri guerrillas were to arise and carry on a war of extermination against Kansans. Up and down the western border numbers of men were waiting for the opportunity to take revenge for real and fancied wrongs that had occurred in the five years before 1861. Thousands of innocent Missourians and Kansans were to pay a bloody and ruinous price for the intemperate prewar acts of a few radical men.

The great irony of this unfortunate situation was that the stereotype of Missourians of the period was not very true. Although sharp sectional antagonism and irregular warfare had become commonplace on the Missouri-Kansas border in the five years preceding 1860, the political attitude of the mass of Missouri voters toward the Union that year was conservative. The evidence is undisputable that most Missourians believed in maintenance of the Union at that time. There was only a small secessionist element in the state, which, however, exerted influence far beyond its numbers. This is borne out by the fact that the Missouri gubernatorial election of August, 1860, was won by Democrat Claiborne F. Jackson, who, in spite of traitorous plans for secession, campaigned on the Douglas-Democratic principles that definitely upheld the Union. In that election 139,000 Missourians voted for an orderly and peaceful interpretation of the question of the expansion of slavery. Only 17,500 men indicated any type of radical views by supporting the Republican or the secessionist Breckenridge-Democratic candidates. In the presidential election of November, 1860, Missouri was the only state which Stephen A. Douglas carried, and only 31,000 men out of the electorate voted for Breckenridge.[4]

Claiborne Jackson, Missouri's new governor in 1860, was a secret secessionist. In his inaugural address he emphasized Missouri's relationship to the South, urged the reorganization of the State Guard, and recommended a convention to consider Missouri's relationship to the Union. The Twenty-first Session of the Missouri General Assembly, reflecting the conservative and placating attitude of the people who had sent it to Jefferson City, refused to be stampeded by the governor. A bill to rearm the State Guard was never brought to vote, and a convention bill was drawn so that no ordinance arrived at by such a body could take Missouri out of the Union without a vote of the people. Commenting on these acts of the legislature the St. Louis *Tri-Weekly Missouri Republican* said they reflected the views of "myriads" of letters received by the representatives.[5] In February, 1861, delegates were elected to the convention, and it was estimated that secessionist candidates had been defeated by eighty thousand votes throughout the state. And, when the convention met it resolved that there was no reason at that time for Missouri to

---

[4] Douglas and Bell, the Constitutional-Union candidate, received 117,000 votes, Lincoln only 17,000. See William M. Pruitt, "The More Definitely Pro-Southern Group in Missouri between August, 1860 and March, 1861," (Master's thesis, University of Missouri, 1932), 8-21; Walter A. Ryle, *Missouri: Union or Secession* (Nashville, 1931), 126-27.

[5] *Tri-Weekly Missouri Republican*, January 23, 1861. Hereinafter cited St. Louis *Republican*.

leave the Union.[6] Thus Jackson's schemes were blocked. Even after Fort Sumter was attacked on April 12 and the governor had indignantly refused to supply the four regiments requested by President Lincoln, hopes for neutrality were observed. There was no surge toward secession.

At this time, however, the direct causes for the great guerrilla struggle on the frontier were created. A few resolute men determined that Missourians must take an active part in either the Union or Confederate cause during the war. Governor Jackson, Lieutenant Governor Thomas C. Reynolds and a small but active group connected with the State Guard were the Confederate marplots. Frank P. Blair of St. Louis, a rising Republican politician whose brother was in Lincoln's cabinet; Captain Nathaniel P. Lyon, soldier-abolitionist; General John C. Frémont, and a procession of Union military commanders were to bring chaos in conducting the course of the Union. All Missouri and the entire frontier were to suffer from the conditions these radical Northern and Southern men created by their schemes, their acts of invasion, their military occupation and the destruction of normal government which they accomplished by martial law and the abrogation of civilized rules of war.

Governor Jackson's complicity with the Confederacy in the spring of 1861 has been firmly established. In April he and his friends began collecting guns and munitions in strategic spots around the state. The United States Arsenal in Clay County was again broken into and a small number of firearms were distributed to local units of the State Guard. The big prize, as the governor saw it, was the federal arsenal at St. Louis which held sixty thousand old muskets, over a million rounds of small arms ammunition, and arms manu-

[6] *Journal and Proceedings of the Missouri State Convention, Held at Jefferson City and St. Louis, March, 1861* (St. Louis, 1861), the *Proceedings*, 15, and the *Journal*, 9, 34, 35.

facturing and repair machinery. Determined to have these, even though men to bear them were not yet in sight, Jackson secretly sent representatives to Jefferson Davis asking for cannon to help in capturing the installation.[7] On April 22, 1861, to implement his plans, he called the General Assembly into special session at Jefferson City and ordered the State Guard into summer encampments. By May 3 some eight hundred local men had reported for duty at Camp Jackson in St. Louis which lay within a half hour's march of the arsenal. Cannon supplied by the Confederate government had been smuggled into this camp.

While Governor Jackson was making these moves Frank P. Blair pursued his course rapidly. Suspecting the governor of duplicity he used political means to have General W. S. Harney removed from command of the Union forces in St. Louis and replaced by Captain Nathaniel Lyon from Kansas. Although there was never any doubt of Harney's complete loyalty to the Union, he was simply too peaceful, too interested in conciliation, for Blair's taste. Blair knew he could count on Lyon in any venture proposed for the Union. Lyon first transferred most of the arms and munitions in the arsenal across the river to Alton, Illinois. On May 10 he and Blair surrounded Camp Jackson with three thousand regular and volunteer troops and without firing a shot obtained the surrender of the State Guard unit. As the Union soldiers were marching their prisoners into the city they were fired on by an unsympathetic mob and in turn they shot back, killing a number of men, women and children. The street fighting in St. Louis was witnessed by three men, then undistinguished, who in a short time became leaders in the western Civil War. On the scene were a short, unkempt

---

[7] United States War Department, *The War of the Rebellion: A Compilation of the Official Records of the Union and the Confederate Armies* (130 vols., Washington, D. C., 1880-1902), Series 1, Vol. I, 688-90. Hereinafter cited *O. R.*

mustering officer from Illinois, U. S. Grant; a nervous red-head, president of the St. Louis Street Railway, W. T. Sherman; and a dapper hot-headed young planter from Lafayette County, Joseph O. Shelby.[8]

The news of Blair's and Lyon's blow at St. Louis spread quickly across the state and alarmed the reluctant legislature at Jefferson City into action. A strong militia bill was passed and large sums were appropriated to arm the state. Sterling Price, an ex-governor and aging Mexican War hero, was persuaded to become major general of the State Guard. He and Jackson set about reorganizing it and appointing pro-Confederate brigadiers over the state's eight military districts.

Peaceful conditions were restored for a few weeks when General Harney again assumed command at St. Louis. He agreed with General Price that the Union would not recruit nor move troops into Missouri so long as the state was peaceful and did not arm for the Confederacy. Harney lasted just as long as it took Frank Blair to arrange his relief through Washington. By the last of May Lyon was again in command at St. Louis, and on June 11, 1861, he told Governor Jackson and General Price to their faces that he would move Union troops about Missouri as he pleased. Jackson then called out the State Guard, and asked for fifty thousand men to resist invasion. The war had come to Missouri.

Nathaniel Lyon, immediately promoted to Brigadier General, was energetic and fearless. An able puritan, he was a military realist. He knew that if war came Missouri had to be held for the Union, that it was the link which would control the entire western theatre of operations. He saw that the state commanded the navigation of the great stream that gave

[8] See James Peckham, *Gen. Nathaniel Lyon and Missouri in 1861* (New York, 1866); Thomas L. Snead, *The Fight for Missouri from the Election of Lincoln to the Death of Lyon* (New York, 1888); Daniel O'Flaherty, *General Jo Shelby* (Chapel Hill, 1954), 51-56; Monaghan, *Civil War on the Western Border*, 129-32.

it its name, as well as the Mississippi, the Illinois, and the Ohio. The North in time of war could never permit the navigation of these vital rivers to be controlled by the Confederacy. Also, Lyon had from the first gauged Governor Jackson and his secessionist associates accurately. He suspected that the governor was secretly preparing for war and looking for an opportunity to bring Missouri into the Confederacy. He was also aware that General Ben McCulloch was grouping troops near Fort Smith, Arkansas, and he believed the Confederacy was preparing to invade Missouri. A Northerner, he knew Missourians only as he had seen them on the Kansas border, and he cared not a whit about the personal loyalties of the average citizen.[9]

At Governor Jackson's call for 50,000 volunteers General Lyon took decisive action and evolved what became the basic Union military strategy in Missouri throughout the war. Before Jackson and Price had the opportunity to assemble the State Guard he moved to occupy the state. Accompanied by 1,700 men, the majority of whom were St. Louis Germans, he went by boat up the Missouri to Jefferson City. There he found the capitol buildings deserted and learned that the governor had fled and the legislature had scattered. Continuing to Boonville on June 17 he routed a small State Guard unit under Colonel John S. Marmaduke in an almost bloodless skirmish.

At the same time he advanced up the river Lyon sent a small force by train down the southern branch of the Pacific Railroad to Rolla. From there Colonel Franz Sigel with some 900 men pressed south and west toward Carthage. Sigel was to intercept Governor Jackson and General Price and to prevent any State Guard units from joining McCulloch and his Confederates in Arkansas. At Boonville Lyon stopped all

9 Wiley Britton, *The Civil War On The Border* (2 vols., New York, London, 1891), I, 32-33; *O. R.*, Series 1, Vol. III, 379-81.

river traffic; Union patrols took over the major crossings and ferries between St. Charles and Kansas City, and the improvised gunboat *John Warner* cruised the stream destroying rafts and boats to prevent enemy forces from crossing south. By these adroit maneuvers Lyon bisected the state through the heart of its most heavily populated slaveholding section.

His next move was to take over the railroads: the Hannibal and St. Joseph which ran east and west across the northern part of the state, the Pacific which extended from St. Louis to Sedalia and Rolla, and the North Missouri which ran from St. Charles west and north to Macon on the Hannibal and St. Joseph. The lines north of the Missouri River were occupied by Union troops called in from Kansas, Illinois, and Iowa. The control of these water and rail transportation routes enabled Lyon, in co-ordination with flanking forces from Kansas, to put into effect an enveloping movement against General Price and Governor Jackson which forced them into southwest Missouri.

General Lyon's strategy paralyzed State Guard recruiting. Many State Guard companies and two small brigades commanded by Brigadier Generals Thomas A. Harris and Martin E. Green in north Missouri were stranded and dispersed. In November General Price wrote Jefferson Davis that he had been forced to leave between five and ten thousand recruits in central and northern Missouri because of Lyon's swift movements.[10] Time after time Price was to send officers into the Missouri River counties to gather these recruits and lead them south to his colors. His only offensive action during the summer of 1861 was based on these recruiting parties which were also ordered to destroy rail and telegraph communications wherever possible. General Lyon was successful in stamping out most of them as soon as they were formed.[11]

[10] *O. R.*, Series 1, Vol. III, 734-36.
[11] *O. R.*, Series 1, Vol. VIII, 496-97.

Lyon's actions were decisive in capturing Missouri, but because of their swiftness they left a hard core of men potentially or actively in opposition to the Union behind the
battle lines. A variety of factors would make numbers of
these men Confederate guerrillas as the war and the Union
occupation of the state progressed.

With north Missouri secure, Lyon advanced down to
Springfield where on August 10, 1861, hopelessly outnumbered, he audaciously and cleverly attacked Price and Mc-
Culloch at Wilson's Creek. There, in one of the severest
battles of the war from the point of casualties among men engaged, the Union force was beaten and forced to retreat to
Rolla. General Lyon, gallantly leading his men, was shot
dead on the afternoon of the battle.

Following Wilson's Creek Price begged McCulloch to go
back with him to central Missouri and recapture the state.
McCulloch refused. He felt the State Guard was undisciplined, officered by politicians, and, in his own words, that
the people of Missouri were so against the Confederacy, "we
had as well be in Boston so far as the friendly feelings of the
inhabitants were concerned." [12] General Price started north
from Springfield with only his Missourians, the news of his
victory at Wilson's Creek bringing him only a few recruits
as he progressed through the state. By September 13 he
reached Lexington on the Missouri River where with some
ten thousand men he overwhelmed a small Union garrison.
At Lexington he was joined by Generals Harris and Green
with light forces from north of the river.

On July 3, 1861, General John C. Frémont had been given
command of the Union Department of the West with headquarters at St. Louis. Frémont's actions, both military and
political, were to confuse the people on the western border.
A few days after Lexington fell he had begun to surround

12 O. R., Series 1, Vol. III, 722, in a letter to General W. J. Hardee.

that town with forty thousand men, and by the last of October with a vast "Army of the West" he had forced Price back to Springfield without a fight.

Now occurred a change in Union strategy which enabled General Price to return to south-central Missouri during the winter of 1861 and to promote guerrilla warfare throughout the state. For lack of aggressiveness General Frémont was removed from his command, and his army was given to General David Hunter. The Department of the West was taken over by Major General Henry W. Halleck. Hunter and Halleck felt the winter too near for a campaign, and on November 11 General in Chief of the United States Armies, George B. McClellan, advised Halleck that the Army of the West should be withdrawn to interior points in the state for future use on the Mississippi.[13]

Price took advantage of the situation quickly, and by mid-November moved up to Osceola on the Osage River where he could send recruiting parties and guerrilla saboteurs into north Missouri. Conditions were desperate for General Price during the fall and winter of 1861. Even though Governor Jackson had called the state legislature into session at Neosho in October to pass an ordinance of secession, Missouri was not accepted as the twelfth Confederate state until November 28. It was commonly known that the Neosho assembly lacked quorums in both houses and that the proxies offered for secession were illegal. Price was still only a major general of state troops allied by treaty to the Confederacy. There was growing indication that his military abilities were held in serious doubt by the authorities at Richmond.[14] As winter came down on the rough camps on the Osage it was also obvious that many of the State Guardsmen were summer

13 *O. R.*, Series 1, Vol. III, 533, 568-69.
14 Arthur R. Kirkpatrick, "Missouri, the Twelfth Confederate State" (Doctoral dissertation, University of Missouri, 1955).

soldiers with very little interest in the Confederate cause. In describing his situation in mid-November General Price complained that the enlistment period of three-fourths of his command was expiring and that many were going home to provide for their families. Most of his men were scantily clad and had never been paid for their summer campaign.[15]

A dangerous feeling of tranquility and a spreading desire for peace also seemed to exist. The state convention to consider Missouri's relationship to the Union had reconvened on July 20 at Jefferson City, and, over the protest of a number of its members that the legislature should be allowed to act, had declared the offices of governor and lieutenant governor vacant. The convention then proceeded to fill these offices with its own members and finally, abolishing the legislature, set itself up as the provisional government of Missouri. To insure the loyalty of all state and county officials, and all voters, an oath of allegiance to the United States and the provisional government itself was required. The convention also established its right to remove all officials at will and to disfranchise any man believed disloyal to the Union. This extralegal government, in other words, took over every aspect of executive, legislative and judicial power in Missouri and then qualified the electorate. There were no constitutional or legal precedents for these acts of the convention. They were based on fear, distrust and emergency. Unfortunately, but as might have been anticipated, they were also based on political expediency, for in spite of numerous dates proposed to terminate the provisional government it maintained itself in autocratic power until 1864 when a new radical constitution could be guaranteed.[16]

15 *O. R.*, Series 1, Vol. VIII, 729-31, in a letter to General Leonidas Polk.

16 *Journal of the Missouri State Convention Held at Jefferson City, July, 1861* (St. Louis, 1861); *Journal of the Missouri State Convention Held at the City of Saint Louis, October, 1861* (St. Louis, 1861); *Journal of the Missouri State Convention Held in Jefferson City, June, 1862* (St. Louis, 1862).

Hamilton Gamble was chosen as provisional governor and his selection was a happy one. A man of integrity and a moderate in all things, he genuinely desired peace and conciliation. In the winter of 1861 he represented stability for all the people of Missouri, but he was soon plunged into conflict with the Union military commanders of the state and the radicals of his own government.

The dissatisfaction in Price's army became so public that Gamble attempted to send an emissary to open negotiations to disband it and turn its allegiance to the new government. General John Pope, who commanded the Union forces on Price's front during the long winter of 1861, also believed the circumstances of the State Guard so hopeless that most of the soldiers would lay down their arms, take any oath required, and return home if they felt they would not be arrested.[17]

Even the new commander of the Department of Missouri, Major General Halleck, thought the chance for more hostilities remote. "Old Brains" Halleck was a military oddity. A West Point graduate, scholar, and authority on international law, Halleck became a prominent military figure in the Civil War because great things were expected of him. A pedant, and a mystery to most of his associates, Halleck apparently earned much of his reputation in the early days of the war from the voluminous and detailed correspondence and directives which steadily flowed from his headquarters. The command of the Department of Missouri in 1861 seemed ideal for a man of his nature and ability. Here was an area in which order was rapidly being restored militarily and politically; an enemy whose forces appeared to be disintegrating without the necessity for further bloody battles. When General Sherman visited Missouri and warned Hal-

---

[17] *O. R.*, Series 1, Vol. VIII, 399, 420-21, in a letter to Halleck asking permission for Gamble's representative to go through his lines.

leck that he could expect more trouble from Price, "Old Brains" informed his wife that Sherman was insane, giving support to a current rumor.[18] With a new Department of Kansas created and placed under General Hunter, and with that troublesome state off his hands, Halleck believed Price could be expelled easily and the western border returned to peace.

[18] Monaghan, *Civil War on the Western Border*, 208.

2

Sterling Price's Guerrillas

||||||||||||||||||||||||||||||||||||||||||||||||||||||||||||||||||||||||||||||||||||||||||||

IN order to save his army, to attempt desperately to build its strength, Sterling Price started a guerrilla war on the western border. He was too weak and demoralized to strike a major blow, even to move actively against the Union forces who had established a line along the border of eastern Kansas and through Kansas City, Sedalia, and Rolla to Cape Girardeau in Missouri. Explaining his position in a desperate proclamation to the people of Missouri on November 26, 1861, he hysterically cried

FELLOW-CITIZENS:

In the month of June last I was called to command a handful of Missourians, who nobly gave up home and comfort to espouse, in that gloomy hour, the cause of your bleeding country, struggling with the most causeless and cruel despotism known among civilized men. When peace and protection could no longer be enjoyed but at the price of honor and liberty your chief magistrate called for 50,000 men to drive the ruthless invader from a soil made fruitful by your labors and consecrated by your homes.

To that call less than 5,000 responded; out of a male population exceeding 200,000 men, one in forty only stepped forward to
defend with their persons and their lives the cause of constitutional liberty and human rights. . . .

Where are those 50,000 men? Are Missourians no longer true
to themselves? Are they a timid, time-serving, craven race, fit only
for subjection to a despot?

. . . .

But where are our Southern-rights friends? We must drive
the oppressor from our land. I must have 50,000 men. Now is the
crisis of your fate; now the golden opportunity to save the state;
now is the day of your political salvation. The time of enlistment
for our brave band is beginning to expire. Do not tax their pa-
tience beyond endurance; do not longer sicken their hearts by
hope deferred. They begin to inquire, "Where are our friends?"
Who shall give them an answer? Boys and small property holders
have in the main fought the battles for the protection of your
property, and when they ask, "Where are the men for whom we
are fighting?" how can I, how shall I, explain?[1]

Very few Missourians came to Price as a result of this plea,
and those who did had great difficulty in passing through
the Union lines. Hoping to attract soldiers, he sent recruiting officers into central and northern Missouri, and entered
on an energetic plan to destroy the excellent interior Union
rail and telegraphic communications on his front. By doing
this he might divert the enemy and weaken the federal lines
so that recruits could come down to him.

Most of General Price's recruiting parties came to grief.
It was the Union tactic to allow them to build to noticeable
size and then to pounce on them. In rapid order in mid-
December 1861, General John Pope attacked parties in
Henry and Johnson counties, scattering 2,000 men gathered
at Chilhowee, capturing 150 more and sixteen wagons loaded

[1] O. R., Series 1, Vol. VIII, 695.

with supplies at Clinton, and taking and paroling 1,300 men at Knob Noster. Other Union cavalry dispersed camps in Saline and Howard counties, and there was sharp fighting at Mount Zion Church in Boone where 25 "rebels" were killed and 150 were wounded.[2]

Price's railroad bridge burners performed a more successful mission. In July, 1861, his supporters had succeeded in burning the Salt River bridge on the Hannibal and St. Joseph road and destroyed culverts on the North Missouri near Centralia. Traffic on both lines was stopped for a time, and when it was resumed, the transportation of troops by rail became hazardous as the cars were shot into. One train was hit by almost a hundred bullets fired from the right of way on a trip between Hannibal and St. Joseph. On September 3 the Platte River bridge on the Hannibal and St. Joe line collapsed under a train, killing some twenty passengers and injuring sixty, many of whom were civilians. The pilings of the bridge had been burned almost through before the train reached it. Newspapers all over the state voiced disapproval, but the sabotage was so well done the St. Louis *Republican* stated that St. Louis was almost cut off from the rest of Missouri. Bridges were out on all of the major rail lines, including the Pacific, which had its big span over the Lamine River destroyed.[3]

Now in December, Price's guerrillas intensified their attacks on the railroads. The large bridge over the Chariton River in Macon County on the Hannibal and St. Joseph was burned, and dozens of culverts were torn out on the North Missouri above Mexico in Boone County. Miles of telegraph wire along the lines were ripped down and carried away. Isaac H. Sturgeon, president of the North Missouri, stated that during the fall and winter of 1861 over a hundred miles of his road was demolished. At one time or another every

[2] *O. R.*, Series 1, Vol. VIII, 37-39, 34-35, 49-50.
[3] St. Louis *Republican*, July 15, August 8, 12, September 4, 7, 13, 19, 1861.

bridge and culvert had been set ablaze, ties had been re-moved, fires built, and rails bent in them. Thirty-odd cars and one engine had been completely destroyed.[4]

General Halleck was frankly at a loss as to how to stop the damage to the railroads. Price's guerrillas and disaffected people living near the lines could so easily demolish bridges and track and then fade into the civil population. And al-though Halleck had ten thousand troopers guarding the rail lines, there were simply not enough men available to watch every foot of track. Worse, the general complained that when persons suspected of sabotage were arrested, the civil courts were unreliable in punishing them. He wrote his friends that he felt his army to be in almost as hostile a country as Mexico had been in the last war. He was of the opinion that there was no alternative but to severely enforce martial law.[5]

Halleck's way of solving the problem, of course, was to write detailed punitive orders. On December 22, 1861, he published General Order Number Thirty-two from his head-quarters at St. Louis. This order, directed against the guer-rilla bridge burners, stated in part:

Insurgent rebels scattered through the northern counties of this State, which are occupied by our troops, under the guise of peaceful citizens, have resumed their occupation of burning bridges and destroying railroads and telegraph wires. These men are guilty of the highest crime known to the code of war and the punishment is death. Anyone caught in the act will be immedi-ately shot, and anyone accused of this crime will be arrested and placed in close confinement until his case can be examined by a military commission, and, if found guilty, he also will suffer death.[6]

By this order Halleck established the treatment for parti-san Confederate soldiers caught behind the Union lines.

4 *O. R.*, Series 1, Vol. XXXIV, Part 4, pp. 548-49.
5 *O. R.*, Series 1, Vol. VIII, 475-76.
6 *O. R.*, Series 1, Vol. VIII, 463-64.

From this time on, guerrilla prisoners could be shot at the discretion of local commanders. Firing squads were to be kept busy along the border between 1861 and 1865. Never content with only one directive on a subject, Halleck published an additional order on January 1, 1862, concerning the treatment to be accorded captured guerrillas. Its ninth paragraph stated:

And, again, while the code of war gives certain exemptions to a soldier regularly in the military service of an enemy, it is a well-established principle that insurgents, not militarily organized under the laws of the State, predatory partisans, and guerrilla bands are not entitled to such exemptions; such men are not legitimately in arms, and the military name and garb which they have assumed cannot give a military exemption to the crimes which they may commit. They are, in a legal sense, mere free-booters and banditti, and are liable to the same punishment which was imposed upon guerrilla bands by Napoleon in Spain and by Scott in Mexico.[7]

"Old Brains" had taken care of pro-Southern guerrillas on the western border by these two orders. Their application was to reap a bloody return. If pro-Confederate partisans were to receive no quarter, they were to give none.

General Price learned soon of these punitive orders. On January 12 he wrote Halleck from Springfield that he had received information that his discharged State Guardsmen were being arrested and imprisoned, and that his recruiting agents and the guerrillas he had sent to destroy communications were being tried under the penalty of capital punishment when captured. Price sent this letter through the Union lines and demanded that Halleck explain his action in violating the laws of war.[8]

[7] O. R., Series 1, Vol. VIII, 476-78. This was General Order Number One, Department of Missouri.

[8] O. R., Series 1, Vol. VIII, 496-97.

Halleck called for his pen and paper. In an elaborate letter he informed Price that so long as uniformed, duly organized and enrolled men were sent behind the Union lines to perform military acts, "we shall try to kill them if possible, in open warfare, or, if we capture them we shall treat them as prisoners of war." Halleck went on:

But it is well understood that you have sent numbers of your adherents, in the garb of peaceful citizens and under false pretenses, through our lines into Northern Missouri, to rob and destroy the property of Union men and to burn and destroy railroad bridges, thus endangering the lives of thousands, and this, too, without any military necessity or possible military advantage. Moreover, peaceful citizens of Missouri, quietly working on their farms, have been instigated by your emissaries to take up arms as insurgents, and to rob and plunder and to commit arson and murder. . . . You certainly will not pretend that men guilty of such crimes, although "specially appointed and instructed by you," are entitled to the rights and immunities of ordinary prisoners of war.[9]

Guerrilla fighting and the destruction of railroad and telegraph lines went on. Having set these forces in motion, Price could not have stopped them had he desired to. Indeed, he had very little actual control over them, and was to exert less and less as time went by.

General Halleck knew now that Price's forces must be pushed from Missouri. Brigadier General Samuel R. Curtis, a West Point graduate, Iowa congressman, and engineer, was ordered to assemble an army at Rolla and destroy the State Guard. Curtis was tough, dogged, and not afraid to fight. By the last of January he had caused Price to retreat to Springfield with only twelve thousand men. From there he pursued him to Pea Ridge, Arkansas, and on March 7, 1862, attacked and defeated the combined forces of Price and Mc-

9 *O. R.,* Series 1, Vol. VIII, 514-15.

Culloch, this time led by General Earl Van Dorn. After the battle at Pea Ridge, General Price and those of his men who would join the Confederate army, were moved east of the Mississippi to take part in the Corinth campaign. The spring of 1862 began with most organized Confederate military units on the western border defeated or dispersed. However, for a variety of reasons, serious forces of insurrection were building up behind the Union lines from Arkansas to Nebraska.

The essential factor for any successful guerrilla campaign, a war fought hundreds of miles behind the front lines of the active belligerents, is a sympathetic supporting civil population and men of military age. On such a population guerrilla forces must depend for subsistence, shelter, information, and recruits. As has been indicated, there was a small but active pro-Confederate element of people in Missouri in 1861 willing to engage in and support guerrilla warfare against the Union. Because of the peculiar political and military conditions on the western border, this resistance group was to grow and become violently active between 1861 and 1865.

During his stay in Missouri during the winter of 1861 General Sterling Price's inability to attract recruits to his cause was not his only serious problem. During that time the six-month enlistment period of many of his State Guardsmen terminated. Large numbers of them returned to their homes legally discharged. Others simply deserted, bored with military routine and cold-weather hardship, no doubt feeling, as Price stated in his recruiting proclamation, that it was a rich man's war and a poor man's fight. Missouri's admission to the Confederacy in November 1861 did not help the General in gaining recruits or holding the men he had. Apparently many State Guardsmen were willing to resist invasion of Missouri from any source, but were most unwilling to leave the state and serve as regular Confederate soldiers. For example, when Price resigned his commission and command over the State Guard to accept a belated appointment as a major general in the Confederate army at Des Arc, Arkansas, in April, 1862, only about four thousand of his men went with him at that time into regular Confederate service.[10]

The failure of General Price and Governor Jackson to draw Missourians to the Confederacy meant several things in view of the people's predominantly Southern background. The most important fact was that many men of Southern origin were simply unwilling to engage in a war against the Union. The wealthier class of slaveholders, it may be presumed, were not so foolish as to trust their lives or property to the Confederacy with the state firmly in the hands of Union military forces. As long as the western border and Missouri remained tranquil, as long as the abolition of slavery was not a primary issue in the war, as long as men of Southern background and origin would be recognized in their loyalty to the Union and were able to conduct their lives and affairs in normal peace and security, there was little reason for serious strife on the border once Price had left it. If these conditions were violated, as they soon were to be, insurrection and guerrilla warfare could be expected as a matter of course.

A considerable potential enemy military population began to build up behind the Union lines in Missouri as soon as Price and the State Guard joined the Confederacy in the spring of 1862. Many of these men were deserters and returnees from the State Guard. Desertion from service in the State Guard and the Confederate armies was eagerly encouraged by both the provisional government of Missouri and the Union military authorities. Following the liberal amnesty policies determined upon by President Lincoln, numerous proclamations and orders were circulated through

10 *O. R.*, Series 1, Vol. VIII, 756-57.

the state in late 1861 authorizing the peaceful return of men who had been in pro-Southern military service. In October, 1861, the State Convention of Missouri had gone on record to offer its full protection to all men who would give up allegiance to the Confederacy and take an oath of loyalty to the Union and provisional governments.[11]

In most instances the man who had been a pro-Southern soldier had to report to a local military post where he swore and signed an oath of allegiance in the form of a parole certificate. He was also required to put up a bond for his future loyalty, and was then allowed to return home and go about his normal business.

One way or another, several thousand Missourians seem to have left the State Guard or Confederate service in the winter and spring of 1861-1862. Military posts throughout the northern and central parts of the state did a land office business paroling ex-Southern soldiers. In the spring of 1862 *The Liberty Tribune*, a weekly newspaper at Liberty, the county seat of Clay County, published long lists of men who were returning to the Union fold. Among those who took the oath and posted a thousand-dollar bond, the *Tribune* reported on May 2, was a tall, raw-boned, blank-faced youth of nineteen, Alexander Franklin James. Young Frank James had joined a home guard company in Clay County in May, 1861, and had fought at Wilson's Creek. He had deserted the State Guard, or left its service because of illness, and returned to his home.[12] Had the times allowed boys such as Frank James to remain neutrals, perhaps there would have been no guer-

[11] William E. Parrish, "The Provisional Government of Missouri 1861–1865" (Master's thesis, University of Missouri, 1953), 76; See also Hamilton R. Gamble Papers, Missouri Historical Society, St. Louis, Missouri, Gamble to Dr. John R. Moore, November 30, 1861. Hereinafter cited Gamble Papers.

[12] *The Liberty Tribune*, May 10, 1861, May 2, 1862; William A. Settle, "The Development of the Jesse James Legend (Doctoral dissertation, University of Missouri, 1945), 17, 22-23.

rilla warfare in Missouri in 1862. Unfortunately, mounting conditions of unrest caused by the Union military occupation and control of the state, and the Confederate utilization of guerrillas brought many of them back under arms. Unable or unwilling to live peacefully in their old neighborhoods, many ex-Southern soldiers formed the backbone of the partisan organizations of the western border.

Under these varied political, social, and military circumstances the foundations for a fierce civil insurrection were constructed. Having its center in Missouri, a slaveholding frontier state whose people were predominantly for the Union, this true Civil War was to plunge the entire western frontier into a blood bath.

The most direct factor contributing to the great insurrection which took place on the western border after 1861 lay in the abuses visited upon the civil population of Missouri by the Union military forces. A tragic portion of these abuses came from the inability, or in many instances, from the deliberate disinclination of the Union commanders to prevent outrages by their troops occupying the state. Combined with countenanced outrages and the misuse of military authority at all levels was the almost startling psychological and social ignorance of the top level Union command which regularly committed blind acts of policy that uselessly outraged the people of the state and abetted insurrection.

There was a positive tendency for Union officers and troops who occupied Missouri in the summer of 1861 to consider all of the people of the state secessionists and rebels. The opinion of the St. Louis *Republican* on July 15, 1861, that "since the commencement of these troubles, not a shade of doubt of the fidelity of her people to the Union has ever existed in the mind of any intelligent man," was definitely not shared by people living outside Missouri. Historian Wiley Britton, who served as an ardent Union officer throughout the war on the western border, blamed this generally erroneous impression on the earlier troubles with Kansas. In his words:

The conduct of the Border Ruffians during the troubles between the Free-State and Pro-slavery parties in Kansas before the war, had given the people of Missouri a bad name throughout the North, so that, when the Rebellion came on, there was a marked tendency among the officers and soldiers from the free states on entering Missouri to treat all classes as secessionists.[13]

Governor Gamble, whose devotion to the Union was never doubted, in the spring of 1862 informed the State Convention that "our State has been visited by a class of troops who came with feelings of hostility to our people . . . and who, under the guise of supporting the Union, perpetrated enormous outrages."[14]

In addition to the belief that Missourians were all rebels, the Union command was adamant in insisting that there would be no neutrality in Missouri over the issues of the war. This was hard on many Missourians who had come from the South and had blood ties there. It meant that no passive position was to be permitted, that every view taken by the Union command must be heartily supported by the people. General Halleck, of course, had a statement concerning this: "Those who are not for us will be regarded as against us. . . . There can be no individual neutrality in the rear in Missouri. Let the people where you go distinctly understand this."[15]

The no-neutrality policy of the Union command created many enemies when it was later applied to issues such as the abolition of slavery. It caused even more trouble when ap-

13 Britton, *The Civil War on the Border,* I, 117.

14 Edward C. Smith, *The Borderland in the Civil War* (New York, 1927), 369, citing the Convention *Journal* of June, 1862.

15 *O. R.,* Series 1, Vol. VIII, 439, in a letter to Colonel J. W. Birge, December 16, 1861.

plied to those persons who had served, or who had relatives serving, in the cause of the Confederacy.

The first major outrages perpetrated by Union troops in north Missouri took place along the Hannibal and St. Joseph Railroad in July, 1861. The military districts of that area were under the command of Brigadier General John Pope, whose troops were composed of volunteer regiments from Kansas, Illinois, and Iowa. Pope was a fascinating military false-front. A Kentuckian by birth, he had been graduated from West Point in 1842, commissioned in the engineers, and had served ably in the war with Mexico. Following his service in Mexico he had performed duties as a topographical engineer in the west, and when the war broke out, was working on lighthouses in the east. When he assumed command in north Missouri in 1861 he was thirty-nine years old, handsome, inclined to corpulence, a fine military figure, but also a loud-mouthed braggart, insecure in his own mind as to his ability to command any large number of troops. To cover this insecurity John Pope was to bluster his way from one command to a higher one until, leading the Union Army of Virginia, he was finally polished off by Jackson and Lee at the second battle of Bull Run in August, 1862.

Pope's actions in north Missouri in the summer of 1861 have been described as those of a tyrant or a madman.[16] Having routed a small force of State Guardsmen near Monroe City in the middle of July, the general then took the peculiar view that the disturbances in that neighborhood were purely local, and that the people were fighting each other in order to satisfy long-standing feelings of personal hostility. In other words, the Union people of the area were about as guilty as the secessionist element. In essence Pope held all the citizens along the Hannibal and St. Joseph and North Missouri railroads, Union and secessionist alike, responsible for the dam-

16 Britton, *The Civil War on the Border,* I, 145.

age created by General Price's guerrillas. On July 21, 1861, he notified the district that his investigations indicated that the destruction of bridges and culverts on the rail lines made it manifest that if the inhabitants of the towns along the roads were not responsible for the damages, they had done nothing to prevent them. He then notified each town that it would be responsible for the security of the track of its environs, and that if further damage took place, a levy of money or a levy on property would be made to pay for it.[17] Having established community guilt and responsibility, General Pope considered the matter solved. Railroad sabotage, however, continued. Guerrillas destroyed culverts and bridges and escaped detection. Troops sent out on patrol found only men working quietly in the fields.

Exasperated by the railroad incendiaries and the resentment his *particeps criminis* policy aroused, Pope worked up a new plan to bring peace to his entire district. He decided to withdraw his troops from the rail lines to central camps and force the civil population of the district to do their own guard and police work. To do this he visited all of the major towns and established Committees of Safety which were to enforce the law by raising guard units. Both Union men and known secessionists were put on these committees, and they were held responsible for policing the railroads, local peace, and for any damage done by the guerrillas.[18] When the committee at Palmyra failed miserably to prevent guerrillas from shooting into trains near that town, Pope ordered the county court to pay the damages done to engines and cars. In addition, he demanded money with which to ration and quarter the troops he was forced to order in to guard the line. When

[17] *O. R.*, Series 1, Vol. III, 402, 403-405. Pope felt this solution so sound that he sold it to General Halleck who repeated this technique in General Order Thirty-two, dated December 22, 1861. See *O. R.*, Series 1, Vol. VIII, 463-64.

[18] *O. R.*, Series 1, Vol. III, 403-405, 423-24.

the county court failed to pay up, the city council of Palmyra was ordered to. When it refused, General Pope instructed his men to take what they needed from merchants and citizens of the town and along the railroad. They did so.[19]

North Missouri was soon in a state near anarchy. Pope's Illinois and Kansas troops looted, burned, and generally mistreated Missourians as they came across them. The Second Kansas and the Sixteenth Illinois infantry regiments especially distinguished themselves in knavery. Drunken soldiers ran the trains and stole horses and other livestock. They shipped these by rail to Illinois for sale. In their trips up and down the lines the soldiers shot at men working in the fields. It was commonly believed that these drunken, lawless acts were known and countenanced at General Pope's headquarters.[20] Reporting these outrages on July 22, 1862, the St. Louis *Republican* acidly remarked that vagabond Union troops entering Missouri were creating secessionists everywhere.

The railroads at first had been delighted to have the protection of Pope's soldiery, but, as the summer went on it became obvious to their officials that while the lines might be saved, at the rate things were going, there would soon be no supporting population able to live along them. On August 13, writing about the conditions along the Hannibal and St. Joe, J. T. K. Hayward, the pro-Union general agent of the line, sent the following remarks to official John W. Brooks, who forwarded them to Secretary of War Edwin M. Stanton:

When there is added to this the irregularities of the soldiery— such as taking poultry, pigs, milk, butter, preserves, potatoes, horses, and in fact everything they want; entering and searching houses, and stealing in many cases; committing rapes on the negroes and such like things—the effect has been to make a great many Union men inveterate enemies, and if these things continue

19 *O. R.*, Series 1, Vol. III, 458-59.
20 Britton, *The Civil War on the Border*, I, 145-46.

much longer our cause is ruined. These things are not exaggerated by me, and though they do not characterize all the troops, several regiments have conducted in this way, and have also repeatedly fired on peaceable citizens—sometimes from trains as they passed —and no punishment, or none of any account has been meted out to them. . . . If the thing goes on this way much longer, we are ruined. I fear we cannot run the road or live in the country except under military protection. It is enought to drive a people to madness, and it is doing it fast.[21]

Hayward also wrote to General Frémont, protesting the atrocities being committed by Pope's troops, and told him that, as a result of them, there were far fewer Union men in north Missouri than there had been two months previously. He bluntly informed Frémont that Pope's tactics might work in a foreign enemy country, but in Missouri they were alienating friends and making enemies more bitter.[22] General Pope was apparently ordered to correct the collapse of discipline of his troops, for in mid-September he wrote Frémont that:

The drunkenness, incapacity, and shameful neglect of duty of many officers of rank in this district have brought matters to a sad state in North Missouri. . . . I have sent Colonel Blair, Second Kansas, and Major Hays and Captain Ralston, Sixteenth Illinois, to Saint Louis in arrest. Charges will be transmitted as soon as there is a moment's leisure to make them out.[23]

With all north Missouri in clamorous outrage, Commanding General Frémont blundered into the act. On August 30, 1861, he declared martial law over the entire state. In his proclamation he ordered the real and personal property of all persons in arms against the United States confiscated and their slaves freed. Then, establishing an arbitrary battle line

[21] *O. R.*, Series 1, Vol. III, 457-59.
[22] *O. R.*, Series 1, Vol. III, 433-35.
[23] *O. R.*, Series 1, Vol. III, 487-88.

from Fort Leavenworth to Cape Girardeau, he stated that all
persons taken in arms behind that line were to be tried by
court martial and shot.[24]

Frémont's martial law proclamation raised a violent storm.
If pro-Union Missourians cared little about what happened
to the property of men fighting the United States, many were
violently opposed to any aspect of abolition or the promis-
cuous freeing of slaves. Governor Gamble had assured the
people on August 3 that "no countenance will be afforded
to any scheme or to any conduct calculated in any degree to
interfere with the institution of slavery existing in the
state."[25] And, if Frémont personally felt safe in his palatial
St. Louis headquarters, there were many of his troops in the
field who could see quick retaliation from the Confederacy
if they started shooting prisoners. President Lincoln recognized this and pointed it out to Frémont, but he had to order
the always nearly insubordinate general to modify these two
provisions of his proclamation.[26]

North Missouri was not the only area harassed by out-state
Union troops during late 1861 and 1862. In the area south of
the Missouri River and along the Missouri-Kansas line ruthless depredations by pro-Union troops reached tragic proportions. With organized pro-Southern forces gone from that
part of the state, the people found themselves at the mercy
of three of their most unrelenting old enemies of the earlier
Kansas troubles: James H. Lane, Charles R. Jennison, and
James Montgomery.

Jim Lane, the Grim Chieftain of Kansas as he was called,
can, even in kindness, be described only as eminently un-
scrupulous. A citizen of Indiana where he had been lieu-

24 *O. R.*, Series 1, Vol. III, 466-67.

25 Buel Leopard and Floyd C. Shoemaker (eds.), *Messages and Proclamations
of the Governors of the State of Missouri* (16 vols. to date, Columbia, Missouri,
1922–1951), III, 512-17.

26 *O. R.*, Series 1, Vol. III, 469-70, 485-86.

tenant governor and congressman, Lane had been a leading pro-slavery Democrat. An evil-looking creature with the "sad, dim-eyed, bad-toothed face of a harlot," Lane represented the worst aspects of fanaticism so current during the Civil War.[27] He had arrived in Kansas in 1855, very likely with the hope of founding and rising with the Democratic party there. Viewing the Kansas situation with cynical objectivity he had become a Republican, a Free Soil party military and political leader, and a screaming abolitionist. Blessed with fierce magnetism and high qualities of leadership, Lane doublecrossed his way through the Republican party in Kansas to become one of the first senators of that state. In the summer of 1861 he had returned from Washington to Kansas and had proceeded, independently of the state government, to recruit "Lane's Brigade," composed of the Third and Fourth Kansas Volunteer infantry regiments and the Fifth Kansas Cavalry.[28] During Price's raid on Lexington in September, 1861, Lane had developed a unique type of warfare. Rather than strike at Price, the Grim Chieftain had determined to follow in his rear and punish all Missourians who had welcomed the State Guard as it marched north to the river. Informing his troops, largely composed of the most desperate raiders and fighters of the earlier border troubles, that "everything disloyal, from a Shanghai rooster to a Durham cow, must be cleaned out," Lane left Fort Lincoln near Fort Scott and leisurely followed Price's army.[29] As soon as the Kansans entered Missouri, they determined that not a person loyal to the Union lay in their line of march; all should be punished. Passing out General Frémont's martial law-emancipation proclamation in its original form, the

[27] Margaret Leech, *Reveille in Washington, 1860-1865* (Garden City, New York, 1945), 59; Monaghan, *Civil War on the Western Border*, 24.

[28] William E. Connelley, *A Standard History of Kansas and Kansans* (5 vols., Chicago, New York, 1918), II, 876-77, 886. Hereinafter cited Connelley, *Kansas*.

[29] Monaghan, *Civil War on the Western Border*, 195.

column turned into nothing but a looting expedition. Anything that could be carried comfortably was taken: horses,
cows, furniture, fowl, clothing, jewelry, and slaves. No family was spared, the homes of men serving with Union forces
being robbed with all others. On September 22, 1861, Lane's
thieves reached Osceola, the county seat of St. Clair County,
a little town of some two thousand people, where Price had
from time to time had his headquarters.

As Osceola the Kansas Brigade established its outlaw reputation on the border. When military supplies and munitions
were found in warehouses, they furnished Lane with the excuse to destroy the town. Teams and wagons were first
stolen and then loaded with the movable goods of the community. Nine citizens were courtmartialed and shot, and
then all but three buildings in the town were set on fire,
including the courthouse which burned to the ground with
all the county records. The Kansans left Osceola with 300 of
their force drunk in wagons, 350 horses and mules, and 200
Negroes. A million dollars' worth of property had been
stolen or destroyed, and Osceola, one of the largest towns
in western Missouri, had ceased to exist. The "Grim Chieftain" led his force as rapidly as he could toward the Kansas
line and Lawrence, where the loot was divided, burning
houses as he went. His raid was condemned in the strongest
terms by Governor Charles Robinson of Kansas, and by
Major W. E. Prince, who commanded Federal troops at Fort
Leavenworth.[30]

The Fourth Kansas Regiment of Lane's Brigade was led by
Colonel William Weer, the Third by Colonel James Montgomery, the notorious border raider of the 1850's. Along
with Lane, Jim Montgomery was to become one of the most

30 *Ibid.*, 195-96; Britton, *The Civil War on the Border*, I, 148; *O. R.*, Series
1, Vol. III, 469, 482; Wendell H. Stephenson, *The Political Career of General
James H. Lane* (Topeka, 1930), 110-17.

hated men in the border. Born in Ohio in 1814, he had taught school in Kentucky, and in 1852 moved with his family to Pike County, Missouri. Tall, black bearded, beady eyed, Montgomery was a rabid abolitionist and a sometime Campbellite preacher. He soon found that he could not stand the slaveholding society of Missouri, and in 1853 moved to Jackson and then Bates County to await the opening of the Kansas Territory which he was determined should be free. In 1854 he purchased a claim near Mound City, Kansas, and in a short time was leader of the free-state men in that vicinity. In 1857 he formed a "Self Protective Company" and raided in Kansas and Missouri until forced to disband by Federal troops. Jim Montgomery was a fanatic; he saw himself to be the hand of the Lord in striking down slavery and all those who supported it.[31]

Dr. Charles R. Jennison was one of Jim Montgomery's closest friends. Born in New York, Jennison was reared in Wisconsin where he studied and practiced medicine for a time. In 1857 he moved to Mound City where he found himself in sympathy with John Brown and Montgomery. He, too, formed a vigilante committee and gained free-soil notoriety in 1860 by hanging two Missourians he caught trying to recover slaves in order to obtain rewards offered for them in Missouri. Dapper and intelligent, his bearing was ostentatious and vain. An abolitionist, "Doc" Jennison was more venal than Montgomery and had a reputation along the border as a peerless horse thief. For many years the pedigree of good horses of doubtful title in Iowa and Illinois was described as "out of Missouri by Jennison," a sour joke for Missourians. In February, 1861, Jennison was made captain of the Mound City guards, and in the spring took his command on occupation duties into Missouri. In September he was commissioned a lieutenant colonel, and his gang was

[31] Connelley, *Kansas*, II, 693-94; III, 1274-75.

named the Seventh Kansas Volunteer Cavalry, commonly called Jennison's "Jayhawkers." [32]

Lane, Montgomery, and Jennison. A fantastic set of zealots and scoundrels. These were the men who would occupy Missouri and represent the Union military forces along the Kansas border during the summer and fall of 1861 and 1862. These were the men who would start the guerrilla war on the western border.

[32] Connelley, *Kansas,* III, 1274-75.

3

The Union Military Occupation of Missouri

J IM LANE, Jim Montgomery, and Doc Jennison hated Missourians because of the border war of 1857. Whenever they came into Missouri, or were ordered into Missouri, they came primarily for revenge and loot. For the most part, they seemed incapable of seeing that thousands of Missourians were loyal to the Union, in her armies, and entitled to her protection. Taking advantage of the defenseless border in the summer and fall of 1861, these armed Kansas gangs swarmed through western and central Missouri. Cloaked with the authority of the Union army, and dressed in blue uniforms as rapidly as they could obtain them, these men created chaos and hatred that existed for years.

If any of these units could be described as the worst, it was

Jennison's "Jayhawkers." Wherever they went, and they were at first completely unopposed, there was a field day of riotous revenge, murder, looting, and arson. Most of the troopers of the Seventh Kansas Cavalry were simply thieves, a fact admitted by the highest United States army officers on the border in 1861 and 1862.

The Jayhawkers first made their appearance in Missouri around Kansas City in June, 1861. At that time, having only the status of a home guard unit, they were ordered out of the state by Captain W. E. Prince, who commanded the United States troops in that area. In July Jennison's men were employed as advance guard by Major Robert T. Van Horn on an expedition against Harrisonville, Cass County, where pro-Southern forces were supposedly gathering. The Jayhawkers advanced so rapidly on Harrisonville, which held not an enemy soldier, that they had most of the stores broken into and robbed before Van Horn's main body arrived. Included in their loot were all of the papers of the Cass County sheriff and a considerable amount of county money. Large quantities of merchandise were packed into stolen wagons and dispatched to Kansas. Colonel Henry Younger, a wealthy Jackson County stock raiser and farmer, lost four thousand dollars in carriages and wagons and forty saddle horses from a livery stable he operated in the town. Henry Younger, the father of Coleman and James Younger, who would shortly be heard from along the border, was a staunch pro-Union man completely opposed to secession.[1]

According to George Caleb Bingham, famous Missouri artist, and unconditional Union man, the Harrisonville raid was only an appetizer for Jennison. Bingham, who at the

[1] James S. Rollins Manuscript Collection, State Historical Society of Missouri, Columbia. Letter from George C. Bingham to Rollins, dated February 12, 1862. Hereinafter cited Rollins Papers. See also John N. Edwards, *Noted Guerrillas, or the Warfare on the Border* (St. Louis, 1877), 136-38. Hereinafter cited *Noted Guerrillas*.

time was a captain in Van Horn's command and later was state treasurer of the provisional government, was outraged when Jennison was made a lieutenant colonel and authorized to recruit the Seventh Cavalry. Writing in protest to Missouri's congressmen, James S. Rollins and William A. Hall, the fiery painter said:

Up to the period of these transactions at Harrisonville, the brigand leader had been murdering and stealing "upon his own hook," having been repelled whenever he attempted to find shelter for his crimes under color of governmental authority. . . . But we next contemplate him as having undergone a complete transition from the condition of an outlaw, abhorred and avoided by honorable minds, to that of an officer in the United States Army, empowered to raise a regiment of cavalry, with a view, as it seemed, to test, upon a more extensive scale, the efficacy of indiscriminate pillage and rapine in crushing out rebellion.[2]

For a time in the late summer of 1861 Lane's Brigade and Jennison's men had stayed in Kansas where they belonged, but they presented a continuous threat. Governor Robinson of Kansas, entirely unable to control them, wrote General Frémont of his fears in September.

It is true small parties of secessionists are to be found in Missouri, but we have good reason to know that they do not intend to molest Kansas in force until Jackson shall be reinstated as governor of Missouri. . . . But what we do have to fear, and do fear, is that Lane's brigade will get up a war by going over the line, committing depredations, and then returning into our State. This course will force the secessionists to put down any force we may have for their own protection, and in this they will be joined by nearly all the Union men of Missouri.[3]

In November, 1861, Jennison was ordered to march his regiment from Leavenworth into Jackson County, Missouri,

[2] Rollins Papers. This letter was written from Jefferson City on February 12, 1862.

[3] *O. R.*, Series 1, Vol. III, 468-69.

following a guerrilla attack on a government train proceeding from Kansas City to Sedalia. This was what the Jayhawkers had been waiting for, and to pave their way, Doc Jennison whipped up a proclamation for the people of western Missouri:

I have come among you with my command, under the authority of the General Government, for the purpose of protecting the Supply Trains and all other property of the United States Government.

For four months our armies have marched through your country; your professed friendship has been a fraud; your oaths of allegiance have been shams and perjuries. You fed the rebel army, you act as spies while claiming to be true to the Union.

But neutrality is ended. If you are patriots you must fight; if you are traitors you will be punished. The time for fighting has come. Every man who feeds, harbors, protects, or in any way gives aid and comfort to the enemies of the Union will be held responsible for his treason with his life and property.[4]

When this proclamation was printed in the *Liberty Tribune* on November 22, 1861, the editor commented rather gingerly that the border counties were quiet and no trouble had been anticipated from secessionists. George Bingham pointed out, "As but a limited number, comparatively, of any community are in a condition for service as soldiers, it is to be seen that he thus carefully left much the largest portion, even of our loyal citizens, as subjects upon which to indulge in his favorite pastime of murder, robbery and arson."[5] The proclamation must have sent a feeling of despair through thousands of Missourians who had at one time supported the Jackson administration or served in the State Guard, but had returned to take oaths of allegiance to the Union and posted heavy bonds for their loyalty.

When Jennison marched his Seventh Kansas Cavalry

[4] *Liberty Tribune*, November 22, 1861.
[5] Rollins Papers, letter to J. S. Rollins and W. A. Hall, February 12, 1862.

through Kansas City toward Independence, that pro-Union town treated the Jayhawkers as though they were a funeral procession. The most shocking aspect of Jennison's retinue to the people of Kansas City was an entire company of Negroes, armed, mounted, and uniformed as soldiers of the Union. They were led by a slave who had been enticed away from a master who was widely known for unwavering loyalty to the Union.[6] The sight of uniformed Negroes was a blow to Missourians. Here was a perfect example of what Southern radicals for years had maintained would happen if slaves were given any liberty. The fear of an armed slave insurrection was real and always present in slaveholding communities.

The Jayhawkers moved on toward Independence, burning a mill and five or six dwellings on the way. Surrounding the town, the county seat of Jackson County, Jennison's men converged, forcing all male inhabitants of the village at bayonet and saber point into the courthouse square. A resident of the town was then selected to separate secessionist from Union citizens. This impromptu judge must have been afflicted with badly crossed eyes, as George Bingham, describing the event, stated, "notwithstanding a very remarkable obliqueness of vision by which he was distinguished, no gross injustice was done in the performance of the delicate task which had been imposed upon him." Those men who were determined to have, or to have had, secessionist proclivities were then forced to take an oath to support the Union. While the male population of Independence was gathered at the courthouse square, the rest of the "Self Sustaining Regiment," as it was locally known, robbed the private homes of the place. Watches, jewelry, shawls, scarfs, comforts, blankets, and counterpanes were packed up and carried off. Kansas winters were cold.[7]

6 Rollins Papers, letter from Bingham to Rollins and Hall, February 12, 1862.

7 Rollins Papers, letter to Rollins and Hall, dated February 12, 1862.

The Seventh Kansas Cavalry stayed in Jackson County throughout December, 1861. During that time they stole wagonloads of dry goods, groceries, and drugs, and every horse, mule, and conveyance they could lay hands on. Farmers were held up in daylight and their purses taken, men were beaten, and where resistance was met, homes were burned—even those of men in the Union service. The Jayhawkers did not shy at cold-blooded murder. While at Independence they killed at least two men, one for refusing to give them liquor, the other for trying to save his mules by swimming them across the Missouri River. On their march back to Kansas City they arrested and then shot Joseph Williams, a former citizen of Clay County, whom the *Liberty Tribune* on November 22, 1861, stated was "a quiet useful citizen, honestly favoring (merely in sentiment) the South."

The outrages committed by Lane's Brigade and Jennison's Jayhawkers filtered back to Halleck at his St. Louis headquarters. "Old Brains" reacted typically, and began corresponding with almost everyone who might be concerned with the situation. In December, 1861, he wrote General McClellan:

The conduct of the forces under Lane and Jennison has done more for the enemy in this State than could have been accomplished by 20,000 of his own army. I receive almost daily complaints of outrages committed by these men in the name of the United States, and the evidence is so conclusive as to leave no doubt of their correctness. It is rumored that Lane has been made a brigadier-general. I cannot conceive of a more injudicious appointment. It will take 20,000 men to counteract its effect in this State, and, moreover, is offering a premium for rascality and robbing generally.[8]

On January 18, 1862, Halleck informed Lorenzo Thomas, Adjutant General of the United States Army, that he had

[8] *O. R.*, Series 1, Vol. VIII, 448-49.

ordered General Pope to drive Lane's Brigade and Jennison's men, who were then stationed in Jackson and Lafayette counties, out of Missouri. He bluntly stated,

I have directed General Pope to drive them out, or, if they resist, to disarm them and hold them prisoners. They are no better than a band of robbers; they cross the line, rob, steal, plunder, and burn whatever they can lay their hands upon. They disgrace the name and uniform of American soldiers and are driving good Union men into the ranks of the secession army. Their conduct within the last six months has caused a change of 20,000 votes in this State. If the Government countenances such acts by screening the perpetrators from justice and by rewarding with office their leaders and abettors it may resign all hopes of a pacification of Missouri.[9]

By the dawn of 1862 the Kansans were under attack by almost every Union man of influence in Missouri. The day before Christmas, 1861, Governor Gamble had written General Halleck, calling attention to the ravishment of the western border of Missouri, and begging for stronger discipline over the Kansans.[10] Through the efforts of United States Representative James S. Rollins, the situation was brought to the attention of Secretary of War Stanton, and Assistant Inspector Major A. Baird of the United States army was ordered out to the border to report on conditions. On February 11, 1862, General McClellan wrote Secretary Stanton that Baird's report indicated that Lane's Brigade and Jennison's Jayhawkers would not obey orders to desist from stealing property and committing outrages in Missouri. Baird recommended that the Kansas troops be removed to another theatre of the war.[11] The situation was ticklish at Washington, however, as Jim Lane was a powerful Republican sena-

9 *O. R.*, Series 1, Vol. VIII, 507.
10 See Gamble Papers.
11 *O. R.*, Series 1, Vol. VIII, 552.

tor, and it was late in the spring of 1862 before Jennison was arrested and relieved of his command and Montgomery was transferred to the East and put in charge of Negro volunteers. Jennison became a Radical Republican hero and pet and was reinstated to command on the border in 1863. Worse, the personnel of Lane's Brigade and Jennison's regiment remained on duty in Missouri and along the Kansas line throughout most of the war. Their new commanders were not much more interested in discipline than the old ones had been.[12]

General Halleck was promoted out of command of the Department of Missouri on March 11, 1862. He realized at last the tragedy which had taken place in Missouri. In a letter to General McClellan, in which he attempted to place the blame for the terrible situation in his command on the authorities in Washington, he whined:

I am satisfied that the authorities in Washington do not understand the present condition of affairs in Missouri. The conduct of our troops during Frémont's campaign, and especially the course pursued by those under Lane and Jennison, has turned against us many thousands who were formerly Union men.[13]

Other men in Missouri could see a little more plainly than Halleck what had really happened along the western border. On January 22, 1862, George Bingham informed Representative Rollins that Jennison should be executed, for "if he were hung Price would lose thereby the best recruiting officer he has ever had." Union Brigadier General Richard C. Vaughan, who commanded various subdistricts in central Missouri, wrote United States Attorney General Edward Bates describing conditions:

12 Connelley, *Kansas,* II, 886-87, III, 1232, 1274-75; *Liberty Tribune,* April 25, 1862; *The Daily Kansas City Western Journal of Commerce,* April 20, 1862. Hereinafter cited *K. C. Journal.*
13 *O. R.,* Series 1, Vol. VIII, 818-19.

It is a fact well known to me that hundreds of people of Jackson and Cass Counties are true and loyal men; they have already been robbed of their property, insulted and in many cases murdered by these troops from Kansas. The policy has caused hundreds of good men to leave their homes and fly to the bushes for protection, while others have actually joined the guerrillas as a measure of safety, believing they would be less liable to danger there than at their homes. Others, I regret to say who were in the beginning disloyal, have, under the various proclamations of the President and the Governor, returned to their homes, and, after doing so, have been ruthlessly shot and hung by the soldiery.[14]

The population which was to create and support guerrilla warfare against the Union had grown larger and larger during the summer and winter of 1861–1862 because of the outrages perpetrated against the people of Missouri by occupying Union forces.

Brigadier General John M. Schofield took over the Department of Missouri from Halleck. Only thirty-one, John Schofield had made a brilliant record at West Point, and was on leave of absence from the army, teaching at Washington University at St. Louis when the war broke out. Serving first as Lyon's adjutant, and later as the commanding general of Governor Gamble's new Missouri State Militia, Schofield inherited an explosive situation. A plump young man with very thin full whiskers and a pious look, Schofield was competent, fair, and knew the temper of Missourians and Kansans.

Schofield was fearful of open fighting between Kansas and Missouri Union forces. He believed that the key to restoring peaceful conditions along the border, and especially in Missouri, lay in removing all out-state troops and keeping them out. To police the department Schofield bent all of his energies toward building up the Missouri State Militia, and by April, 1862, had recruited nearly fourteen thousand men

[14] *O. R.*, Series 1, Vol. XXII, Part 2, pp. 484-85.

into that force. He then revised the old military districts of Missouri to expedite his command function and to define more clearly the areas of authority and control of his subordinates.

Unfortunately, General Schofield's Union state militia, in many instances, proved as insubordinate and lawless as the troops from Kansas, Illinois, and Iowa. Most of the depredations of the Missouri militia units came from the fact that they were raised locally, and normally performed duty in their own neighborhoods. If out-state troops did not know, or misjudged, the sympathies of the people in the areas in which they served, the militia did intimately. It knew the relationships, history, and the political and economic background of most of the people in the districts in which it served. As the guerrilla war increased in fury and bitterness between 1862 and 1865, the militia became ruthless in rooting out suspected disloyalty to the Union. The militia also served as an excellent vehicle for local factions to settle old grudges which in many cases had little to do with the issues of the war. Most of the officers and men were not trained or experienced, and although they became fighting units in time, many of their mistakes were based on ignorance and the fact that they did not have the supervision of soldierly superiors. Many Missouri militia units were guilty of vicious outrages, and were to burn, loot, and murder throughout the war.

The lawless acts of the militia in 1861 and 1862 were aggravated and often caused by the fact that Missouri had not sufficient arms, uniforms, and subsistence to provide the men. As a consequence, the militia was frequently ordered to live off the country while on active duty. Provisions, horses, guns, and forage were obtained from "disloyal" people or by establishing levies.[15] Naturally the local militia group de-

15 O. R., Series 1, Vol. XIII, 13, 550-51, Series 1, Vol. VIII, 343.

termined who was loyal and who was not; injustice, hardship, and unnecessary brutality became commonplace.

So the spring of 1862 arrived with all of the northern and western parts of Missouri ready to burst into flaming irregular warfare—a warfare that would burn up and down the entire border. Military bungling and ineptitude, the revengeful acts of Union forces, and plain criminality had turned an area with good prospects for peace into a powder keg. Although not a single regular Confederate soldier stood on Missouri soil, a vast population disloyal to the Union had either been created or augmented. The time was ripe for insurrection and guerrilla activity. Adult pro-Southern men unable to join the Confederate armies in Arkansas, men who desired to remain neutral in the war, very young boys not considered of real military age, men who had served the Southern cause and been paroled, and those who had suffered wrongs at the hands of the Union military were to swarm into the brush as guerrillas in the winter of 1861 and the spring of 1862. Joined by unstable and lawless border elements, they were to become formidable enemies. Behind them and around them was a large sympathetic population of relatives and friends who would eagerly and secretly maintain and support them.

Courtesy of the State Historical Society of Missouri

GENERAL HENRY W. HALLECK

Courtesy of the State Historical Society of Missouri

GENERAL SAMUEL R. CURTIS

"ORDER NUMBER ELEVEN" BY GEORGE CALEB BINGHAM

WILLIAM C. QUANTRILL

Courtesy of the State Historical Society of Missouri

"BLOODY BILL" ANDERSON

BILL ANDERSON AND TWO OF HIS BOYS

"LITTLE ARCHIE" CLEMENT

FLETCHER TAYLOR, FRANK AND JESSE JAMES

4

William Quantrill's Guerrillas

‖‖

THE irregular Confederate military groups of the western border arose from two circumstances. Certain of them were deliberately organized and placed in operation by the Confederate commanders of the Trans-Mississippi, while others came into existence spontaneously in response to local conditions.

Of the latter type, the most notorious was the band of guerrillas raised and led by an enigmatic young man named William Clarke Quantrill. Quantrill literally wrote his name in blood across the western border between 1861 and 1863, and from his parent organization came those companies of desperate young boys captained by Bill Anderson, George Todd, William Gregg, and David Pool.

Quantrill was one of the most romantic and controversial figures of the Civil War in the west. Even today his name is far better known to the people of the midwest, especially

Missourians and Kansans, than the names of the Northern and Southern generals who led armies up and down the border. The official records of the Civil War contain hundreds of accounts concerning his activities or mentioning his name, yet this man, little more than a boy, seldom led over two hundred men. A mysterious figure, he had a brief, bloody, and tragic career. Quite evidently a courageous natural leader, he was loved by his men and by thousands of other Missourians, who never knew really who he was or where he came from. To those people who supported and fought for the Union he was a vicious reptile which had risen on the scene. In a cold military sense he was the equivalent of a small army to the western Confederacy.

William C. Quantrill, the oldest of twelve children of Thomas Henry and Caroline Clarke Quantrill, was born at Canal Dover, Ohio, on July 31, 1837. He lived only twenty-seven years, dying of wounds in a hospital at Louisville, Kentucky, on June 6, 1865. Quantrill was not a Southerner and never lived in the South. There is no substantial evidence to indicate that his people were anything but decent, above-average Ohioans. His father was a high school teacher, and there is abundant proof that Quantrill had received a much better education than the average young man on the Missouri-Kansas border. At sixteen he had become a teacher, and had taught for two years at schools in and near Canal Dover, at Mendota, Illinois, and Fort Wayne, Indiana. In 1857 at the age of nineteen he moved out to Miami County in eastern Kansas upon the urging of family friends.[1]

Quantrill arrived in Kansas Territory during its wildest period, and was soon swept up by violent currents. By all accounts Bill Quantrill was a handsome and extremely personable boy, with the typical vanity, temper, and weakness

[1] William E. Connelley, *Quantrill and the Border Wars* (Cedar Rapids, Iowa, 1910), 25-29, 35, 42, 49-50, 58, 471-83. Hereinafter cited Connelley, *Quantrill*.

of a young man cast loose in an unstable society. A slight but compactly formed boy, about five feet nine inches tall, Quantrill had fair reddish hair, was quiet spoken, sober, and had neither a fierce nor vicious outward appearance. His eyes were his only unusual feature. Cold, pale, blue, they stared flatly from beneath heavy upper lids that gave his face an almost Mongol appearance.[2] But if Quantrill looked handsome only in a commonplace way, ferocious and dangerous qualities underlay his personality. Bold and physically courageous, he was also a sham and almost completely amoral.

Upon arriving in Kansas, Quantrill seems to have found the onerous duties of frontier farming not in agreement with his education or basic personality. In the fall of 1858 he joined an emigrant party and travelled out to Salt Lake City. On this trip it may be imagined that he carried and became proficient in the use of the frontier Bowie knife, Sharps rifle, and Colt revolving pistol. In mid-summer 1859 he returned to Lawrence and then kept a rural school near the free-soil community of Osawatomie, Kansas, until the spring of 1860. During this period he wrote his mother regularly. His letters, which were preserved, show fine penmanship, a sound command of grammar, and real literary ability at descriptive writing.[3] In March, 1860, his school closed, and for the remainder of the year he seems to have roamed the border in the company of Indians and free-soil toughs who made a living by gambling and theft. Some of his associates were young Lawrence abolitionists.

In the winter of 1860 Quantrill was suspected, and later

[2] Unpublished manuscript written by William H. Gregg, State Historical Society of Missouri, Columbia, Missouri, p. 2. This handwritten manuscript was written from memory by Gregg about 1900. He served as Quantrill's lieutenant from 1861 to 1864. After the war Gregg was a prominent farmer and deputy sheriff of Jackson County, Missouri.

[3] Connelley, *Quantrill*, 75.

placed under charges (which were dismissed), of stealing a horse in Lykins County, Kansas.[4] In December, fearing the law, he determined to leave Kansas, and the method he took indicated a part of his true character. During the first week of December, 1860, he joined five young Quaker abolitionists from Lawrence on a slave-stealing "freedom raid" into Jackson County, Missouri. Charles Ball, John Dean, Chalkey T. Lipsey, Albert Southwick, and Edwin Morrison composed the party. Armed with pistols and knives, these men plotted a raid on the farm of Morgan Walker, a wealthy planter. They hoped to carry Walker's twenty-six slaves back to liberty in Kansas. Bringing a wagon in which some of the Negroes were to be transported, this party crossed the state line, and on December 10, 1860, arrived in the Blue Springs neighborhood. Quantrill, ostensibly out to reconnoiter the area, traitorously rode to the Walker farm and informed Andrew Walker, the son of Morgan, of the raid. Andy Walker called in four young farm neighbors, John Tatum, Lee Koger, D. C. Williams, and one other, and with Quantrill's help arranged an ambush for the Kansans. At dusk on December 10 this self-appointed anti-slave-thief association, believing they were dealing with Montgomery, armed themselves with buckshot-loaded guns and hid in the loom room on the porch of the Walker home.

When it was quite dark Quantrill led his unsuspecting Kansas friends to the Walker home to demand the slaves. By prearrangement he was admitted, and when he was out of the line of fire, Andy Walker and his friends shot into the five men left on the porch and in the yard. Morrison fell dead. Lipsey and Dean were wounded, Lipsey seriously. Dean and Southwick fled to their horses and finally got back to Lawrence. Charles Ball returned under fire and carried Lipsey to a nearby patch of woods where the two men were hunted

[4] Connelley, *Quantrill*, 103-39, 191-95.

down and killed by Walker, Quantrill, and other men of the neighborhood a day or two later.

The bloody fight at the Walker farm was reported in the Kansas City newspapers with approval. The young Quakers were mentioned as being part of Montgomery's gang. Quantrill was referred to as a stranger who had learned of the raid and had given timely warning.[5]

Bill Quantrill became a hero to the slaveholding citizens of Jackson County and was widely received. An ingenious young man, he manufactured a tale to remove the onus of informer and turncoat from himself. He told his new Missouri friends that he was a native of Maryland who had come to Kansas to join a brother on a trip to Pike's Peak. Enroute they had been attacked by Montgomery's raiders; his brother had been killed, and he had been wounded. After recovering from his wounds he had joined Montgomery's Jayhawkers under an assumed name to seek revenge. This story was repeated up and down the border, and most of Quantrill's men always believed it to be true.[6]

Quantrill remained in Jackson County during the winter of 1860-1861, making furtive visits to Kansas where the legal and moral climate had become most unhealthy for him. As a result of the Walker raid a minuteman organization was created in Jackson County to police every township, and it is likely that Quantrill served on these patrols with other young men of the neighborhood. In the spring of 1861 he is reported to have wandered down into the Cherokee Nation where he became a friend of Joel Mayes, a war chief of the Cherokees, and to have fought with them under General Mc-Culloch at the battle of Wilson's Creek. He is also said to have taken part in the battle of Lexington in September,

[5] *Kansas City Enquirer and Star*, December 15, 1860; Kansas City, Missouri, weekly *Western Journal of Commerce*, December 30, 1860. Hereinafter cited *K. C. Journal.*
[6] *K. C. Journal*, December 13, 1860; Gregg Ms., 2-4.

1861, apparently deserting Price's army at Osceola on its retreat south. By November, 1861, with other young men, he had returned to Jackson County, tired of or disgusted with organized military service.

In mid-December Quantrill joined Andy Walker and eleven other young farmers of the Blue Springs neighborhood in the pursuit of a squad of Jennison's Jayhawkers who were out looting. Walker and his men surrounded and captured the Kansans at the house of Strawder Stone, where one of them had just struck Mrs. Stone with a pistol for protesting their robbery. To the Missourians—to most men of the West—this was a final outrage. During the entire Civil War on the border there were few reported incidents of physical violence toward women. Both guerrillas and Union soldiers rigidly maintained the frontier code of respect for white females. Bill Quantrill drew his pistol and killed the man who had struck Mrs. Stone. Two other Kansans were fatally wounded.[7]

Quantrill's skill and cold-blooded willingness to use his pistols, and, it may be presumed, his intelligence and education, soon caused him to become the ruling spirit of a few young Jackson County farmers who were being driven into armed resistance by the outrages committed by the Kansans under Lane, Montgomery, and Jennison. By Christmas, 1861, he had gathered about him ten men who were to become the first full-duty members of his pro-Confederate guerrilla organization. These were William Haller, George Todd, Joseph Gilcrist, Perry Hoy, John Little, James Little, Joseph Vaughan, William H. Gregg, James A. Hendricks, and John W. Koger. Only half of these boys were to survive the terrible guerrilla war which would soon explode on the border. Throughout January and February, 1862, Quantrill and his men rode about Jackson County, recovering cattle and horses

[7] Connelley, *Quantrill,* 200-201.

stolen by Jennison's and Montgomery's Kansans. When the opportunity was favorable they ambushed and attacked the Jayhawk patrols. In turn, they were driven into the brush and pursued by all Union troops stationed in the area. As the depredations of the Kansans increased in viciousness and scope, so did the number of recruits coming in to join the guerrillas. William Quantrill, traitor, informer, and turncoat, was becoming the symbol of Southern resistance to Union-Kansas invasion on the border. Where else could men who desired to strike a blow against the enemy go?

The first skirmish with Quantrill's guerrillas mentioned in official Union records took place near Blue Springs in Jackson County on February 1 and 2, 1862. It is evident, however, from the letter written by Captain W. S. Oliver, Seventh Missouri Infantry, to General John Pope at Otterville, that Quantrill's men had been causing trouble for a long enough period to have become notorious. Oliver's report stated:

GENERAL: I have just returned from an expedition which I was compelled to undertake in search of the notorious Quantrill and his gang of robbers in the vicinity of Blue Springs. Without mounted men at my disposal, despite numerous applications to various points, I have seen this infamous scoundrel rob mails, steal the coaches and horses, and commit other similar outrages upon society even within sight of this city. Mounted on the best horses of the country, he has defied pursuit, making his camp in the bottoms of the ——————— and Blue, and roving over a circuit of 30 miles. I mounted a company of my command and went to Blue Springs. The first night there myself, with 5 men, were ambushed by him and fired upon. We killed 2 of his men (of which he had 18 or 20) and wounded a third. The next day we killed 4 more of the worst of the gang, and before we left succeeded in dispersing them. I obtained 6 or 7 wagon loads of pork and a quantity of tobacco, hidden and preserved for the use of the Southern Army, and recovered also the valuable stagecoach, with 2 of their horses. I was absent a week, and can say that no men were ever more earnest or subject to greater privations and hardships than both the mounted men and the infantry I employed on this expedition.

Quantrill will not leave this section unless he is chastised and driven from it. I hear of him to-night 15 miles from here, with new recruits, committing outrages on Union men, a large body of whom have come in to-night, driven out by him. Families of Union men are coming into the city to-night asking of me escorts to bring in their goods and chattels, which I duly furnished.[8]

Captain Oliver succinctly analyzed the tactics of Quantrill's early guerrilla organization. The maneuvers which he observed were to become standard against Union forces on the western border. Knowing the country intimately, operating in numerous small bands, able to group and disperse quickly, the guerrillas could ambush greatly superior forces. Mounted on the best horses in the country, which they took from Union men or which were given them by Southern friends rather than have them go to Union cavalry, fed, protected, and kept informed by a large sympathetic population, they were able to tie down large forces of the enemy. A dirty, tricky total warfare was emerging on the border, a type of combat in which no quarter was asked or given, and in which every person was forced to take some side.

Quantrill's band increased in size at a steady rate in the early spring of 1862. The original members of the group, with the exception of George Todd who was a bridge mason, were farm boys, most of them in their teens. They came from some of the best rural families of western Missouri, the majority of them driven to insurrection by the treatment their people had received from the Union troops that occupied the area. Here was a type of service that attracted reckless youths and gave them a chance to play a deadly game over the roll-

[8] *O. R.*, Series 1, Vol. VIII, 57.

ing hill land and heavily wooded streams of Jackson County. Here was the opportunity to strike at a hated enemy by Indian stealth and ambush, to serve with friends and neighbors in a fighting unit without formal restrictive military discipline. Here was a service that eliminated all but the wildest rider, the best pistol shot, the boy with the least regard for personal safety.

Many young men rode with Quantrill for sheer excitement, others sought merciless revenge. Into the guerrilla camp in 1862 came Coleman Younger, eighteen years old. Cole had special reason to hate Union soldiers. In the fall of 1861 he had seen his father's liquid fortune stolen at Harrisonville and carried off to Kansas. He had not been with Quantrill long before his father, old Henry Younger, was brutally murdered by a Union officer. Colonel Younger, after attending a cattle sale at Independence, was followed from town by a squad of the Fifth Missouri Militia Cavalry under the command of a Captain Walley, shot dead, and robbed. General Ben Loan, who commanded the Central District of Missouri at the time, had Walley arrested, and ordered his court-martial at Independence. The court was not held because "Bud" Younger, as Cole was nicknamed, and others of Quantrill's men ambushed and killed the witnesses while they were on the way to the trial. Before the year was out Cole saw his home burned and his mother and her family turned out into the winter by Union soldiers. In 1864 his sixteen-year-old brother Jim joined him in the brush.[9]

Another boy recruit seeking revenge was Riley Crawford. Jeptha Crawford, Riley's father, was taken from his home near Blue Springs and shot by the Jayhawkers. After Crawford was killed Mrs. Crawford brought Riley to Quantrill's camp and asked Quantrill to make a soldier of the fourteen-

9 O. R., Series 1, Vol. XXII, Part 2, p. 80; Coleman Younger, *The Story of Cole Younger by Himself* (Chicago, 1903), 9-31.

year-old child. Little Riley Crawford was to kill every Union soldier who fell into his hands until he was shot dead at the age of sixteen in Cooper County in 1864.[10]

Many of Quantrill's men had served in the State Guard and now found they could not remain at peace. Automatically suspect, they and their families received the most brutal treatment from the Union troops. In midsummer of 1862 Quantrill's ranks were swelled by such recruits, some of whom were to become famous. Nineteen-year-old Frank James, rail thin, with flat grey eyes, crossed the river from Clay County and joined the guerrillas. In 1864 his seventeen-year-old brother, Jesse Woodson James, joined him.[11] John McCorkle, the only guerrilla to turn author, was another ex-Guardsman. In the spring of 1862 he had determined he would either have to leave the border or join Quantrill. He lived through three years of desperate fighting to write of his adventure.[12]

In addition to the men who entered Quantrill's guerrillas for protection or revenge, there is evidence that many of his troopers were, or became, neurotic and criminal. The irresponsible and undisciplined nature of guerrilla service naturally attracted the worst elements of the border society as it gave opportunity for robbery and unwarranted cruelty not present in regular military duty. Moreover, as the bloody, no-quarter warfare grew, there was a noticeable increase in the number of twisted and vicious boys such as the revenge-crazed Bill Anderson and his seventeen-year-old murderous executioner and scalper, Archie Clement.

All of these types, then, were drawn together under the baleful command of William Quantrill, a terribly dangerous

[10] Walter B. Stevens, *Centennial History of Missouri* (3 vols., St. Louis, Chicago, 1921), I, 853; Gregg Ms., 50-52.

[11] Settle, "The Development of the Jesse James Legend," 32-33.

[12] John McCorkle, *Three Years with Quantrill: A True Story* (Armstrong, Missouri, n.d.).

leader, as he was himself amoral, vicious, and ambitious. Only one question was asked them: "Will you follow orders, be true to your fellows, and kill those who serve and support the Union?" Under Quantrill's direction these young men were to shock an entire nation and to plunge the western border into three years of ghastly irregular warfare.

Quantrill's first military acts in western Missouri in the early spring of 1862 were feeble and merely harassing in nature, but as his band grew he became bolder and his objectives enlarged. On February 22, believing that there were no Union troops in the town, he rode into Independence with fifteen men. Dashing up the streets the guerrillas ran head on into a column of Union cavalry. Instead of retreating, Quantrill charged into them and began shooting right and left. From the confusing melee that resulted, William Gregg was to remember a Union cavalryman following him down the street, hacking at him unsuccessfully with a saber. The guerrillas scattered, Gabriel George and Hop Wood were shot dead from their saddles. Quantrill was wounded in the leg, but had the audacity to attend George's funeral a day or so later, calmly leaning on a cane.[13]

In late January Jennison's men had burned the little towns of Dayton in Cass County and Columbus in Johnson County, and had driven the inhabitants away.[14] In retaliation Quantrill determined to raid a town in Kansas, and on March 2 led his band to Aubry in Johnson County. Riding into the little village at night, screaming and shooting as they came on, the guerrillas looted the place of all they could carry, burned one house, and rode through Union patrols back to Missouri.[15] Kansas was now to have a taste of the medicine Lane, Jennison, and Montgomery had been giving

13 Gregg Ms., 11; Connelley, *Quantrill*, 225-28.
14 *O. R.*, Series 1, Vol. VIII, 45-47.
15 *O. R.*, Series 1, Vol. VIII, 335-36.

Missouri for months. From this date Kansas towns were considered fair game for the guerrillas.

On March 18, 1862, with Union forces combing the Jackson County area for him, Quantrill took forty men, crossed the Missouri River to Clay County and raided a small Union recruiting post at Liberty. After a fight which went on for three hours the post of eight men surrendered; a Captain Hubbard, who commanded it, was severely wounded. Quantrill paroled the Union soldiers, evidently trying to follow the rules of warfare, but an unarmed soldier named Owen Grimshaw was shot through the head when he refused to tell the guerrillas in what building the post was located. Quantrill permitted no looting or burning at Liberty, which had a large pro-Southern population, and the newspaper reports concerning this "independent armed band" indicate that they were viewed with something close to enthusiasm.[16]

Union cavalry swarmed north over the river into Clay County at about the same time the guerrillas crossed back into Jackson. On March 22, numbering nearly a hundred men, they rode up the Independence-Kansas City road and burned the bridge over the Blue River. Guarding the bridge was a Union sergeant and a tollkeeper named Allison, both of whom were captured and then shot. Allison was murdered before the eyes of his small son, and it was reported that Quantrill personally pistoled the sergeant because news of Halleck's General Order Number Two had just reached him.[17]

On March 13 Halleck had published this order from his St. Louis headquarters, specifically charging General Price with having issued commissions to "certain bandits" to form guerrilla organizations in Missouri. Order Number Two stated flatly that "every man who enlists in such an organiza-

16 *Liberty Tribune,* March 21, 1862.
17 Connelley, *Quantrill,* 238; *K. C. Journal,* March 23, 1862.

tion forfeits his life and becomes an outlaw. All persons are hereby warned that if they join any guerrilla band they will not, if captured, be treated as ordinary prisoners of war, but will be hung as robbers and murderers."[18]

Halleck's extermination orders were now being applied to Quantrill's men, and the Union troops began shooting them when they were captured. Knowledge that execution would follow capture caused the guerrillas to fight to their deaths. Few persons were taken by either side after the spring of 1862, and the most minor skirmishes were of a desperate nature.[19]

Following the killings at the Blue River bridge, Quantrill took some of his men to the farm of David Tate, about three miles from Little Santa Fe in Jackson County. News of the murders and the burned bridge soon put Kansas cavalry on his trail. Detachments of the Second Cavalry under Colonel Robert B. Mitchell and the Fourth Cavalry under Colonel William Weer and Major Charles Banzhaff were sent into southern Johnson County after him. Following their usual custom, the Kansans established headquarters at Santa Fe and then sent out patrols to arrest and question local citizens about the guerrillas. At ten o'clock on the night of March 22 a squadron of the Second Kansas, under the command of Major James M. Pomeroy, was dispatched to arrest Tate at his home. Arriving at the house Pomeroy dismounted his men, surrounded the place, and foolhardily beat on the front door demanding entrance. His answer was a Minié ball through the portal, the large soft lead slug tearing a gaping wound through his right thigh. The Major crawled from the house, and his men fired volleys into it. These shots brought screams from women and children inside, and Pomeroy or-

18 *O. R.*, Series 1, Vol. VIII, 611-12.

19 Gregg Ms., 8-9, stated Quantrill took prisoners and paroled them until March 20, 1862, when Halleck's order was applied to his men.

dered the firing stopped. Several women and children came out, and the firing was resumed. After a short time two men jumped from a window, and with their hands in the air begged to surrender. These men told the Kansans that they were not guerrillas, but that Quantrill and twenty-six of his men were inside with no intention of giving up. Seriously wounded, Pomeroy saw his chance to stamp out the guerrilla gang. The Tate house, constructed of brick, had a blind wooden ell at its rear. The ell was set on fire, and soon the whole structure was blazing, lighting up the surroundings as if it were day. The Kansas cavalry ceased firing and settled back on their carbines to pick the guerrillas off if they came out or to watch them burn. Suddenly the whole lower wall of the blazing ell was kicked out. Through the flying embers the guerrillas charged, firing their revolvers into the faces of the startled Kansans. In seconds they had broken through the Union line and were in the dense woods surrounding the place. They left only two of their number sprawled in the yard, and killed one Union trooper in their wild dash to safety. Major Pomeroy believed he saw the bodies of five more men lying in the ashes of the Tate house. Chagrined at the escape of the guerrillas, the Kansas troops closed in on the neighborhood and burned houses and outbuildings on adjacent farms. Six suspicious men were arrested and sent to Fort Leavenworth. Over twenty-five horses were captured.[20]

The fight at the Tate house was a disaster for the guerrillas. On foot they slipped through the countryside, scattering to obtain more horses. On March 26, 1862, they were mounted again, and on the afternoon of that day over two hundred of them swept down on the Union post at Warrensburg, the county seat of Johnson County, Missouri. Warrensburg was held by Major Emory Foster and a detachment of sixty men of the Seventh Missouri Cavalry. Foster had forti-

[20] *O. R.*, Series 1, Vol. VIII, 347; *Daily K. C. Journal*, March 26, 27, 1862.

fied the brick county courthouse and had his men posted behind a thick board stockade surrounding the building. A surprise charge failed, and Quantrill was beaten off into the dusk, leaving nine of his men dead on the square and carrying away at least seventeen wounded. At dawn of the twenty-seventh the guerrillas made another half-hearted attempt to rush the position, but failed to carry it again. Major Foster and ten of his men were wounded, two were killed. The guerrillas raced back into Jackson County and disbanded.[21] Quantrill had learned his first lesson about attacking brick walls and stockades, but the border was shocked over the surprise blow at a major Union post.

On March 30 the guerrillas held a rendezvous at the farm of Samuel C. Clark, three miles southeast of Stoney Point in Jackson County near the hamlet of Pink Hill. There they were attacked by Captain Albert P. Peabody with sixty-five men of D Company, First Missouri Cavalry. On nearing Pink Hill Peabody split his force, and as he and his troop passed the Clark house, they were fired on. Peabody dismounted and attacked. The guerrillas, evidently feeling that the odds were about even, held and fought. A runner was sent back to bring up the other half of the Union patrol, and when it arrived, Peabody began to rush the house. Outnumbered and separated from their horses, the guerrillas dispersed into the woods on foot. Six of them were found dead in and near the house; the others took their wounded off with them. Peabody had only three men wounded, but by the time the guerrillas retreated, the shooting had so aroused the countryside that the captain found himself in a very hot spot. Coming in from all directions, the Clarks' neighbors began to snipe at the Union force from long range with Sharps rifles. Captain Peabody estimated that by the time the guerrillas had escaped, his force was being shot at by over a hundred men.

21 *Daily K. C. Journal,* April 2, 1862; *Liberty Tribune,* April 4, 1862.

The Union patrol sullenly backed off to Pink Hill, taking twenty captured horses and, no doubt, wrote the Clark neighborhood off as of not much value to the Union. As a sop they burned Sam Clark's house and outbuildings.[22]

As a result of the violent skirmishing of the preceding two weeks a mass meeting was called at Independence on April 19 by Colonel Egbert B. Brown, commanding the Missouri militia in Jackson and Cass counties. The activities of Quantrill and Jennison were discussed, and Colonel Brown pled for a return to quiet and order. He assured the gathing that Union troop depredations would cease, and offered in evidence Jennison's arrest and removal from command. Resolutions were passed requesting all men of Jackson County to put down their arms and leave law enforcement to the Missouri State Militia.[23] Unfortunately, the role of Southern guerrilla soldiers was much too appealing to many western Missouri boys.

Quantrill answered the Independence mass meeting with a proclamation of his own in which he advised the Union settlers in the county not to plant crops, as they would not be around to harvest them when autumn came. The cheek of the guerrilla leader jolted the commander of the Central District, Brigadier General James Totten, into official notice of the insurrection that was rapidly sweeping the western half of his district. "Old Bottle Nose" Totten, as he was affectionately known by his soldiers because of a handsome red proboscis and his extremely convivial habits, sighted down on Quantrill with a special order on April 21. It stated in part:

I. It is represented on reliable authority at these headquarters that bands of jayhawkers, guerrillas, marauders, murderers, and every species of outlaw are infesting to an alarming extent all the

[22] O. R., Series 1, Vol. VIII, 357-58; K. C. Journal, April 5, 1862.
[23] K. C. Journal, April 20, 1862.

southeastern portion of Jackson County, and that persons of influence and wealth in these vicinities are knowingly harboring and thus encouraging (if not more culpably connected with) these bands of desperadoes. A prairie known as the "Doctor Lee Prairie," its borders and surroundings, are mentioned as the haunts of these outlaws, and the farmers generally in these neighborhoods are said to be knowing to and encouraging the lawless acts of these guerrillas, &c., as mentioned above. Murders and robberies have been committed; Union men threatened and driven from their homes; the U. S. mails have been stopped; farmers have been prohibited planting by the proclamation of a well-known and desperate leader of these outlaws by the name of Quantrill, and the whole country designated reduced to a state of anarchy. This state of things must be terminated and the guilty punished. All those found in arms and opposition to the laws and legitimate authorities, who are known familiarly as guerrillas, jayhawkers, murderers, marauders, and horse-thieves, will be shot down by the military upon the spot when found perpetrating their foul acts.[24]

Quantrill's men were particularly successful in disrupting Union communications in western Missouri during the spring of 1862. By the middle of April Jackson County was for weeks almost isolated from the rest of the state. On April 18, 1862, the *Kansas City Journal* remarked that an entire company of Union cavalry was being detailed to escort the mail to Pleasant Hill in northern Cass County, and complained, "We have had no mail from St. Louis for three weeks." Putting the mail carriers under troop escort, however, simply gave Quantrill's men additional targets to shoot at from ambush. This type of warfare was dangerous, harassing, and demoralizing. The Union patrols never seemed able to put their fingers on a skulking, deadly enemy that killed their men and then disappeared. Every bush and tree, every pass and ravine, every stream ford carried the threat of hid-

24 *O. R.*, Series 2, Vol. III, 468.

den enemy riflemen observing each blue-clad trooper over open sights. A report written by a Captain Cochran of the Seventh Missouri Cavalry illustrates the stark deadliness of the situation. Detailed on June 11, 1862, to carry the mail between Independence and Harrisonville in Cass County, Cochran and twenty-four troopers were ambushed. Cochran's report read:

We had proceeded some 10 miles when I learned that some of Quantrill's men had been seen in the vicinity. I proceeded very slowly and cautiously, with six men riding by file as an advance. They had proceeded only a short distance when they were fired upon, 2 of them being killed on the spot and 3 dangerously wounded. I was about fifty yards in the rear with 18 men. We charged in the brush and routed them and then dismounted and searched the brush, and fired at them a number of times. I do not know what their loss was, as I had to leave to take care of the mail. The mail is safe.[25]

Lieutenant Colonel James T. Buel, commanding the Seventh Cavalry at Independence, was outraged. Evening after evening his patrols came in with one or two of his troopers slung dead over their horses and others held wounded in their saddles by their comrades. This was not warfare; this was butchery. Reporting the Cochran ambush to Central District Headquarters at Jefferson City, Buel wrote:

The mail arrived safely at Harrisonville, but the carrier dared not come back with escort. I am unwilling that any more of my men shall be murdered escorting this mail. I have therefore ordered it to be carried for the present by secessionists. I shall hold them accountable for its safe transmittal. Have also cautioned the postmaster not to send any valuables or important dispatches in this mail, but by the way of St. Louis. I am keeping my troops constantly on the move, leaving the post at times so much exposed that it gives me some uneasiness.[26]

[25] O. R., Series 1, Vol. XIII, 121-22.
[26] O. R., Series 1, Vol. XIII, 121.

It may be presumed that the "secessionists" whom Colonel Buel drafted as mail carriers soon decided that they would be about as safe in the brush with Quantrill as they were in Union mail employment.

Throughout June and July Quantrill's men ran wild in western Missouri. Their number increased each day. They ambushed the Little Blue River ferry, mail escorts and patrols in Jackson, Johnson, and Cass counties. June 22 saw them swarming on the Missouri River steamboat *Little Blue,* which they caught by surprise at a landing near Sibley. Forty sick and wounded Union soldiers were threatened and shoved around, and a large quantity of military supplies was carried away. Major Eliphalet Bredett, commanding the Seventh Cavalry post at Lexington, Lafayette County, was sent after the guerrillas. On July 3 he informed his adjutant that as a result of a week's scout into western Lafayette and eastern Jackson counties he had arrested and brought in to the provost marshal at Lexington 107 prisoners, all "except two or three" of whom could be proved guilty of treason. He had recovered articles taken from the *Little Blue* from cellars, outhouses, and haystacks at Sibley, Wellington, and Napoleon on the Missouri River. He had not run across an armed guerrilla. Quantrill was reported twelve miles south of his line of march.[27] The *Little Blue* was not damaged, but it gained the distinction of being the first of a long list of Missouri River boats that the guerrillas were to attack or capture as the war went on.

The mysterious success of Quantrill's band in operating under the noses of the Union forces was explained in a typical editorial fashion by the *Kansas City Journal* on June 17, 1862. Remarking that the guerrillas were harbored and supplied by pro-Southern men who had taken loyalty oaths and given bond to the Union, the paper stated that ". . . the

27 *O. R.,* Series 1, Vol. XIII, 131-32.

banditti have a complete system of espionage over the infested district. Their spys [*sic*] may frequently be seen upon high points going through such gyrations as to leave no doubt that they have a perfect system of signals among them, by which the approach of troops is instantly communicated over a large tract of country."

As the tempo of the partisan war in western Missouri quickened, so did the ferocity and the number of men engaged increase. On July 8, 1862, Major James O. Gower, commanding a detachment of the First Iowa Cavalry at Clinton, Henry County, learned that Quantrill with some two hundred men was in camp on Sugar Creek near Wadesburg, Cass County. Gower sent out a patrol of ninety men led by Lieutenants R. M. Reynolds, Foster, Bishop, and Wisenand. Their orders were to strike the guerrilla bivouac in a surprise dawn attack.

At sunrise of July 9 the Iowa Cavalry arrived on Sugar Creek and found Quantrill's camp. Lieutenant Bishop led a charge with the advance party of the patrol without waiting for the main body to come up. The guerrillas beat him off easily. Another charge was mounted against the now thoroughly alerted partisans which cost the Union force several wounded. Realizing that they were involved with a superior enemy that was beginning to encircle them, the Iowans broke off the action and limped back to Clinton.

When his chewed-up patrol rode into Clinton with their wounded slung over their horses, Major Gower was infuriated. He rushed dispatch riders to Harrisonville, Cass County, and Warrensburg in Johnson County, ordering the Union posts at those towns to send all available troops to join him the following day at the Lotspeich farm near the guerrilla camp. Gower's tactics were excellent, for he was concentrating cavalry on Quantrill from all directions of the compass. At five o'clock on the morning of the tenth, Gower, with four officers and seventy-five men of the First Iowa, arrived at the Lotspeich farm. There he found a detachment of sixty-five men of the First Iowa under Captain William H. Ankeny, and sixty-five men of the Seventh Missouri Cavalry led by Captain William A. Martin. These troops had come from Harrisonville to meet him. In an hour his force was joined by sixty-three additional men of the First Missouri Cavalry from Warrensburg, commanded by Captain Martin Kehoe. The four units moved cautiously through the dense woods along Sugar Creek to Quantrill's camp and found it vacated. Gower then split his command into its original components in an attempt to pick up the line of the guerrillas' march. At two o'clock a messenger rushed in to him from Kehoe, who reported that he was pursuing Quantrill east of Rose Hill in Johnson County along the Big Creek bottom. Gower called in his elements and galloped through a fiery July afternoon to join Kehoe at 7:00 P.M. on the Hornsby farm at the edge of Cass County. Riding in an arc Quantrill and his men had eaten at Hornsby's, and with their horses badly jaded had gone on north into the dusk to camp. Major Gower, having ridden nearly fifty miles that day, bivouacked. He felt certain that he could strike the guerrillas with a rested force early the next morning.

July 11 dawned clear and blistering hot. Martin Kehoe and his Missouri cavalry were the first to saddle in the Union camp. It is quite likely that, having chased the guerrillas all the preceding day, Kehoe was determined his men were to have the honor of striking the initial blow at the hated Quantrill. At any rate, in direct disobedience of Major Gower's orders, he and his company slipped out of the Iowa bivouac and went up the guerrilla trail. Six miles west of Pleasant Hill in Cass County he came on the Quantrill pickets, exchanged shots, and sent a messenger back to Gower reporting the enemy on the farm of a man named Sears.

Kehoe pressed on rapidly, and seeing only a few men near the Sears house, which was located in a clearing in the timber, ordered a charge. The little column of the First Missouri was halted, sabers were drawn, and with a cheer the blue-shirted cavalrymen spurred up a lane toward the Sears house. Captain Kehoe rode at the head of his men, waving them on with his sword.

Quantrill's men ran about wildly in the yard of the Sears place, pretending surprise at the Union charge. The wily guerrilla had, of course, prepared an ambush. As Kehoe and his men roared up the lane, they were suddenly fired upon from all sides. Part of the enemy was in the brush on his flanks, others raised up from the front yard and shot over a rail fence. The guerrillas had held their fire until the first Union troopers were nearly to the house. One ripping volley knocked the first six men in the charge dead from their saddles. Nine others were wounded, including Kehoe, who was shot through the shoulder. At guerrilla William Gregg's suggestion, Quantrill personally opened the yard gate and the riderless Union horses galloped into the lot.[28]

Kehoe and his men fell back down the lane in disorder, shooting right and left at an unseen enemy. The wounded Captain got his men dismounted and opened fire on the guerrillas at short range with his carbines. The Sears clearing was too open to fight from, so Quantrill mounted his men and fell back into a series of ravines at the rear of the place. He did not know heavy Union reinforcements were coming up to support Kehoe.

For nearly three hours the guerrillas and the First Missouri exchanged shots, the Union forces desperately outnumbered.

At eleven o'clock Major Gower and his men pounded up. A detachment of the First Iowa was sent around to flank

28 Gregg Ms., 17.

Quantrill, and the entire Union command was then dismounted and ordered to advance on the ravines. The resulting clash was furious and bloody. No quarter was asked or given.

Gower's men rushed the heavy brush in small squads. As soon as they entered the undergrowth, an equal number of the guerrillas would rise with pistols to meet them. The Union cavalrymen used their sabers and carbines, Quantrill's men revolvers, Bowie knives, and, as their ammunition ran low, clubs and rocks. Within two hours the superior discipline and handling of the Union force told on Quantrill, who was out of his element fighting on foot. A few at a time, his desperate thirst-crazed men broke out of the ravines. Retreating on foot and horse, they took most of their wounded toward the Blue River. Major Gower did not follow them up. His force was used up by the long march, the fierce heat, and the bloody fighting. Proportionately his losses were heavy, twenty-six men killed and thirty-five wounded, many badly. Because of the undergrowth and rough terrain it was believed many of the dead would not be located until the crows and buzzards came in. The Union force held the field, but Quantrill and most of his men had managed to escape.[29] On July 12 Gower's command limped back to Pleasant Hill where he buried his dead and set up a hospital for his wounded. No guerrilla prisoners were taken, and the *Liberty Tribune* reported that signed loyalty oaths were found on the bodies of five of Quantrill's men.[30]

29 *O. R.*, Series 1, Vol. XIII, 154-60.
30 *Liberty Tribune*, July 18, 1862.

5

Porter Raids in North Missouri

‖‖‖

TOWARD the first of July, 1862, General Thomas C. Hindman, who had succeeded Van Dorn as the commander of the Confederate District of Arkansas, activated strategic plans which were to intensify the tragedy of the war on the border. Tom Hindman was the most able general to serve in the Trans-Mississippi Department. Unlike the officers who followed him, he realized that the Confederacy needed a third front west of the Mississippi, and he set about energetically to make Arkansas a strong military base. Hindman conceived his strategic plan in three phases. First, he would gather the munitions and supplies of war to provide the logistical support necessary for a major army. Second, he would acquire and train the men to form an army. Third, with an army he would invade Missouri and flank the Union forces on the Mississippi.[1]

[1] Monaghan, *Civil War on the Western Border*, 251; O'Flaherty, *General Jo Shelby*, 129-31.

To obtain men for his army, Hindman put the draft into rigid effect in Arkansas, and rounded up the many deserters in that state. At the same time he sent officers north into Missouri to recruit and enroll troops, sponsor guerrilla warfare, and finally, to bring back as many men to Arkansas as was possible by fall.

Tom Hindman believed in the military value of guerrilla warfare. He had utilized it against General Curtis' march across Arkansas to Helena following the Confederate defeat at Pea Ridge. Now he intended to set the border ablaze with guerrilla organizations, and to explode occupied Missouri in General Schofield's face. In order to do this, he had to follow, on the surface at least, the detailed directives of the Confederate War Department concerning partisan warfare. A more important task was to accomplish his mission before it came too much to the attention of President Jefferson Davis, who took a personal, and usually a crippling interest, in all Confederate military affairs.

Jefferson Davis did not believe in guerrilla warfare. Such service was too disorganized, too free of restriction and control, too lacking in petty detail for him to recognize its merit in the western theatre. Davis had not in any way approved of General Price's use of guerrillas in Missouri in the summer and fall of 1861. In December of that year he had informed W. P. Harris, a Missouri delegate to the Confederate Congress, that the future conduct of the war in that state "is therefore to be on a scale of very different proportions than that of the partisan warfare witnessed during the past summer and fall."[2] However, in an act approved April 21, 1862, by the Confederate Congress, President Davis was authorized to commission officers with authority to form bands of partisan rangers. By order of the War Department on April 28, this Partisan Ranger Act was interpreted in such a manner as to give the commanders of the Confederate military de-

[2] *O. R.*, Series 1, Vol. VIII, 701.

partments in which such units were employed the first opportunity to pass on all applications for irregular service.[3]

The Confederate Partisan Ranger Act was just what General Tom Hindman needed for his district. For its best application west of the Mississippi the general felt it should be liberalized a bit, and adapted a little more closely to local conditions. Accordingly, on July 17, 1862, Hindman published at his headquarters at Little Rock his own guerrilla act. This order was to give Quantrill and others like him some legality for organizing partisan bands. It read:

I. For the more effectual annoyance of the enemy upon our rivers and in our mountains and woods all citizens of this district who are not subject to conscription are called upon to organize themselves into independent companies of mounted men or infantry, as they prefer, arming and equipping themselves, and to serve in that part of the district to which they belong.

II. When as many as 10 men come together for this purpose they may organize by electing a captain, 1 sergeant, 1 corporal, and will at once commence operations against the enemy without waiting for special instructions. Their duty will be to cut off Federal pickets, scouts, foraging parties, and trains, and to kill pilots and others on gunboats and transports, attacking them day and night, and using the greatest vigor in their movements. As soon as the company attains the strength required by law it will proceed to elect the other officers to which it is entitled. All such organizations will be reported to these headquarters as soon as practicable. They will receive pay and allowances for subsistence and forage for the time actually in the field, as established by the affidavits of their captains.

III. These companies will be governed in all respects by the same regulations as other troops. Captains will be held responsible for the good conduct and efficiency of their men, and will report to these headquarters from time to time.[4]

---

3 *O. R.*, Series 4, Vol. I, 1094, 1098.

4 *O. R.*, Series 1, Vol. XIII, 835. Citizens of Missouri were not subject to conscription as there was no Confederate government in the state. However, the

With Confederate War Department red tape thus neatly cut, Tom Hindman proceeded to select the officers he wanted to send to Missouri to start guerrilla activities. Among those he chose were Colonel Upton Hays, Colonel John T. Hughes, Colonel Joseph C. Porter, Colonel J. Vard Cockrell, Colonel John T. Coffee, Colonel Gideon W. Thompson, Colonel Warner Lewis, Colonel J. A. Poindexter, and Captain Joseph O. Shelby. These men were to commission guerrilla officers and organizations wherever possible. Singly, or with small commands, they passed through the Union lines and made their way into Missouri during the summer of 1862.

General Schofield, commanding the Union Department of Missouri, soon learned of their arrival in the state. In a few weeks he found that their operations, combined with the furious activity of the guerrillas, were plunging his quiet department into insurrection. In reporting local conditions at that time, he wrote General Halleck:

About this time commenced the execution of a well-devised scheme of the rebel Government to obtain large re-inforcements from Missouri and ultimately to regain possession of the State. A large number of Missourians in the rebel army were sent home with commissions to raise and organize troops for the rebel army. Many of them succeeded in secretly passing our lines and in eluding arrest. Some were arrested and others voluntarily surrendered themselves, professing their desire to return to their allegiance, and were permitted to take the oath of allegiance and return to their homes as loyal citizens. These emissaries spread themselves over the State, and, while maintaining outwardly the character of loyal citizens or evading our troops, secretly enrolled, organized, and officered a very large number of men, estimated by their friends at from 30,000 to 50,000.[5]

Conscription Act was not officially suspended in Missouri by act of the Confederate Congress until October 2, 1862.

[5] *O. R.*, Series 1, Vol. XIII, 10, from General Schofield's departmental report for 1862.

District of the Northeast

Schofield's first action was to outlaw the Confederate partisan forces being released in the center of his command. On May 29, 1862, in General Order Eighteen, he stated,

The time is passed when insurrection and rebellion in Missouri can cloak itself under the guise of honorable warfare.

The utmost vigilance and energy are enjoined upon all the troops of the State in hunting down and destroying these robbers and assassins. When caught in arms, engaged in their unlawful warfare, they will be shot down upon the spot.[6]

The "extermination policy" toward Confederate partisans pronounced by Generals Halleck and Schofield was copied at once by their subordinates in the subdistricts of Missouri. Tough Colonel Egbert B. Brown of the explosive Central District ordered his troops to execute guerrillas on the spot, even though they professed to be acting "under the authority of the so-called Confederate States of America."[7] General Ben Loan of the District of North Missouri directed that any person, regardless of Confederate commission, who attempted to assemble a force to act in opposition to Union authority was to be "promptly executed by the first commissioned officer to whom he may be delivered."[8] Quantrill's men had received no quarter; Hindman's recruiting officers were not to be given any either.

Colonel Joseph C. Porter was the first of Hindman's guerrillas to cause trouble. Joe Porter was born in Kentucky in 1819, but had moved to Lewis County, Missouri, with his family as a child. A farmer of strong Southern sympathies, Porter left his wife and five children in the summer of 1861 and joined General Martin Green's State Guard unit where he was made a lieutenant colonel. A natural leader, Porter fought bravely at Lexington and Pea Ridge. Because of his

6 O. R., Series 1, Vol. XIII, 402-403.
7 O. R., Series 1, Vol. XIII, 420, General Order Seven, dated June 6, 1862.
8 O. R., Series 1, Vol. XXII, Part 2, pp. 64-65.

excellent character and many acquaintances, he was chosen
to raise guerrilla forces in northeast Missouri. Although this
duty was not his personal choice, Porter obeyed his orders
and returned to Missouri where he set up a secret recruiting
organization. He made his presence known for the first time
on June 17 when he captured a detachment of state militia
in the western part of Marion County, took their equipment,
and paroled them.[9] By July 13 he had gathered together
nearly two hundred men from Pike, Ralls, Marion, Shelby,
Knox, and Lewis counties, and on that date this force of
poorly armed farm boys raided Memphis, the county seat of
Scotland County. Porter took the town without serious resistance, capturing a hundred badly needed muskets and a
number of Union uniforms which he issued to his command.
Considerable looting in stores owned by Union men took
place. Dr. William Alward, an ardent pro-Union man with
some reputation as an informer, was taken from his home by
Porter's men and was never seen again. It was believed he
was hanged and the body disposed of that night.

The attack on Memphis was a surprise to the Union command in north Missouri. General John McNeil of the Northeast District put all his troops in the field, and on July 18 the
first battalion of his own elite cavalry guard, Colonel Lewis
Merrill's Horse, came upon Porter's rear guard near Vassar
Hill in Scotland County. With a complete lack of caution
the Union advance guard charged the guerrillas. As Porter's
men fell back, the Union cavalry pushed into a carefully prepared ambush. Eighteen of the twenty-one troopers in the
advance party were dropped from their saddles by the first
volley. Major John Y. Clopper, who commanded the unit,
brought up his main body immediately, and an undecisive
skirmish took place in the heavy woods. In three hours the
Union force lost eighty-three men killed and wounded.

[9] Joseph C. Mudd, *With Porter In North Missouri* (Washington, 1909),
24-26. Mudd was one of Porter's men.

Clopper gave the guerrillas credit for fighting savagely. On July 19, being reinforced, he cautiously took up pursuit again.[10]

Moving southward Porter entered Florida, Monroe County, on the morning of July 22. A detachment of fifty men of the Third Iowa Cavalry held the town, which was Mark Twain's birthplace. A brisk skirmish ensued, and after an hour's shooting, the Third Iowa retreated, leaving twenty-six men, more than half its force, killed, wounded, or missing. The Iowa Cavalry fell back to Paris, the county seat, where Major H. C. Caldwell called upon McNeil in St. Louis for immediate reinforcements. The Confederate forces in northeast Missouri were building up with frightening rapidity.[11]

The initial Union reverses in McNeil's command, the success of Porter's recruiting, and the savage guerrilla fighting in western Missouri greatly alarmed General Schofield. Missouri, which had been peaceful in the spring, was now blazing with warfare throughout its most heavily populated areas. Losing the calmness and objectivity he normally maintained under all circumstances, Schofield obtained authorization from Governor Gamble to put into effect a drastic manpower draft. On July 22, 1862, he published General Order Nineteen which in part stated: "Every able-bodied man capable of bearing arms and subject to military duty is hereby ordered to repair without delay to the nearest military post and report for duty to the commanding officer. Every man will bring with him whatever arms he may have or can procure and a good horse if he has one."[12] The drafting of the total manpower of Missouri, the order went on, was "for the purpose of exterminating the guerrillas that infest our state."

10 O. R., Series 1, Vol. XIII, 163; Mudd, *With Porter in North Missouri*, 83-87.
11 Mudd, *ibid.*, 132.
12 O. R., Series 1, Vol. XIII, 506.

Order Nineteen came as a lightning bolt to the explosively tense situation throughout the state. Its all-inclusive scope created the greatest excitement. Wealthy men in high places saw themselves in the field carrying muskets on, to say the least, hazardous military errands. Far worse, the order sent hundreds of men into hiding or into the guerrilla organizations. Soldiers of Price's State Guard who had returned and been granted amnesty, men who had remained neutral but who would never strike a blow against the South, boys whose Southern families had persuaded them not to join the armies, and many men whose minds were not made up over the issues of the war found themselves faced with compulsory Union military service against friends, relatives, and principles.

The guerrillas were quick to capitalize on the confusing situation. Word came out of the brush that a choice of active military service must now be made. In Schofield's rueful words: "The first effect, and which was to be expected, was to cause every rebel in the State who could possess himself of a weapon of any kind to spring to arms and join the nearest guerrilla band, thus largely and suddenly increasing the force with which we had to contend, while thousands of others ran to the brush to avoid the required enrollment."[13]

The order which was designed to quell the guerrilla war resulted in its vast acceleration. Down in the Central District "Bottle Nose" Totten advised the Missouri Adjutant General on July 30 that "General Order No. 19 aroused not only the loyal militia of this division, but also, and particularly, the rebels and guerrillas. . . . that element is now thoroughly awake and actively concentrating, and will very soon cease defending themselves and commence attacks upon our numerous weak posts."[14]

[13] *O. R.*, Series 1, Vol. XIII, 10-11, 557.
[14] *O. R.*, Series 1, Vol. XIII, 522-523.

In addition to its rigid drafting provisions, Order Number Nineteen, and the orders that supplemented it, had other stipulations which were to prove harassing to Missourians. To arm the militia, the order provided for the random seizure of guns. This offered an excellent excuse for Union patrols to enter private homes to search for arms, and to loot generally while searching. As the militia increased in strength during the last of July and the first part of August, the problem of subsistence and forage for men on active duty became acute. Schofield solved this by General Order Nine, dated August 12, 1862, which directed that "during active operations in the field in pursuit of guerrillas, the troops of this command will not be encumbered with transportation of supplies, but will, as far as possible, obtain subsistence from the enemy and those who aid and encourage the rebellion."[15] The end of the summer of 1862 saw large sections of Missouri stripped by Union and Confederate foraging parties. On both sides hatred was built up as men saw their hard-earned and vitally necessary crops and stores of food hauled away by rapacious soldiery. The state militia abused the foraging authority to such an extent that General Schofield was forced to publish an additional order on September 22 which sadly commented: "The general commanding has learned with much regret, that in various parts of the State, under pretense of carrying out General Orders, No. 9 . . . there has been perpetrated pillage and marauding of the most unsoldierlike and disreputable character."[16]

Schofield's draft, however, was successful in bringing out the Union men of the state. If it stirred up the guerrilla war, it also provided the forces to defeat the Confederate elements operating in Missouri in 1862. By the close of the year 52,056

15 U. S. War Department, Record and Pension Office, *Organization and Status of Missouri Troops, Union and Confederate, In Service During the Civil War* (Washington, 1902), 57. Hereinafter cited *Missouri Troops.*

16 *Missouri Troops,* 58.

men and officers had been formed into sixty-nine regiments, three battalions, and fifty-eight independent companies.[17]

Greatly assisted in his recruiting mission by General Schofield, Joe Porter now tried to get his men south across the Missouri River and down to Arkansas. On July 24 he pushed through a detachment of the Third Iowa Cavalry near Santa Fe, Monroe County, and on into northern Callaway County. There he proceeded down Auxvasse Creek, gathering men as he went. On July 25, 1862, he was joined by Alvin Cobb and seventy-five Montgomery County guerrillas, and by sixty-five men from the Blackfoot region of Boone County. Cobb was a welcome addition. A fierce and murderous man, he had earned a frightening local reputation because of an amputated hand which had been replaced with a curved and sharpened hook. Porter, his force now numbering 400 men, pressed on south toward the river. At dusk of July 27 he found his way blocked at Brown's Spring on the Auxvasse by Colonel Odon Guitar of the Ninth Missouri Cavalry. Guitar had 186 men of his regiment, a company of the Third Iowa, and one section of the Third Indiana Artillery. Believing the odds favorable, Porter determined to fight early the next day. On July 28 Guitar was reinforced by 547 men and officers of Merrill's Horse, the Third Iowa, the Tenth Missouri Cavalry, and an independent company, the "Red Rovers." Guitar hurled this force on Porter at Moore's Mill and was ambushed. For a time it seemed that the guerrillas had a good chance of breaking through the Union line, but in a few hours Porter, heavily outnumbered, found himself fighting for the life of his command in the heavy timber and underbrush along the Auxvasse Creek. Odon Guitar, who was to become one of the toughest field officers in the Missouri Union command, rallied his men and then led them in a fearless and aggressive manner. Ranging on horseback

[17] *Missouri Troops*, 53.

back and forth before his dismounted troops, Guitar's swearing and hoarse commands to "bring on them cannon," could be heard by Porter's men above the heavy firing. By the middle of the sweltering July afternoon Porter's force was completely smashed. His men had fought like demons, believing they would be executed if captured. Fifty-two lost their lives on the field, and more than a hundred were wounded. Guitar lost thirteen men killed and fifty-five wounded. Porter and a few of his men disappeared to the north; Cobb escaped to the east.[18]

There was general rejoicing by Union men throughout Missouri when the news of the Union victory at Moore's Mill became known. It was thought that Porter's campaign had been smashed. Guitar, famous because of his victory, was assigned to take his Ninth Cavalry after Confederate Colonel A. J. Poindexter who was recruiting in the vicinity of Glasgow, Howard County.

Porter moved back up into north Missouri. General McNeil again took up his pursuit, for the guerrilla leader was far from finished. General Schofield's draft sent men to him from all directions as he became a symbol of resistance. On August 1 he captured Newark in Knox County, after a sharp skirmish at the seventy-man post of the Second Missouri Cavalry. The Union troopers fortified themselves in the Presbyterian church and other brick buildings, which were set on fire. The garrison then surrendered, and Porter paroled his prisoners. He had eight men killed and thirteen wounded, several mortally. The Second Cavalry lost four killed and seven wounded.[19] Between August 1 and 4 he sent patrols to Canton, Lewis County, and to Kirksville, Adair County, to obtain arms and recruits. By August 5, 1862, he had nearly

18 Mudd, *With Porter in North Missouri*, 159-214; *O. R.*, Series 1, Vol. XIII, 189.
19 Mudd, *ibid.*, 241-46.

a thousand men with him at Kirksville. On the morning of August 6 General McNeil with five hundred men and six cannon found the guerrilla force there ready to fight for the town.

McNeil's command, although numerically inferior, was well trained, and the excellent use of his artillery terrified Porter's recruits. By mid-afternoon house after house had been shelled, and short charges had sent the Confederate irregulars retreating across the Chariton River to the west. McNeil lost only five men killed and thirty-two wounded. He estimated Porter's casualties at 150 killed and 300 to 400 wounded. Forty-seven guerrillas were captured. McNeil shot fifteen of these prisoners whom he determined had been in arms before and had violated their oaths of loyalty to the Union. On September 25 he executed ten more of Porter's men at Macon.[20]

The Union cavalry pressed on after the disorganized Confederate partisans. On August 9, almost surrounded, the guerrilla disbanded his men and they fled in all directions. Porter went into hiding in Monroe County. He struck only once more, a small raid on Palmyra, Marion County, on September 12. Union forces closed swiftly on him this time, and he retreated rapidly to the Missouri River, taking as many men as possible with him. On October 16 about three hundred of his guerrillas crossed the river at Portland, Callaway County, on the steamboat *Emilie,* which they had commandeered. As the boat arrived on the south shore, Union cavalry appeared on the north.[21] Joe Porter crossed the Missouri by row boat at Providence, Boone County, joined Jo Shelby in Wright County and was killed in a small skirmish near Marshfield on January 10, 1863. His campaign in north

[20] *Ibid.,* 258-67, 304, citing Colonel McNeil's official report to Assistant Adjutant General George M. Houston, September 17, 1862.
[21] *Ibid.,* 436-39.

Missouri had failed because he had violated the guerrilla tactic of never fighting open battles.

The Confederate plans in northeast Missouri had come to disaster, but the whole region had been brought into insurrection. Many of Porter's men who were captured were executed by General McNeil, and that really competent officer gained a name for barbarity. On October 18 he ordered, in an excess of butchery, the shooting of ten prisoners at Palmyra in retaliation for the disappearance of a Union man named Andrew Allsman, thought to have been killed by Porter's men. Hoping to recover Allsman, he had the following letter placed in local newspapers and given to Mrs. Porter.

PALMYRA, Mo., October 8, 1862

JOSEPH C. PORTER.

SIR:—Andrew Allsman, an aged citizen of Palmyra, and a noncombatant, having been carried from his home by a band of persons unlawfully arrayed against the peace and good order of the State of Missouri, and which band was under your control; this is to notify you that unless said Andrew Allsman is returned unharmed to his family within ten days from date ten men who have belonged to your band, and unlawfully sworn by you to carry arms against the Government of the United States, and who are now in custody, will be shot as a meet reward for their crimes, among which is the illegally restraining of said Allsman of his liberty, and if not returned, presumably aiding in his murder. Your prompt attention to this will save much suffering.

Yours etc.
W. R. STRACHAN
Provost-Marshall General
    District N.E. Missouri
Per order of Brigadier General
    Commanding McNeil's Column[22]

22 *Ibid.*, 299-300.

The ten days passed without the appearance of Allsman; that unfortunate never did turn up. Five of Porter's men were selected by lot from the Hannibal prison, and Provost Marshall "Beast" Strachan picked the other five from prisoners at Palmyra. It was widely rumored that Strachan made a substitution on his list when the wife of one of the men agreed to allow the provost marshall to use her sexually in return for her husband's life.[23]

On October 18 the ten hostages were shot by firing squads. The story of the "Palmyra Massacre" shocked the Confederacy and the British press. Jefferson Davis demanded that Mc-Neil be handed over by the Union, and ordered that if he were not, the first ten Union officers to be captured in the Trans-Mississippi Department were to be executed.[24] McNeil was retained in command and became a hero of the Radical Republican element in Missouri and the North.[25]

Over in central Missouri Colonel Guitar and his Ninth Missouri Cavalry picked up Confederate Colonel A. J. Poindexter's trail near Renick, Randolph County, on August 8. In the following seven days the tenacious Guitar rode 250 miles, fought Poindexter three times, and completely annihilated the guerrilla force. Poindexter, apparently trying to join Porter in Macon County, was pushed west into Chariton County and then north into Linn County. On the night of August 10, Guitar caught Poindexter as he was crossing Grand River in Chariton County with some 1200 recruits, and in a savage attack, killed, wounded, and scattered the guerrilla command.[26] Poindexter was captured in Chariton County at the end of August, hiding without followers. Colonel Lewis Merrill planned his execution by drumhead

[23] Ibid., 300.

[24] Ibid., 302-307. Davis, in a letter to Lieutenant General T. H. Holmes on November 17, 1862, who then commanded the Trans-Mississippi Department.

[25] Ibid., 304-305.

[26] O. R., Series 1, Vol. XIII, 225, 547.

court-martial, but the Confederate officer was finally tried by a military commission. Apparently no sentence of execution could be obtained, for Poindexter was paroled.[27]

By September 1, 1862, the Union had put down the insurrection in northeast Missouri, but it had been a bloody summer that left a vast residue of malignant hatred.

[27] *O. R.*, Series 1, Vol. XIII, 621.

6

From Independence
to Arkansas

I F military affairs went well for the Union command in the guerrilla war in northeast and north central Missouri during July and August, 1862, the situation was generally reversed along the Kansas border. The Confederate plan in western and central Missouri, as determined by its evolution, was to have Colonel Upton Hays move up from Arkansas into the Jackson County area in June, where in liaison with Quantrill, he was to recruit and then strike at any Union target he could find. Confederate cavalry units were then to be thrown north around the first of August to assist in recruiting and to escort the men back when the mission was completed. These supplementary units arrived all along the Missouri River in August, commanded by Colonels

John T. Coffee, J. Vard Cockrell, John T. Hughes, Gideon W. Thompson, and Captain Jo Shelby.

William Quantrill and Upton Hays began to consolidate their forces during the first week in August, learning that the cavalry columns of Coffee, Cockrell, and Shelby were moving northward toward them.[1] On August 8 Colonel E. C. Catherwood, Sixth Missouri Cavalry, notified the Adjutant General of Missouri from Sedalia that there were five hundred organized guerrillas in eastern Jackson County. Catherwood begged for reinforcements.[2]

By August 11 the Confederate partisans were ready to strike as a major force. The week preceding had seen greatly heightened guerrilla activity in Jackson County. Confederate Colonels Hughes and Thompson had arrived there about August 1 to aid Hays with recruiting. These officers had established a headquarters almost under the guns of the Union garrison at Independence, locating their camp on the prairie near Lee's Summit. Their Confederate battle flag set on a tall pole could be seen from the Jackson County courthouse.[3]

Independence was held at the time by Lieutenant Colonel James T. Buel, commanding three companies of his Seventh Missouri Cavalry, one company of the Second Missouri Cavalry, and one company of the Sixth Missouri Infantry, a total force of about three hundred men. These troops were stationed in an unfortified tent camp a half mile west of the courthouse square. Colonel Buel had more comfortable headquarters in the stone Southern Bank building on the south side of Lexington Street just off the square. His guard company was quartered in a building immediately across the street, and his provost marshal and guard were at the county jail on North Main Street, a block north. By this casual ar-

---

1 *O. R.*, Series 1, Vol. XIII, 221.
2 *O. R.*, Series 1, Vol. XIII, 547.
3 Connelley, *Quantrill*, 260.

rangement Buel was isolated from the main body of his troops. In spite of the visual evidence of Confederate activity near his post, Buel did not have patrols out on August 9 and 10 to observe the enemy. From the disposition of his troops it was evident that he did not fear or expect an attack. Buel was a qualified guerrilla fighter, and it is very likely that his experience made him feel that Quantrill and Hays would never attack his large garrison.

On August 10 Hughes and Thompson, who had gathered in about seventy-five recruits, were joined by Hays and Quantrill, with a surprising force of nearly 325 horsemen. It was decided that Independence would be raided on the eleventh. Colonel Hughes was to command this partisan group, and from his plan of attack it is apparent that the town had been ably scouted. The disposition of Buel's men was known perfectly by the irregular Confederates. Quantrill's men were given two major tasks separate from the main force. They were to lead the raid into town, approaching north up Spring Street, and were to cut down the guards Buel would have out there. They were then to attack his headquarters, kill him if possible, and if not, keep him isolated from his camp while Colonel Hughes led the main assault.[4]

At four-thirty on the morning of August 11, 1862, headed by Quantrill, the Confederate partisans swept into the sleeping village of Independence. Dawn was just breaking, and in the semidarkness the Union post was taken completely by surprise. The guards on Spring Street were run over and killed by Quantrill's men, who proceeded on a screaming dash for the square. Colonel Buel was awakened in his bedroom on the second floor of the bank building by Rebel yells and a series of pistol shots which smashed his window. His life was saved by an alert sentry who called out his guard

4 Connelley, *Quantrill*, 263.

company across the street. These half-dressed men grabbed their muskets and cartridge boxes, fired into the milling guerrillas, and soon were able to cross the street and barricade the headquarters building. A detachment of Quantrill's men then raced up to the provost marshal's office at the jail. The provost guard fired one wild volley and ran westward for Kansas City. The guerrillas released the prisoners in the jail and pistoled the Independence city marshal who was conveniently incarcerated at the time on a murder charge. The main Confederate force under Colonel Hughes charged into the Union tent camp, scattering undressed, half-awake soldiers back to a stone fence at its rear.

As the sun rose, Colonel Buel found himself in a miserable position. Quantrill's men, their revolvers popping, swarmed over adjacent buildings and lay at the street corners firing at the windows of his headquarters. The main body of his command was cut off from him, disorganized and under heavy attack. At about eight-thirty Quantrill, tired of sniping at the stone bank building, ordered firing ceased, set an adjoining store on fire, and shouted to Buel that if he would not surrender, he could roast.

While the attack on the headquarters was going on, Colonels Hughes and Thompson had defeated the Union troops at the tent camp. Only a few units resisted fiercely, the rest fled across country toward Kansas City. Colonel Hughes was killed leading one of the final charges. By nine o'clock the Southern Bank building was beginning to be very warm. Colonel Buel raised a white flag and asked for a parley. Colonel Thompson agreed to talk with him. Upon being assured that he and his men would not be turned over to Quantrill and executed, and that they would be treated as prisoners of war, Buel surrendered. He had lost 37 men killed, 63 wounded, and over 150 captured. The remainder of his command had run away. The Union colonel and his

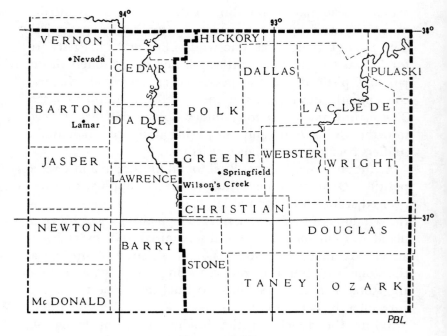

Districts of the Frontier and the Southwest

troops were all paroled and accorded excellent treatment, in sharp contrast to the way Porter's men were shot when captured in north Missouri. The Confederate partisans also had suffered heavily, having thirty-two killed and many wounded. They had captured some twenty wagons of supplies and enough muskets and sabers to arm all the recruits. Much of the loot was given to Quantrill. Colonel Thompson hastily marched his men out of town that evening toward Blue Springs.[5]

The capture of Independence was a fearful blow to all western Missouri. Out of nowhere a sizeable guerrilla force had sprung to destroy a major Union post. Telegraph lines were kept busy throughout the central part of the state. There were rumors that Kansas City and Lexington would be attacked next, and it was three days before a Union scout gingerly approached Independence.

General Schofield calmly informed General Halleck of the situation on August 12. He told Halleck that Porter's and Poindexter's guerrillas had been almost eliminated, and that Quantrill's success at Independence, and Coffee's advance northward presented only limited threats, as he had ordered heavy troop concentrations toward the Jackson County area.[6] On the same day he wired General Ben Loan of the Northwest District that the remnants of Poindexter's guerrillas must be prevented from joining Quantrill and Thompson. All the border garrisons in the District of Kansas were ordered to group at Fort Scott and to move in from the west on the Confederate irregulars. The Union posts on the Missouri River were instructed to prepare to march, and arms and ammunition were forwarded to them on the gunboat *John Warner*.

[5] For accounts of the fight at Independence see *Daily K. C. Journal*, August 12, 13, 14, 1862; *O. R.*, Series 1, Vol. XIII, 225-27; Britton, *The Civil War on the Border*, I, 322-25.

[6] *O. R.*, Series 1, Vol. XIII, 560-61.

John Schofield's plans were put into motion on August 15, 1862. Early on the morning of that day Major Emory S. Foster led a cavalry column of eight hundred men and two cannon out of Lexington, Lafayette County, in the direction of Lone Jack in southeastern Jackson County. He was to be joined there on the morning of the sixteenth by General Fitz Henry Warren and the First Iowa Cavalry from Clinton, Henry County. Foster and Warren were to wait in southern Jackson County until Brigadier General James G. Blunt, commanding the Department of Kansas, joined them with a large cavalry and infantry column from Fort Scott. Once this grand juncture was accomplished, the combined Union forces were to turn northwest, compressing Coffee, Thompson, and Quantrill against the Missouri River. The Confederate partisans were to be prevented from fleeing to the west by another Union force from Fort Leavenworth, commanded by Colonel John T. Burris.

The Union encirclement was excellently planned, but was not correctly timed or co-ordinated. General Blunt did not leave Fort Scott until August 16, and then his column of two thousand Kansans moved slowly due to the fact that he hauled his infantry in prairie wagons drawn by four mules.[7] Major Foster did not meet General Warren at Lone Jack on the sixteenth, Blunt did not arrive in the area until the seventeenth, and Colonel Burris did not move east toward Independence until the twenty-first. However, Foster did run on to Confederates Coffee, Hays, and Thompson. After camping in the streets of Lone Jack on the night of August 15, his small unit was swamped at sunrise the next day by two thousand howling Missouri guerrillas. The battle of Lone Jack was a savage frontier engagement, fought hand to hand in the houses, streets, and gardens of the hamlet. Believing they were being attacked by Quantrill and would

---

[7] Britton, *The Civil War on the Border*, I, 327-28.

receive no quarter, Major Foster and his men fought like fanatics. By afternoon the Union force had lost its cannon, 43 men killed, 154 wounded, and 75 missing. Foster, seriously wounded, surrendered when he learned that his men would be treated as prisoners of war and paroled.[8] The Confederates, with 118 men killed and many wounded, began a hasty retreat south on the seventeenth. They were joined by Captain Jo Shelby and 1000 men he had recruited in Lafayette County in only four days. Blunt's Kansans and Warren's Iowa Cavalry trailed them to the Osage River.

The Union command blamed a portion of Foster's smashing defeat upon Quantrill's guerrillas, but the partisan leader did not take part in the battle of Lone Jack. Following the capture of Independence on August 11 he had taken his company of 150 men to the Morgan Walker farm where they set up a hidden camp. Evidently he feared swift pursuit and retaliation for the raid. On August 14, 1862, he decided to form a Confederate partisan ranger company. He and his men were sworn into the Confederate service by Colonel Gideon W. Thompson, and then held an election which resulted in his being made captain, William Haller, first lieutenant, George Todd, second lieutenant, and William H. Gregg, third lieutenant.[9] Quantrill was then given a commission as captain, apparently signed by Thompson, who had authority from General Hindman to do so.[10]

On August 16 Quantrill decided it would be safe to return to Independence to pick up military supplies left there in his hasty withdrawal on the eleventh. Leaving sixty men in camp under Haller, he took the rest of his force back to town and thus missed the battle of Lone Jack. Haller and his guerrillas were called into the fight by Upton Hays on the

[8] O. R., Series 1, Vol. XIII, 238; Britton, ibid., 326-35.

[9] McCorkle, Three Years With Quantrill, 33 (McCorkle was present); Gregg Ms., 23.

[10] O. R., Series 1, Vol. XIII, 33.

afternoon of the sixteenth, and Cole Younger distinguished himself by his bravery under fire.[11]

Quantrill and Upton Hays did not retreat south with Coffee and Shelby. They remained in Jackson County, doubtlessly hoping to pick off small Union units engaged in the grand pursuit.

Arriving belatedly in the Independence area on August 21, Lieutenant Colonel John Burris and his Fourth Kansas Cavalry made no haste in pursuing Coffee. His first act was to burn the houses of known guerrillas and to arrest the editor and scatter the type of the *Border Star,* "a treasonable sheet" published at Independence. On the morning of the twenty-second, Burris moved his column out of Independence south toward Harrisonville. Near the headwaters of the Little Blue River he learned from a Negro, to what must have been his considerable surprise, that Quantrill and Hays "with 1000 men" were camped four miles up the stream in a dense wood. As it was dusk, Burris bivouacked, determining to attack the next day. At dawn he moved up to the farm of Charles Cowert near the guerrilla camp, where his two pieces of artillery could be effective. He then sent forward two companies of cavalry to draw Quantrill into the open. The guerrillas, their number greatly exaggerated by Colonel Burris' slave informant, retreated deeper into the woods. Burris quite evidently had no stomach for a fight with the partisans in the dense timber. In typical Kansas fashion he burned Cowert's "house and outbuildings and the immense ricks of grain and hay found on the premises," and turned away from the enemy to the west.[12] Quantrill emerged from the timber in front of him while he was performing these tasks, and both sides formed a line of battle. A few rounds from the Union cannon broke the guerrilla ranks

[11] Gregg Ms., 25.
[12] *O. R.,* Series 1, Vol. XIII, 251.

and they retreated south. Burris did not press them. He followed them south only to Pleasant Hill and then fell back to more peaceful surroundings at Independence. On August 27 he returned to Fort Leavenworth, his Fourth Cavalry taking along "about 80 loyal colored persons."[13]

Upton Hays took his recruits toward Arkansas following the skirmish at Cowert's. Before leaving, he turned a Lieutenant Copeland, whom he had captured at Lone Jack, over to Quantrill. On the afternoon of August 28 Quantrill read in a newspaper that one of his men, Perry Hoy, a Union prisoner, had been executed at Fort Leavenworth. Quantrill had hoped to exchange Copeland for Hoy, and now in a rage he had the lieutenant shot. He then ordered his men to saddle, and they galloped toward Kansas with the intention of killing ten more Union men for Hoy. William Gregg wrote casually that ten were killed before the state line was reached.[14]

On the morning of September 6, 1862, Quantrill led his guerrillas in a raid on Olathe, Kansas. Pouring into the town at dawn, the partisans surprised and captured a garrison of 125 men. Three civilians were killed, the town was thoroughly looted, and the community newspaper, the *Mirror,* was destroyed. Quantrill strutted around the streets displaying his Confederate commission and asking old acquaintances to call him Captain, not Bill. Paroling the Union soldiers, the guerrillas returned to Missouri with several wagon loads of booty. The Olathe raid brought Burris and his Fourth Kansas Cavalry down from Fort Leavenworth again. On the morning of the tenth he came upon Quantrill on the north branch of the Grand River in Cass County. The guerrillas fled, and a wild horse race took place over Jackson, Johnson, and Lafayette counties, which lasted until Quantrill's men

---

13 *O. R.*, Series 1, Vol. XIII, 255.
14 Gregg Ms., 29; Connelley, *Quantrill*, 270-71.

disbanded on September 21. During this ten-day running skirmish Burris recovered most of the Olathe spoils, including six wagons, a hundred muskets, ten thousand rounds of ammunition, clothing, and groceries. Only two guerrillas were killed. Burris had one man dead and three wounded. The Fourth Kansas got in some good looting. Burris marched back to Fort Leavenworth after burning a dozen houses. He took with his column a hundred horses, four yoke of oxen, and "upward of 60 loyal colored persons, tired of the rule of rebel masters."[15]

Smarting from his four-county chase, Quantrill called his men together again at Sibley on the Missouri River in Jackson County on October 5. By the sixth Captain Daniel H. David, with parts of four companies of the Fifth Missouri Cavalry, numbering eighty-eight men, was on his trail. David and his cavalry were scouring the country between Fire Prairie and the Sni River when he noticed ominous mounted pickets observing his march from the hills near Sibley. He moved cautiously into the little town where he was given false information that the guerrillas, numbering three hundred, were camped at a mill two miles west. Feeling himself outnumbered, the captain sent a messenger back to his post at Independence for reinforcements. He then moved his squadron toward Big Hill above Sibley with the idea of holding there until help should arrive. While carrying off this movement, he rode squarely into an ambush. Over a hundred guerrillas rose from the brush and fired a volley into the blue-coated column. Captain David found himself surrounded by wounded troopers and horses. Somehow he managed to get his men dismounted, had them draw sabers, and bravely led them into the timber against the guerrillas. A short hot fight followed, and again Union discipline told. Quantrill's men fell back before David's carbines, leaving

[15] *O. R.,* Series 1, Vol. XIII, 267-68; Connelley, *Quantrill,* 271.

behind, fatally wounded, one of their best boys, Richard Chiles. The partisans finally broke and retreated south, impressing buggies and wagons to carry their wounded. Reinforced, stout Captain David followed them, and throughout the seventh carried on an indecisive running battle down to Pink Hill in southern Jackson County. The guerrillas scattered and concentrated throughout the day, and toward evening turned north toward Independence. David and his men were forced to give up pursuit. The Fifth Cavalry troopers had been in the saddle for three days, and their captain wistfully reported: "We do not believe that guerrillas can ever be taken by pursuit; we must take them by strategy."[16]

From October 8 to 16 Quantrill moved freely through Jackson County with some 150 men under his command. He was reported at a dozen different places, and Union posts were on continuous alert. On October 17 the guessing concerning his whereabouts and plans ended. On the morning of that day he and his men, screaming and shooting, swooped across the prairie toward Shawneetown, Johnson County, Kansas. Just outside that community they ran into a Union wagon train proceeding toward Kansas City. Indian fashion, they circled the train, killed fifteen of the escort and drivers, scattered the rest, and burned the wagons. Entering Shawneetown, they shot ten men and looted and put torches to the stores and houses. For every house burned in Missouri one was to be burned in Kansas. Shawneetown was erased from the map, and the guerrillas dashed back into hiding in Missouri.[17]

The Shawneetown raid was made primarily to obtain clothing, an item the guerrillas were chronically short of. As Confederate uniforms were not available to Quantrill and his men in 1862, even had it suited their purpose to wear

16 *O. R.*, Series 1, Vol. XIII, 313-14.
17 Connelley, *Quantrill*, 274-75; Gregg Ms., 36-37.

them, they developed a dress peculiar to themselves which became known up and down the border. Its distinguishing item was a "guerrilla shirt." This shirt, patterned after the hunting coat of the Western plainsman, was cut low in front, the slit narrowing to a point above the belt and ending in a rosette. The garment had four big pockets, two in the breast, and ranged in color from brilliant red to homespun butternut. They were made by the mothers, wives, and sweethearts of the guerrillas, and many were elaborately decorated with colored needlework.

With their brilliant shirts, wide-brimmed slouch hats of the plains, and mounted on the finest horses in western Missouri, Quantrill's boys made a colorful appearance. There were few beards on the faces of the guerrillas; most were too young, but this hirsute lack was made up for by abundant locks and curls which they wore to their shoulders. The real secret of their success in combat against their more numerous Union enemy, aside from their guerrilla tactics, lay in their superior weapon, the Colt revolving pistol. The revolver was the primary weapon of Quantrill's men, and there is abundant evidence that they were deadly with this frontier weapon. It became customary for the guerrillas to carry from two to eight revolvers in their belts and on their saddles. These rapid firing, five- and six-shot weapons, in addition to the customary Sharps carbine, gave them a tremendous volume of fire power. As the majority of the Union cavalry on the border in 1862 was armed only with single-shot muzzle-loading carbines, or muskets and sabers, Federal officers complained continually of their weapons and begged for revolvers for their men.

November 3 found Quantrill in camp on Big Creek in Cass County. The bracing fall weather was turning into the raw gloom of a Missouri winter. It was decided that a move down to the Confederate army in Arkansas was advisable.

Quantrill mounted his men and they galloped south. At the same hour that Quantrill turned his band toward Arkansas, Colonel E. C. Catherwood, commanding the Sixth Missouri Cavalry at Harrisonville, had dispatched an ox-drawn military train of thirteen wagons toward the Pacific railhead at Sedalia. Lieutenant Newby and twenty-two troopers of the Sixth were sent along as escort. The line of march of the train lay northeast across that of the guerrillas who were moving south between Harrisonville and Rose Hill. Held down to the crawl of the oxen, Newby and his men loafed along, not believing there was an enemy in the vicinity. Suddenly the train was surrounded by 150 yipping guerrillas who circled and closed in, Comanche fashion, until they swept over the defenders. Newby and four privates were captured, four soldiers and six teamsters were killed, three men were wounded, and the others dispersed. Quantrill burned the wagons, turned the oxen loose on the prairie, and went on south.

Shortly after Colonel Catherwood had sent out his train, a scout came in to Harrisonville and informed him that Quantrill was moving down the county near Rose Hill. The Colonel knew at once that his train was liable to attack. He mounted all the available men at his post, 150, and galloped out toward Rose Hill where he found the smoking remnants of his wagons and the riddled bodies of his troopers and wagoneers. In savage anger he turned his column on the guerrilla trail, caught up with them, and in a fierce running fight, scattered them. Lieutenant Newby was cut free from his captors and rescued; six of Quantrill's men were shot or sabered. Catherwood chased the guerrillas until his horses were exhausted.[18]

Surprised by the violent Union counterattack, Quantrill spent hours collecting his men and then raced on down the

[18] O. R., Series 1, Vol. XIII, 347-48; 781-89.

border through Bates and Vernon counties, avoiding the
military posts at Butler and Nevada. On November 5 he was
in northern Barton County where he fell in with Colonel
Warner Lewis of the Confederate army with a group of three
hundred recruits. Lewis and Quantrill decided to attack the
Union post at Lamar, the county seat. Lamar was held by
Captain Martin Breeden with a company of the Eighth Missouri Cavalry who had been warned of a raid. Quantrill and
Lewis planned a night attack, with the guerrillas charging
the town from the north, the Confederate colonel from the
south.

At 10:00 P.M. Quantrill's men, their pistols blazing, roared
down the pitch-dark streets of Lamar and on to the courthouse square. Warner Lewis and his men did not put in their
appearance, and the guerrillas found Martin Breeden and
his men waiting for them behind the brick walls of the fortified courthouse. Milling around the square, Quantrill's men
began to drop from their horses as shot after shot was fired
into them from the dark windows of the structure. Quantrill
kept up the attack for an hour and a half and then bitterly
broke off the fight with six men dead and many wounded. In
chagrin he set a third of the houses in Lamar on fire, and,
carrying his wounded, limped off over the prairies to the
south. The guerrilla chief was beginning to have his fill of
fortified brick buildings.[19]

From Lamar Quantrill led his men west into Kansas, thus
avoiding heavy Union troop concentrations waiting for him
in Jasper and Newton counties. He then proceeded down the
Fort Scott–Fort Gibson Road through the Osage Nation, and
in mid-November joined Brigadier General John S. Marmaduke whom Hindman had made cavalry commander of the
District of Arkansas. Quantrill and 150 men were assigned
to Jo Shelby's Brigade at Cross Hollows, Arkansas, the re-

[19] O. R., Series 1, Vol. XIII, 348; Gregg Ms., 41-42.

markable Shelby having been made a colonel for his summer exploits in Missouri.[20]

Energetic General Tom Hindman had been demoted from command of the Confederate Trans-Mississippi Department in July, 1862. His strictness in enforcing the draft, his administrative skill in making Arkansas a vast training center, his promotion of guerrilla warfare in Missouri, and his ambitious plans for an active third front west of the Mississippi were too much for the Confederate powers at Richmond. He had been replaced by deaf, doddering Major General Theophilus H. Holmes, who was awarded command of the vast Trans-Mississippi apparently in reward for his blunders at Malvern Hill.[21] "Old Granny Holmes," as he was disrespectfully called by his soldiers, had made Tom Hindman commander of the army in northwestern Arkansas, and had given him orders to protect the state and forget about operations in Missouri.

Hindman, Marmaduke, and Shelby welcomed Quantrill and his boys. In a departmental report concerning his activities in the summer of 1862, Tom Hindman frankly informed the Confederate Adjutant General of the success of his guerrillas and their type of warfare in Missouri and along the border. A portion of this report stated: "With the view to revive the hopes of loyal men in Missouri and to get troops from that State I gave authority to various persons to raise companies and regiments there and to operate as guerrillas. They soon became exceedingly active and rendered important services, destroying wagon trains and transports, tearing up railways, breaking telegraph lines, capturing towns, and thus compelling the enemy to keep there a large force that might have been employed elsewhere." Hindman praised Quantrill as being "extremely zealous and useful," and

20 Gregg Ms., 42.
21 O'Flaherty, *General Jo Shelby*, 122.

added that "the victory won at Lone Jack by Colonels Cockrell . . . aided by Captain Quantrill, was one of the most brilliant affairs of the war."[22] Quantrill glowed with pleasure at
the reception he got, but he must have found out quickly
that "Granny" Holmes at Little Rock had no sympathy for
his grandiose plans for a vastly accelerated guerrilla war on
the border.

With the bloody haze of the past summer behind them the
Union military authorities in Missouri paused for an ac-
counting of the guerrilla insurrection that had taken place.
General Schofield had been replaced by Major General Samuel R. Curtis on September 21, 1862, promoted and sent
down to command operations in Arkansas. Schofield believed
his military campaign had gone well. The partisan organizations of Porter, Poindexter, and Cobb had been destroyed,
and Hays and Quantrill had left the border. However, the
Union victories had been expensive in many ways. More
than sixty thousand soldiers had been on duty in Missouri to
fight an enemy that never numbered more than three or four
thousand. Had it not been for the guerrilla war, these troops
and the money required to support them would have been
potentially available for use elsewhere where the Union was
desperately pressed. In a social sense the summer war had
created chaos in western and central Missouri, and had established ugly patterns of military behavior and government
that would bear ghastly fruit in 1863. In his usual candid
way, General Schofield described the situation bluntly and
precisely: "The border of Kansas and Missouri has been the
scene of the most revolting hostilities during the past two
years."[23]

Over in the Department of Kansas the departure of the

---

[22] *O. R.*, Series 1, Vol. XIII, 33.

[23] *O. R.*, Series 1, Vol. XXII, Part 1, p. 15. From his General Report of December, 1863.

guerrillas southward relaxed public tension and gave the signal for new raids into Missouri. In mid-November the entire Twelfth Kansas Cavalry Regiment, four hundred strong, entered Jackson and Lafayette counties. Commanded by Colonel Charles W. Adams, and Lieutenant Colonel J. E. Hayes, the Twelfth Kansas was surrounded by Brigadier General Richard C. Vaughan with a large force of Union militia of the Central District. At cannon point the Kansans were forced to release forty Negroes, one hundred horses, six or eight ox teams and wagons, and several two-horse teams, all of which were loaded with the household goods of Missouri farmers. The Twelfth Regiment was escorted to the state line at gunpoint. Adams and Hayes were arrested and sent to St. Louis with court-martial charges drawn against them, but General Sam Curtis restored them to duty.[24]

24 *O. R.,* Series 1, Vol. XXII, Part 1, pp. 39-40, 796-97, 821-22.

7

Lawrence is Destroyed

||||||||||||||||||||||||||||||||||||||||||||||||||||||||||||||||||||||||||||||||||||||||||||||

A FTER reaching General Shelby's camp at Cross Hollows in November, 1862, William Quantrill disappeared from the military scene for several months. Both Major John N. Edwards, who was Shelby's adjutant and the historian of his brigade, and William Connelley report that the guerrilla leader went to Richmond in the winter of 1862-1863 to obtain permission to raise a partisan ranger unit in Missouri.[1] It is certain that he was absent from his company during its service with the Fourth Missouri Confederate Cavalry. General Shelby stated that Quantrill's "famous company" was led by Lieutenant William H. Gregg at the battles at Cane Hill and Prairie Grove, Arkansas, and Springfield and Hartville, Missouri, between November, 1862, and January, 1863.[2] At the battle of Prairie Grove,

[1] Edwards, *Noted Guerrillas,* 156-58; Connelley, *Quantrill,* 278.
[2] *O. R.,* Series 1, Vol. XXII, Part 1, pp. 55, 58, 200; Gregg Ms., 42-43.

Shelby was saved from capture by Frank James and others of Quantrill's band whom he gratefully remembered the rest of his life.[3]

It is most likely that General Holmes refused to countenance Quantrill's ambitious plans for a vast renewal of guerrilla warfare up the border and into Missouri or to recognize the partisan leader as more than a captain. It is also probable that "Granny" Holmes informed the guerrilla that under military regulations final approval for the type of organization he proposed had to come from Richmond. At any rate, Quantrill did go to the Confederate capital during the winter of 1861-1862, and did obtain a commission authorized by Jefferson Davis. In the fall of 1863, when the guerrilla leader took his blood-drenched company down from Missouri to the Confederate lines in Texas, the warm welcome and praise that he had received from the generals of the Trans-Mississippi in 1862 was not forthcoming in all instances. During Quantrill's numerous collisions with various Texas district commanders over orders issued to him, he several times produced his independent commission. For example, Brigadier General Henry E. McCulloch, who held the guerrilla in abhorrence, wrote General H. P. Bee, District of the Coast, on February 9, 1864, that "Captain Quantrill has been ordered to the coast and will send report to General Magruder. His company could not have been moved to that point if I had not promised to use my influence to keep him in the independent partisan service to which he is entitled by his commission from the President."[4] McCulloch was trying to get Quantrill and his men out of his Northern Sub-District, and his statement that the guerrilla had a commission for independent partisan service from "the President" could mean only that.

3 O'Flaherty, *General Jo Shelby,* 155-56.
4 *O. R.,* Series 1, Vol. XXXIV, Part 2, pp. 957-58.

As the spring of 1863 returned to the western border, Quantrill prepared to leave the Confederate army in northwestern Arkansas for a renewal of his type of warfare. Up at his headquarters in St. Louis irritable Union General Sam Curtis made plans to receive him. To make certain that everyone on the border understood what the Union attitude toward the guerrilla was, Curtis published General Order Number Thirty on April 22, 1863. This order dealt in a prolix but highly definitive manner with the laws of war concerning spies, partisans, brigands, guerrillas, and other people "disloyal" to the Union. The order was to guide military courts and commissions, and to instruct district commanders in establishing their own policies and directives. General Curtis defined the guerrilla as follows:

4th. *The Guerrilla Proper.*—Guerrillas proper may be defined as—

Troops not belonging to a regular army, consisting of volunteers, perhaps self-constituted, but generally raised . . . by individuals authorized to do so by the authority they acknowledge as their Government. They do not stand on the regular pay-roll of the army, or are not paid at all, take up arms or lay them down at intervals, and carry on petty war chiefly by raids, extortion, destruction, and massacre, and who cannot encumber themselves with many prisoners, and will, therefore, generally give no quarter. They are peculiarly dangerous, because they easily evade pursuit, and, by laying down their arms, become insidious enemies, because they cannot otherwise subsist than by rapine, and almost always degenerate into simple robbers or brigands.

Whoever shall be convicted as a guerrilla under this order shall suffer death, according to the usage of nations, by sentence of a military commission.[5]

Order Number Thirty was simply for the record; privately General Curtis had advised his subordinates that the guer-

[5] *O. R.*, Series 1, Vol. XXII, Part 2, p. 239.

rillas "deserve no quarters; no terms of civilized warfare. Pursue, strike, and destroy the reptiles. . . ."[6]

Sometime toward the latter part of April, 1863, Quantrill and his company left Shelby's brigade and started north up the border. This time all Union military posts were avoided, and the guerrillas kept their movement hidden. Suddenly they appeared in Lafayette County, where on May 5, 1863, Lieutenant Colonel Walter King of the Fourth Missouri Cavalry at Lexington reported that one of his spies had brought in information that Quantrill and his men were back. King stated that the master guerrilla was calling his men together, and, elevated in purpose through his winter association with the Confederate States army, was under orders from Sterling Price to annoy the Union forces in Kansas and western Missouri while the Confederacy invaded the southeast part of the state. King's report was accurate. In a very few days western Missouri began to blaze with guerrilla activity. The houses of Union men went up in flames, mails were robbed again and again, miles of telegraph wire between the Union posts were torn down, federal patrols were ambushed, bridges were burned, steamboats on the Missouri were attacked, and once again no man, soldier or civilian, felt his life or property safe.[7]

On May 24, 1863, General Schofield replaced General Curtis as commander of the Department of Missouri. The renewal of guerrilla activity caused him to create two new districts to combat Quantrill. On June 9 by General Order Forty-eight Schofield set up the District of the Border and that of the Frontier. The District of the Border, where the guerrilla war was centered, was the state of Kansas and the two western tiers of Missouri counties north of the thirty-

6 O. R., Series 1, Vol. XIII, 688-89, in a letter to General Ben Loan, September 29, 1862.

7 Daily K. C. Journal, May 14, 15, 19, 23, 27, 28, 1863.

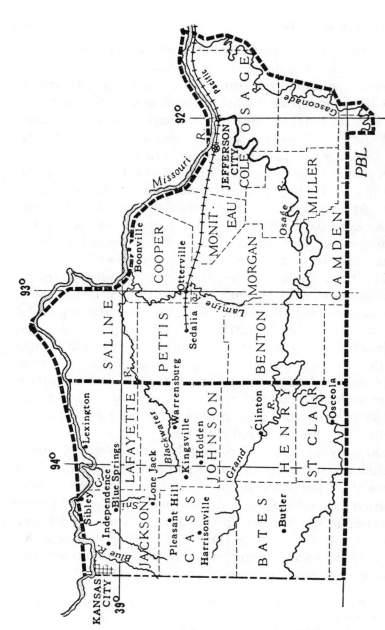

District of the Border and the Central District

eighth parallel and south of the Missouri River. The District
of the Frontier was the rest of Kansas and the two western
tiers of Missouri and Arkansas counties south of the same
parallel. Brigadier General Thomas Ewing, Jr. was given
command of the District of the Border; General James G.
Blunt, that of the Frontier. Tom Ewing, brother-in-law of
General William T. Sherman, had come to Kansas in the
late 1850's to establish a law office at Leavenworth. Handsome, blue-eyed, dark-bearded, Ewing came from a politically
prominent Ohio family, and had soon become active in Republican politics in Kansas. Chief Justice of the Kansas Supreme Court, he had resigned in 1861 to accept a commission
from Jim Lane to raise a regiment. The choice of Ewing to
command western Missouri was unfortunate, even if politically expedient, for General Schofield. Essentially a brave
and honest officer, General Ewing was at the time Lane's
political creature, and was hence obliged to share his master's
views concerning Missourians. His command of the District
of the Border in 1863 was to earn him a lifelong reputation
as a cruel villain. The District of the Frontier was given to
General James G. Blunt, an abolitionist and a real fighter.
Ewing set up his headquarters at Kansas City; Blunt made
Fort Scott his headquarters.

General Ewing quickly took stock of the conditions in his
new district. He believed that the Missouri militia was too
soft in dealing with the pro-Southern population of the area
which was supporting the guerrillas in their war against the
Union. He understood perfectly that the actual basis for the
guerrilla insurrection was the civil population that supported
the partisans. With his "loyal" Kansas troops he determined
to eliminate that sympathetic population. This was the
strategy that Jim Lane had long recommended.

The General began by arresting and confining a considerable number of the wives, mothers, and sisters of some of the

most notorious members of Quantrill's band. From April to August, 1863, these women were picked up by Union soldiers in the towns and on the farms of Jackson, Lafayette, and Cass counties. They were jailed in certain buildings designated as military prisons in Kansas City. When they were charged with specific crime, it was for sheltering guerrillas or for buying percussion caps or clothing for them with stolen money.[8] The confinement of their women served only to enrage Quantrill's men and to crystalize their hatred of Tom Ewing. To make the situation worse, the *Kansas City Journal* carried several stories that the Union command was considering a drastic move to banish all guerrilla families from the area.[9]

Ewing soon recognized the impossibility of confining all of the families of the guerrillas. There simply was not enough prison space available. On August 3 he wrote to Schofield about the desperate situation, and proposed the wholesale removal of the guerrilla families from the western border. His letter is worth citing, for it set the scene for a series of bloody tragedies in the western war:

SIR: About one half of the farmers in the border tier of counties of Missouri in my district, at different times since the war began, entered the rebel service. One-half of them are dead or still in the service; the other half, quitting from time to time the rebel armies, have returned to these counties. Unable to live at their homes if they would, they have gone to bushwacking, and have driven almost all avowed Unionists out of the country or to the military stations. And now, sometimes in squads of a dozen and sometimes in bands of several hundred, they scour the country, robbing and killing those they think unfriendly to them, and threatening the settlements of the Kansas border and the towns and stations in Missouri.

[8] *K. C. Journal*, April 3, 1863; *Daily K. C. Journal*, August 14, 15, 1863; McCorkle, *Three Years With Quantrill*, 78-79.
[9] *Daily K. C. Journal*, April 7, May 6, 1863.

So large a portion of the troops under my command are held fast, guarding the Kansas border and the towns and stations in Missouri, which are filled with refugees, that I cannot put in the field numbers equal to those of the guerrillas. From the character of the country and people, and the great vigilance of the enemy, and the secrecy of their movements, it is rarely practicable to surprise them, and they will never fight unless all the odds are on their side, and they are too well mounted to be run down.

. . . .

About two thirds of the families on the occupied farms of that region are of kin to the guerrillas, and are actively and heartily engaged in feeding, clothing, and sustaining them. The presence of these families is the cause of the presence there of the guerrillas. I can see no prospect of an early and complete end to the war on the border, without a great increase of troops, so long as those families remain there. While they stay there, these men will also stay, if possible. They know they cannot go home and live peaceably because of the fierce feeling against them among the loyal men of the border, who have suffered at their hands. Against these loyal men no amnesty now or hereafter can protect them. They will, therefore, continue guerrilla war as long as they remain, and will stay as long as possible if their families remain. I think that the families of several hundred of the worst of these men should be sent, with their clothes and bedding, to some rebel district south, and would recommend the establishment of a colony of them on the Saint Francis or White Rivers, in Arkansas, to which a steamboat can carry them direct from Kansas City. About one-half of them could take with them no provisions or money of any consequence, and would have to be temporarily supplied by Government. I think it would not do to send them north, because the men would not follow them, while if sent south the men will follow, I think, and there they can live at home if they wish, in safety, and can have amnesty, when the day of amnesty comes.[10]

On August 13, 1863, the *Kansas City Journal* informed its readers, among whom were the guerrillas, that General

10 *O. R.*, Series 1, Vol. XXII, Part 2, p. 428.

Ewing had been at departmental headquarters in St. Louis to obtain authority and make arrangements for the banishment of the families of Quantrill's men from Missouri.

On August 14 a tragedy occurred in Kansas City that was to throw its shadow over the rest of the Civil War on the border; one that was to intensify the ferocious hatred of the guerrillas for the Union forces and to drive all humaneness from their minds. A large three-storied brick building which was being used as a prison for the guerrillas' women collapsed. Confined in the prison were Josephine, Mary, and Jennie Anderson, Susan Vandiver, Mollie Grindstaff, Mrs. Armena Whitsett Gilvey, Mrs. Christie McCorkle Kerr, Nannie Harris, Susan Munday, Martha Munday, and Mrs. Lou Munday Gray. Four of these girls were crushed to death, one was fatally injured, and the others were seriously hurt. One of the dead was Josephine Anderson, a sister of Bill Anderson, who was to become one of Quantrill's most notorious men. Mary Anderson, sixteen, was badly injured. Christie McCorkle Kerr, John McCorkle's sister, was also killed. Her brother and husband were with Quantrill, as were the brothers of Sue Vandiver, Armenia Gilvey, Mollie Grindstaff, and Nannie Harris. Sue Vandiver and Armenia Gilvey were also the cousins of Coleman and James Younger. The building in which the girls had been imprisoned was owned by the wife of painter George C. Bingham, and was located on a ravine in the "Metropolitan Block, McGee's Addition," on Grand Avenue between 14th and 15th Streets.[11] In a dilapidated condition, its floors had been reinforced with wooden girders to keep it from falling. The first floor of the building was a liquor shop; the women were imprisoned on the second story. A large muttering crowd gathered around the dusty debris of the wrecked prison to listen to the screams of the

[11] *Daily K. C. Journal*, August 14, 15, 1863; McCorkle, *Three Years With Quantrill*, 76-77.

injured girls and watch the removal of the bodies. General Ewing called out his guard company to preserve order. In a matter of hours the dark rumor was passed about that Ewing had directed his soldiers to remove the girders under the structure in order to convert it into a deadfall for the deliberate purpose of murder. It was further reported that Dr. Joshua Thorne, Kansas City post surgeon, had inspected the prison a day or so before it fell and had told the general that the women should be removed because of the dangerous condition of the building.[12]

It is impossible to believe that Tom Ewing plotted the murder of the guerrillas' women. They had been well treated and moved from the Union Hotel prison when it became crowded. There is evidence that he was careless of their safety in jailing them in the unsafe structure. A great many people would pay for this carelessness.

When news of the tragedy in Kansas City reached Quantrill's men in the brush, they were wild. Naturally, they believed the stories that Ewing and his men had undermined the prison in order to kill their female relatives. Their rage was increased when Union circles put out the completely unlikely tale that the women had been digging a tunnel to escape and had weakened the prison walls.[13]

Regardless of what caused the collapse of the Kansas City military prison, it had two shocking results. It tore the last thin covering of mercy from the hearts of Quantrill's boys. More serious, from this moment on, Bill Anderson, who until now had been an unknown trooper in the guerrilla company, rose as a demonic leader. Quickly earning the name of "Bloody Bill," Anderson became insane because of the injury to his sisters, and his attitude toward all men who sup-

12 Elmer L. Pigg, "Bloody Bill, Noted Guerrilla of the Civil War," *The Trail Guide* (Kansas City, 1956), 20-21.
13 Connelley, *Quantrill*, 301-302.

ported or served the Union was that of a homicidal maniac.

On the day that the prison collapsed, General Schofield agreed to Ewing's plans to banish the guerrilla families, and directed him to do so, stating however: "On account of the expense and trouble necessarily attendant upon the carrying out of this plan, and also the suffering it may cause to children and other comparatively innocent persons, the number to be transported should be as small as possible, and should be confined to those of the worst character."[14]

On August 18, 1864, General Order Number Ten was sent out from General Ewing's headquarters at Kansas City. It was quite explicit and sealed the doom of many Union men —and Lawrence, Kansas. In part, it stated:

Such officers will arrest, and send to the district provost-marshal for punishment, all men (and all women not heads of families) who willfully aid and encourage guerrillas, with a written statement of the names and residences of such persons and of the proof against them. They will discriminate as carefully as possible between those who were compelled, by threats or fears, to aid the rebels and those who aid them from disloyal motives. The wives and children of known guerrillas, and also women who are heads of families and are willfully engaged in aiding guerrillas, will be notified by such officers to remove out of this district and out of the State of Missouri forthwith. They will be permitted to take, unmolested, their stock, provisions, and household goods. If they fail to remove promptly, they will be sent by such officers, under escort, to Kansas City for shipment south, with their clothes and such necessary household furniture and provision as may be worth removing.[15]

Order Number Ten was a final blow to Quantrill's boys. Those desperate, fear-crazed young men now knew that those persons dearest to them were to be forced from their homes

[14] O. R., Series 1, Vol. XXII, Part 2, pp. 450-51.

[15] O. R., Series 1, Vol. XXII, Part 2, pp. 460-61. Another paragraph of the order stated guerrillas who would lay down their arms might accompany their families.

and banished, with little money and very few possessions, from Missouri. Coupled with the death of their women in Kansas City, Order Number Ten seemed to scream for retaliatory measures. In John McCorkle's words, "We could stand no more."[16]

William Quantrill and his lieutenants had for some time planned a raid on Lawrence, in the eyes of the guerrillas the center of all their troubles and the home of their bitterest enemy, Senator Jim Lane. Now Lawrence was to be destroyed. On August 17 and 18, 1863, Quantrill assembled his men on the farm of a Captain Perdee on Blackwater Creek, Johnson County, Missouri. On August 19 the guerrillas, 294 men, rode west toward Lawrence. Enroute they were joined by Colonel John D. Holt, C.S.A., with 104 recruits, making their total strength about 450.

It is easy to speculate on the thoughts of Quantrill and his men as they galloped west to sack Lawrence. Quantrill's crafty, twisted mind found pleasure, perhaps, in the opportunity to strike at the community which had made him an outlaw. He would make a great name for himself in the Confederacy by wiping out the most famous center of abolitionism in the United States. In Bill Anderson's mad, gleaming eyes there certainly could be seen the desire for blood revenge, a desire shared by John McCorkle, Nathan Kerr, and many, many others. George Todd a murderous killer, looked forward to a hot fight. William Gregg and other more moderate men hoped to get money to distribute to the destitute families of the guerrillas.[17] And, as General Schofield afterwards wrote President Lincoln, all sought vengeance for the "radical" measures the Union had initiated against them and their friends and relatives.[18] Behind these violent, unstable leaders rode a savage host of young men who would

16 McCorkle, *Three Years With Quantrill*, 78-79.
17 Gregg Ms., 47-48.
18 *O. R.*, Series 1, Vol. XXII, Part 2, pp. 482-83.

follow their orders and example with pleasure, boys who had resolved that if they and their people were to be harried from the border, or the earth, they would take some Kansas enemies with them.

The death ride on Lawrence took two days. At dawn of August 20 Quantrill halted his men at the head of the middle fork of the Grand River near the Kansas line. Riding in a column of fours, the guerrillas crossed the line at the southeast corner of Johnson County, Kansas, and then pressed on a mile south of Aubry. Alerted to the approach of the partisans, Captain A. J. Pike, commanding the Union post there, brought out his two companies of cavalry, but when he saw Quantrill's strength, he did not resist him. Worse, the Kansas captain made no attempt to warn other posts of the large force moving westward into the state. As the sun sank on the twentieth, the guerrillas stopped to rest and graze their horses for an hour and then went on to Spring Hill. From that little settlement they turned northwest to Gardiner which they reached at 10:00 P.M. just as the moon went down. With the moon gone, the August night turned black and hot, and Quantrill impressed guides to take him on northward toward Lawrence. Men were awakened on little Kansas farms, forced to lead the rushing column across the prairie, and, if identified by the guerrillas, killed. William Gregg stated that ten guides were shot that terrible night. As the raiders neared Lawrence, they stopped at the farm of Joseph Stone, whom George Todd recognized as the man who had caused his arrest at Independence at the outbreak of the war. Not wishing to make any noise, the guerrilla lieutenant took a musket and beat Stone to death. The silent column galloped on north and west toward Lawrence.

Friday, August 21, 1863, dawned hot and clear. Quantrill's guerrillas halted briefly on the outskirts of Lawrence. The town of some two thousand people lay sleeping before them in the haze of the Kaw River, completely unwarned of the dreadful force about to descend on it. The Missourians were formed in squadrons of forty-five. Bill Quantrill rode along the column and gave each unit its specific mission. Haggard and dusty after a two-day ride, the guerrilla chief still presented a handsome appearance. Wearing a black slouch hat with a gold cord, gray pants and cavalry boots, brown, highly decorated guerrilla shirt, and with four revolvers in his belt, his last order was always the same: "Kill every man big enough to carry a gun."

Then, like a roaring tide, the guerrilla column poured into Lawrence from the southeast at the corner of Delaware and Adams streets. It split on Quincy and Rhode Island streets, and in a few minutes had the town enveloped. The first Kansan to die was the Reverend S. S. Snyder, sometime lieutenant of the Second Kansas Colored Infantry. Milking in his house yard, Snyder was shot dead under his cow.

Quantrill, Bill Gregg, and one squadron galloped up Massachusetts Street, shooting right and left, to the Eldridge Hotel where they established a headquarters—after robbing all the guests. The other guerrillas spread out over town carrying lists of those to be executed and houses to be burned. The Missourians knew most of their enemies. The recruiting camp of the Second Colored Regiment and the Fourteenth Cavalry on New Hampshire Street was overrun and seventeen new soldiers were pistoled to death, several in their blankets. One howling group of guerrillas went to Senator Jim Lane's new house. Quantrill planned to capture him and take him back to Missouri for a public hanging. The worthy Senator, wakened by rebel yells a minute or so before the Missourians arrived at his place, vaulted from bed, thoughtfully removed the nameplate from his premises, and then raced to hiding in a nearby corn patch, his long nightshirt floating behind him. The guerrillas ransacked his house, took his gold sword and general's flag, and set the structure on fire.

Then followed a diabolical, unpardonable massacre, one which has no parallel in the Civil War. Houses and buildings were looted, set on fire, and almost every Kansas man encountered was pistoled down. Saloons were broken into, and many of the guerrillas got drunk, raging up and down the streets with American flags, which they stole from a stationery store, tied to their horses' tails. Some men of Lawrence were chased like rabbits and shot down. Others were torn from their homes and killed in cold blood before their wives and children. Many tried to hide and were burned in their houses. City Mayor Collamore secluded himself in his cistern and suffocated. In two hours at least 150 male citizens of Lawrence were killed, several only young boys. Not one Kansan sold his life dearly; there were no guerrilla casualties. Not one Lawrence woman was injured or physically violated.

At nine o'clock the blood bath ended. Scouts on Mount Oread, the highest elevation in town, reported Union troops approaching from the north and west. Quantrill gathered his men, and loaded with booty they roared out of the stricken, blazing village to the south. One hundred and eighty-five buildings had been destroyed, including most of the business district. The hated newspapers, the *Journal, Tribune,* and *Republican* had been burned out, along with other property worth two million dollars. Eighty widows and 250 orphans were left crying in the dusty streets. Hated Lawrence was almost wiped from the map.

Unfortunately, only a few acts of mercy on the part of the raiders could be recorded. Confederate Colonel John Holt took no part in the massacre and protected several men. Here and there guerrillas helped women remove furniture from burning homes. A widow's house was spared. For the most part, however, Quantrill's men were simply berserkers.

Only one lost his life, drunken Larkin Skaggs, who stayed behind and was shot by an Indian. A mob tore his body apart later in the day. By nightfall of August 22 the exhausted guerrillas were back in Missouri and disbanded, pursued by most of the Union forces in eastern Kansas and western Missouri. Only a few were caught, and they were promptly executed.[19]

The butchery at Lawrence shocked the whole nation. President Lincoln called on General Schofield for an explanation of the frightful event. Kansas Governor Thomas Carney informed the general that he held all Missouri responsible for the raid, as so large a number of guerrillas could not have been raised without common knowledge of their plans. Senator Jim Lane called for a general retaliatory invasion of Missouri, and held hysterical mass meetings to recruit men for the purpose. Schofield tried to mollify Carney by explaining that he could not exterminate Quantrill without five times the cavalry available to him. He also met with Senator Lane, and earned his undying hatred by stoutly informing him that Kansas troops would not be allowed to enter Missouri for general revenge. In Missouri the Lawrence massacre was taken up by politicians, and Governor Gamble and General Schofield were accused by the Radical Republicans of backing Quantrill. A delegation from the United States Congress, headed by Lane, saw Lincoln and unsuccessfully demanded General Schofield's removal.[20]

Jim Lane held General Tom Ewing even more responsible than Schofield for the Lawrence raid. Lane helped Ewing draw up General Order Number Eleven, and bluntly told him that he would be a "dead dog" politically and militarily

19 For details of the Lawrence raid see *O. R.*, Series 1, Vol. XXII, Part 1, pp. 583-85, 572-91; Connelley, *Quantrill*, 303-395.

20 *O. R.*, Series 1, Vol. XXII, Part 1, pp. 572-78; St. Louis *Republican*, August 28, 1863; St. Louis *Democrat*, August 24, 1863.

if he failed to enforce it. Ewing did as he was instructed, but he and Lane were afterwards bitter enemies.[21] Order Number Eleven, issued from Ewing's headquarters at Kansas City on August 25, 1863, completed the ruin of western Missouri. It forced the removal of all people in Jackson, Cass, Bates, and half of Vernon County, living more than a mile from Union military posts. The Missourians were required to vacate the area within fifteen days. The Fifteenth Kansas Cavalry, with the hated Doc Jennison in command, helped to enforce the order, and the revenge-seeking Jayhawkers burned all houses, food, and forage. Jennison and the cavalry robbed and murdered while performing their official duties, and their acts were so brutal that George Bingham later perpetuated their violence in his famous painting "Order Number Eleven," in which Tom Ewing is also a central figure. In two weeks western Missouri was desolated as old men, women, and children were banished from their homes. Only six hundred persons were left in Cass County which had had a population of ten thousand before the war; fewer persons were left in Bates than in Cass. The Union arson was so thorough that only mournful stone chimneys could be seen for hundreds of miles, and for years the area was called the "Burnt District." The people of Lafayette, Henry, and Jackson counties were also so abused by Ewing's soldiers that Schofield was finally forced to remove them from the District of the Border and put them under Egbert Brown's Central District.[22] The condition of the banished Missourians was so pitiful that it turned even the hardest Union heart. On September tenth Colonel Bazel Lazear, commanding the post at Lexington, wrote his wife: "It is heart sickening to see what I have seen since I have been back here. A desolated country and men & women and children, some of them allmost [sic]

[21] Connelley, *Quantrill*, 417-18.
[22] *O. R.*, Series 1, Vol. XXII, Part 2, pp. 570-71.

naked. Some on foot and some in old wagons. Oh God."[23]

In spite of the tragedy he had brought to the border, Quantrill remained exhilarated and active. By September 3 he was back in Jackson County with two hundred men, skirmishing with the Kansans and attacking the Missouri steamboats *Mars, Marcella,* and *Fannie Ogden.* On October 1, 1863, he called his men together in Johnson County preparatory to moving toward winter haven in Texas. Some four hundred guerrillas reported to him at Perdees, and were formed into four companies captained by William Gregg, George Todd, Bill Anderson, and David Pool.[24] This force moved rapidly south, passing west of Carthage in Jasper County. They met no opposition as man or domesticated animal no longer lived on the devastated border.

[23] Vivian K. McLarty (ed.), "The Civil War Letters of Colonel Bazel Lazear," *Missouri Historical Review,* Vol. XLIV, No. 4 (July, 1950), 390.

[24] Gregg Ms., 78. See also *O. R.,* Series 1, Vol. XXII, Part 1, pp. 700-701, in which Quantrill reports other captains, "Estes, Garrett, and Brinker."

8

Quantrill and the Confederacy

███

O N October 6 Quantrill's column reached Union Fort Baxter near Baxter Springs, Kansas, at the edge of the Indian nations. This post was held by two companies of the Third Wisconsin Cavalry and one of the Second Kansas Colored Infantry. The advance guard of the guerrillas decided to attack, and in one desperate charge was beaten off the sod walls of the fort. While the unsuccessful attack on Fort Baxter was taking place, Quantrill was informed that a train of ten wagons was approaching from the north. With half of his command he moved out to meet it. As luck would have it, the train approaching the fort was convoying General James G. Blunt, the swarthy, tough, Union commander of the District of the Frontier, from Fort Scott to Fort Gibson. Blunt was guarded by a hundred men of the Third Wisconsin and Fourteenth Kansas Cavalry. He had with him in a wagon his band, and was accompanied by

128

his adjutant, Major H. Z. Curtis, the son of Major General Samuel R. Curtis. A woman also rode with the general in his buggy, Mrs. Chester Thomas, the wife of an army contractor on the way to join her husband.

Quantrill and 250 of his men formed a line of battle across the path of the approaching train. As many of the guerrillas were dressed completely or partially in Union uniforms, General Blunt decided that they were an honor guard from Fort Baxter, sent out to meet him. He had his cavalry escort dress its ranks, and trotted on toward Quantrill at a leisurely pace. When Blunt's men were sixty yards away, the guerrillas fired a volley into them and launched a screaming charge. The Union cavalry fled in wild disorder. Seventy-nine of the hundred troopers were run down and killed, including all of the bandsmen and Major Henry Curtis. No prisoners were taken. General Blunt and Mrs. Thomas jumped from their buggy onto horses and escaped in a wild race. Mrs. Thomas, her feet in stirrup straps, rode astride, an unheard of position for ladies of that day. She was not, of course, shot at. The deadly revolvers of the guerrillas had paid heavy dividends, for in addition to his dead, Blunt had eight men wounded (who escaped) and five missing. Nine Union soldiers were also killed and ten wounded in Fort Baxter. The guerrillas had only three men killed and four wounded in the affair. Bill Quantrill and his men were jubilant. In addition to the capture of ten loaded wagons, they had taken a fine ambulance and all of Blunt's official correspondence, including his commissions. Quantrill carried off the general's sword and two stands of Union colors. Best of all, they believed one of the dead on the field to be General Blunt. In this they were mistaken, but there were no Union prisoners alive to inform them of their error. The guerrillas looted the train and then burned it. Placing a seriously wounded companion, John Koger, in the ambulance, they thundered on down the old

ILL.

Kirksville • Memphis
Palmyra

St. Joseph
Macon
Hannibal

Atchison •
Plattsburg
Keytesville

Fort Leavenworth •
Liberty

KANSAS CITY
Lexington
Glasgow
Centralia

Topeka   Lawrence •
Independence
Rocheport

Olathe •
Portland
ST. LOUIS

Harrisonville •
Warrensburg

K A N S A S
Sedalia
JEFFERSON
CITY

• Butler

• Osceola
Rolla

Fort Scott • • Nevada

• Lamar

Baxter Springs •
• Springfield

(The Osage)
Carthage

• Neosho

• Cassville

(The Cherokee)
Pea Ridge

INDIAN
• Cane Hill

(The Creek)

Canadian   River
Fort Smith

(The Choctaw)
Arkansas
River

N A T I O N S
LITTLE ROCK •

(The Chickasaw)

Sherman
Bonham

Marshall •
• Shreveport

THE
CONFEDERATE
GUERRILLA   THEATRE
OF
WAR
1861 - 1865

Red   River

L O U I S I A N A

Mississippi River

Missouri River

M I S S O U R I

A R K A N S A S

P.B. Larimore

Texas road into the Indian nations. Between Baxter Springs and the Canadian River they killed 150 Union Indians and Negroes who were gathering ponies. On October 12, 1862, they entered the Confederate lines and joined General Douglas H. Cooper and his Indian soldiers on the Canadian.[1]

Anxious that his glittering victory should be known, Quantrill on October 13 wrote Sterling Price, who was at Camp Bragg, Arkansas, about his exploits. The guerrilla used glowing and detailed terms in describing General Blunt's defeat and supposed death, but made no mention at all about the tragic butchery at Lawrence. Indeed, he dismissed the whole subject with a paragraph at the end of his letter which stated: "At some future day I will send you a complete report of my summer's campaign on the Missouri River." He signed himself as "Colonel, Commanding, &c."[2]

Quantrill and his men remained with General Cooper a few days to rest, and then rode on south, crossing the Red River at Colbert's Ferry. A winter camp was set up on Mineral Creek, approximately fifteen miles northwest of Sherman, Texas, and the guerrilla leader began to renew his association with the Confederate army.

Major General Sterling Price was delighted with "Colonel" Quantrill's report concerning Baxter Springs, but he had reservations about what the guerrilla had done during the preceding summer months. On November 2, 1863, he dispatched the following letter to Quantrill:

Col. WILLIAM C. QUANTRILL,
    Commanding Cavalry:
COLONEL: I am desired by Major-General Price to acknowledge the receipt of your report of your march from the Missouri River to the Canadian, and that he takes pleasure in congratulating

[1] *O. R.*, Series 1, Vol. XXII, Part 1, pp. 688-701.
[2] *O. R.*, Series 1, Vol. XXII, Part 1, pp. 700-701.

you and your gallant command upon the success attending it. General Price is very anxious that you prepare the report of your summer campaign, alluded to by you, at as early a date as practicable, and forward it without delay, more particularly so as he is desirous that your acts should appear in their true light before the world. In it he wishes you to incorporate particularly the treatment to which the prisoners belonging to your command received from the Federal authorities; also the orders issued by General Blunt or other Federal officers regarding the disposition to be made of you or your men if taken or vanquished. He has been informed that orders of a most inhuman character were issued. Indeed, he has some emanating from those holding subordinate commands, but wants to have all the facts clearly portrayed, so that the Confederacy and the world may learn the murderous and uncivilized warfare which they themselves inaugurated, and thus be able to appreciate their cowardly shrieks and howls when with a just retaliation the same "measure is meted out to them." He desires me to convey to you, and through you to your command, his high appreciation of the hardships you have so nobly endured and the gallant struggle you have made against despotism and the oppression of our State, with the confident hope that success will soon crown our efforts.

I have the honor to remain, respectfully, your obedient servant,

MACLEAN,
*Major and Assistant
Adjutant General*[3]

General Price wrote Missouri Governor Thomas C. Reynolds, who had taken office at Claiborne Jackson's death, at his "capital" at Marshall, Texas, on the same date. Stating that the guerrillas were down from Missouri, and enclosing a copy of Quantrill's report, Price praised him warmly: "Colonel Quantrill has now with him some 350 men of that daring and dashing character which has made the name of Quantrill so feared by our enemies, and have aided so much to keep

[3] *O. R.*, Series 1, Vol. LIII, 908.

Missouri, though overrun by Federals, identified with the Confederacy."[4]

The general added that the guerrillas were not willing to join regular Confederate forces since many of them had deserted from the commands of Generals Holmes and Hindman the previous winter because they had been bored with inactivity. Quantrill's men also were afraid to serve under Confederate officers who might make mass surrenders, as they had been outlawed by the Union and were subject to execution if captured.

Quite obviously Sterling Price admired the guerrillas, but knowing what had actually taken place at Lawrence, he was anxious, if possible, to justify their acts, even to putting exculpating words in their mouths. Price's anxiety for Quantrill to appear in the best light possible was probably based on a desire to make his guerrillas acceptable to Lieutenant General Edmund Kirby Smith, who had taken over command of the Trans-Mississippi from old General Holmes. The previous summer Kirby Smith had written Governor Reynolds that the guerrilla war in Missouri was only entailing new persecution and misery for "our friends there," without advancing the Confederate cause in the slightest.[5]

Before writing to Quantrill on November 3, General Price had done a little detective work concerning the legal status of the guerrillas' organization. On October 28 he had communicated with Governor Reynolds concerning the matter. Reynolds had answered his letter on the thirtieth from Shreveport, Louisiana, giving his views. First, the governor informed Price, "Colonel" Quantrill was not, and had never been, a military officer of the state of Missouri. Second, the guerrilla was not known as a Confederate officer at Trans-Mississippi Headquarters. Third, he felt that Quantrill and

4 *O. R.*, Series 1, Vol. LIII, 907-908.
5 *O. R.*, Series 1, Vol. XXII, Part 2, p. 855.

his men should join the Confederate army, and should so do under no stipulations as to type of service or the honorable re-enlistment of deserters. But, Tom Reynolds added, he would like to see Quantrill, and to use him, as he always had a Missouri campaign in mind.[6] On October 31 Governor Reynolds wrote a Judge Watkins that Quantrill had arrived in north Texas "like an elephant won at a raffle," and that no one knew what to do with him or his men.[7]

Because of Quantrill's victory over feared and dangerous General Blunt, he was, when he first arrived in Texas in the fall of 1863, an object of curiosity and approbation. On October fifteenth Brigadier General William Steele, commanding the District of the Indian Territory, wrote Brigadier General Henry McCulloch of the Northern Sub-District of Texas that he was anxious to meet Quantrill. Steele believed that the guerrilla was better posted regarding the disposition of Union forces in Missouri and western Arkansas than anyone else.[8] On the same date Major General J. Bankhead (Prince John) Magruder, commanding the entire District of Texas, published a general order congratulating "Colonel W. C. Quantrill" for defeating Blunt at Baxter Springs.[9]

Other Confederate officers, however, not so pragmatic as Price, Steele, and Magruder, began to eye Quantrill and his blood-drenched gang with something akin to horror when their deeds became known. General Henry McCulloch, who commanded the sub-district which Quantrill and his men entered when they first reached Texas, seems to have been the first general officer to have serious doubts as to the guerrilla's ornamentation to the Confederate service. On Octo-

[6] Reynolds Manuscript Collection, Numbered Letter Books of Thomas C. Reynolds, Library of Congress. Hereinafter cited Letter Book. This citation, Letter Book, 4463, 171-72.

[7] Letter Book, 4463.

[8] O. R., Series 1, Vol. XXII, Part 2, p. 1046.

[9] O. R., Series 1, Vol. XXVI, Part 2, pp. 339-40.

ber 22, 1863, he expressed his official feelings in a letter to Captain Edmund P. Turner, Assistant Adjutant General of the Trans-Mississippi:

CAPTAIN: A good many of Colonel Quantrill's command have come into this sub-district, and it is said he is now within it. He has not reported here, and I do not know what his military status is. I do not know as much about his mode of warfare as others seem to know; but, from all I can learn, it is but little, if at all, removed from that of the wildest savage; so much so, that I do not for a moment believe that our Government can sanction it in one of her officers. Hence, it seems to me if he be an officer of our army, his conduct should be officially noticed, and if he be not an officer of our army, his acts should be disavowed by our Government, and, as far as practicable, he be made to understand that we would greatly prefer his remaining away from our army or its vicinity.

I appreciate his services, and am anxious to have them; but certainly we cannot, as a Christian people, sanction a savage, inhuman warfare, in which men are to be shot down like dogs, after throwing down their arms and holding up their hands supplicating for mercy.

This is a matter to which I wish to call the attention of our commanding generals, and with regard to which I desire their advice and instructions as early as practicable.[10]

On November 1 McCulloch further informed Turner that although "it may be said that Quantrill will help you," he had little confidence in men who fought for booty and whose mode of warfare was like that of the savages.[11]

Kirby Smith believed that he had found a use for Quantrill by the beginning of November. General McCulloch's command had been plagued by gangs of deserters. General Smith proposed that Quantrill and his men be used as a police company to capture them and bring in conscripts. This was a

10 *O. R.*, Series 1, Vol. XXVI, Part 2, p. 348.
11 *O. R.*, Series 1, Vol. XXVI, Part 2, p. 379.

rather unusual proposition, but possibly Kirby Smith believed in the old axiom that it takes a thief to catch a thief. He also gratuitously advised McCulloch about Quantrill's boys:

They are bold, fearless men, and, moreover, from all representations, are under very fair discipline. They are composed, I understand, in a measure of the very best class of Missourians. They have suffered every outrage in their person and families at the hands of the Federals, and, being outlawed and their lives forfeited, have waged a war of no quarter whenever they have come in contact with the enemy. Colonel Quantrill, I understand, will perform that duty, provided rations and forage are issued to his men and horses; this you are authorized to order. In the event you have no immediate service for him and his command, direct him to report in person at these headquarters.[12]

Henry McCulloch evidently decided Quantrill would be of small assistance to him in his district problem, for the guerrilla leader went to Shreveport to report to General Smith. On November 19 Smith advised McCulloch that "Captain" Quantrill was leaving his headquarters and was to report to the general at Bonham before joining his command. On November 21 Smith advised McCulloch again to use Quantrill and his men in rounding up deserters.[13]

While the generals of the Trans-Mississippi were trying to fit Quantrill into their formal military establishment, things were not going well for the guerrilla chieftain at his camp on Mineral Creek. The Texas winter of 1863-1864 saw the dissolution of his original force and his decline as a leader. The reasons for Quantrill's downfall were varied, and their details have been lost in the passage of time. In the first place, if Bill Quantrill refused to place himself under Confederate army authority, his men were reluctant to give him the status

12 O. R., Series 1, Vol. XXVI, Part 2, pp. 382-83.

13 O. R., Series 1, Vol. XXII, Part 2, pp. 1072-73; O. R., Series 1, Vol. XXVI. Part 2, pp. 430-31.

and obedience due a Confederate captain. Quantrill simply could not maintain discipline without accepting discipline himself. Secondly, his men began to realize that their leader, their hero, was viewed with disgust and horror, rather than with praise, by many regular Confederate officers. By December, 1863, Bill Quantrill could no longer control his wild young subordinates.

Bill Anderson and his company were the first to defect, and this could be expected in view of the personality of this strange young man. Anderson, now known as "Bloody Bill" from Missouri to Texas, was to take Quantrill's place in notoriety in 1864. His terrible demoniac deeds were to far exceed those of his captain. In the annals of the border Bill Anderson is truly a mysterious figure, for little is known about the background of this terrible young man, and his career at war was brief. By all accounts "Bloody Bill" was the most handsome of Quantrill's guerrillas. Tall, sinewy, lithe, with long dark hair which curled and fell to his shoulders, Anderson had prominent cheek bones, and large, piercing blue eyes which literally blazed with emotion. An elegant dresser and a dashing figure on horseback, there is little doubt that he was at times insane. Unlike Quantrill, who went into battle with murderous calmness, Anderson approached his enemy crying and frothing at the mouth.[14]

Bill Anderson was reared and educated at Huntsville, the county seat of Randolph County, Missouri. As a young boy he had moved with his father, his brother Jim, and his three sisters to an area near Council Grove, Kansas, where the family was at once caught up in the border war. Bill's father was killed in some forgotten foray, and he and his brother joined the guerrillas.[15] In a letter to the editors of the Lexington, Missouri, newspapers on July 7, 1864, Anderson made

14 Gregg Ms., 90; St. Louis *Democrat*, November 14, 1864.

15 *Columbia, Missouri, Statesman*, July 22, 1864. Hereinafter cited *Statesman; O. R.*, Series 1, Vol. XLI, Part 2, pp. 209, 216, 217.

the following statement concerning his family and his reasons
for being a guerrilla:

I have chosen guerrilla warfare to revenge myself for wrongs that
I could not honorably revenge otherwise. I lived in Kansas when
this war commenced. Because I would not fight the people of
Missouri, my native State, the Yankees sought my life, but failed
to get me. Revenged themselves by murdering my father, destroying all my property, and since that time murdered one of my
sisters and kept the other two in jail twelve months.[16]

In view of "Bloody Bill's" remorseless savagery on the
border during the summer and fall of 1864, these remarks
explain a great deal. He gave every indication of being moti-
vated solely by an insane desire for revenge against all Union
men. He killed every man he saw dressed in a blue uniform,
every man who supported the Union cause.

Anderson's separation from Quantrill at the Mineral Creek
camp seems to have come as the result of romance. In his
early twenties Bill fell in love with and married a Miss Bush
Smith of Sherman. Evidently feeling that the town offered
more private and comfortable possibilities for connubial bliss
than the rough Mineral Creek camp, Bill moved to Sherman.[17] His company came with him, and while Bill pursued
Venus, it was commanded by eighteen-year-old Archie
Clement from Kingsville, Johnson County, Missouri, Anderson's lieutenant and personal executioner. Archie Clement
was a gunman in the true frontier sense. Small, blonde, grey
eyed, with a perpetual smile on his face, he knew and obeyed
only one master, Bloody Bill Anderson. When Anderson said
"kill," Archie Clement killed, with pistol or knife. An un-
feeling savage, this child soldier scalped and mutilated his
victims when it pleased him. As fearless as Anderson, "Little

[16] *O. R.*, Series 1, Vol. XLI, Part 2, p. 75.
[17] Connelley, *Quantrill*, 439.

Archie" Clement was as vicious and as cruel a boy as appeared on the frontier.

Archie was not much of a company commander. Anderson's boys rioted night and day in Sherman. Their favorite sport was shooting up the town, and in a few weeks they had riddled most of the steeples, signs, and saloon doors in Sherman. Drunk on Christmas Day, 1863, they rode their horses into Ben Christian's hotel and broke up all the lobby furniture. Holding their revolvers in their hands, they had their pictures made, but when they saw the proofs, they demolished the photographer's equipment. When they sobered up, they sheepishly paid for the damage, but they soon made a bad name for themselves, and every crime committed in wild north Texas was laid to them. When the citizens of Sherman and the surrounding countryside complained about them to General McCulloch at Bonham, Bloody Bill rode down and informed the general that Quantrill's boys were the guilty parties.[18] On February 3, 1864, McCulloch wrote his immediate superior, General Magruder, in disgust:

Quantrill will not obey orders and so much mischief is charged to his command here that I have determined to disarm, arrest, and send his entire command to you or General Smith. This is the only chance to get them out of this section of country, which they have nearly ruined, and I have never yet got them to do any service.

They regard the life of a man less than you would that of a sheep-killing dog. Quantrill and his men are determined never to go into the army or fight in any general battle, first, because many of them are deserters from our Confederate ranks, and next, because they are afraid of being captured, and then because it won't pay men who fight for plunder. They will only fight when they have all the advantage and when they can run away whenever they find things too hot for them. I regard them as but one

18 Connelley, *Quantrill,* 440-41.

shade better than highwaymen, and the community believe that they have committed all the robberies that have been committed about here for some time, and every man that has any money about his house is scared to death, nearly, and several moneyed men have taken their money and gone where they feel more secure.[19]

McCulloch was completely soured on Quantrill, but on February 9, in his previously mentioned letter to General Bee, he admitted that he could do little with the guerrilla because of his independent presidential commission.

With Anderson and Quantrill at odds, Lieutenant William Gregg departed. Sobered over the butchery of Lawrence and the lack of discipline of the guerrillas in Texas, Gregg left Quantrill in November, 1863, to become a captain in Shank's Regiment, Shelby's Brigade of the Confederate States army.[20] Quantrill had only George Todd left, and that young lieutenant was showing signs of restlessness and jealousy. Apparently Todd had just become more popular with the guerrillas than Quantrill, and fancied himself a better leader. Even less is known about George Todd than Bill Anderson. According to John N. Edwards, who knew most of the guerrillas personally, he was born in Scotland. As a boy he had killed a man in his native country, had fled to Canada, and eventually to Jackson County, Missouri. He and his father were bridge and railroad contractors there before the war. Todd had gotten in trouble with the law at Independence and had joined Quantrill in December, 1861. A round-faced, taciturn, ferocious boy, blonde-headed George Todd was fearless and a tough guerrilla. He rode back to Missouri with Quantrill in the spring of 1864, but at the first opportunity he struck out with an independent command.[21]

[19] O. R., Series 1, Vol. XXXIV, Part 2, pp. 941-943.
[20] Gregg Ms., 88.
[21] Edwards, Noted Guerrillas, 321-22; Connelley, Quantrill, 447.

On March 10, 1864, Governor Tom Reynolds wrote Quantrill that he had obtained permission for him to leave Texas. In a letter to the guerrilla, who was at Sherman, the governor of Missouri advised him:

General Smith is sending instructions partly at my suggestion to allow you to proceed within the enemy lines. I strongly suggest that you refuse to accept any deserter from the Army of Ark. and that you establish a regular command in the regular Confederate service, that you follow all the rules of war and abandon the "no quarter" system you say was forced on you. The history of guerrilla leaders is that they always fail or are killed. You have brilliant ability and can if you do properly look forward to a high future.[22]

Reynolds was prophetic. Quantrill was to be killed little more than a year later, and at the time the governor wrote, his command was falling apart.

The spring of 1864 came on slowly in northern Texas. At Mineral Springs Quantrill and surly George Todd watched the grass turn green and planned their movement north. At Sherman wild-eyed Bill Anderson and smiling Archie Clement made similar preparations. Down at Bonham General McCulloch secretly prayed for the return of the grass so that these troublesome boys would move out of his command. The entire Trans-Mississippi Confederacy was ready to wash its hands of the guerrillas—for the time being.

22 Letter Book, 4464, pp. 119-20.

9

Martial Law

‖‖‖

A S tragic and cruel as the guerrilla insurrection was in Missouri between 1861 and 1865, its principal injury to the people lay in consequential rather than immediate factors. To be sure, several thousand Missourians lost their lives and property as a direct result of the war, but many more suffered because of the complete abrogation of their civil rights. At the present day, when there is apprehension in some circles concerning the weakening of civil law and individual rights and liberty, it is interesting to examine the conditions which existed when the people of an entire state had all the protection afforded them by law and the Constitution stripped away for a period of nearly four years.

The primary evils of the guerrilla insurrection came as a result of sequential events that began in the first days of the struggle for the state. As has been indicated, the Union military commanders of Missouri assumed that widespread disloyalty to the federal government abounded in 1861. This assumption, which seems to have been largely erroneous, led to military occupation, and, from available evidence, the harshness with which the occupation was accomplished contributed greatly to the very unrest the Union captains suspected and feared. The first overt reaction to military occupation took the form of guerrilla warfare. As irregular partisan conflict spread, it, in turn, weakened civil law and order, and caused the Union military authorities to enact a series of severe punitive measures against the people.

In a real sense the Union military command faced a confusing problem in Missouri during the war. There were numerous people disloyal to the Union throughout the State, and there were even more, who if forced to take sides, would become disloyal. There was the baffling question as to the definition of loyalty itself, and also the question of the depth and degree of deviation from this definition. There was the vexing riddle of the various types and shades of disloyalty, and the matter of measures to be taken against men in each instance. There was the problem of guilt; guilt by active resistance to authority, guilt by past act, utterance, and association; guilt by blood relationship and marriage, and guilt suggested by informers or by mischievous or revengeful people. And, of course, if there was guilt, there had to be evidence and punishment appropriate to every case. To further complicate the situation, the Union command also had as its responsibility a very large population that was loyal to the Union. This population had to be protected, supported where possible in its governmental functions, and often catered to or resisted in its own serious factional differences.

All in all the military government of Missouri between 1861 and 1865 required great ability and understanding. Unfortunately, ineptness, confusion, and excess as often characterized that government, and the generals who headed it, as did the finer qualities of justice, temperance, and good

sense. Abraham Lincoln's magnificent personality and sense
of calm fairness was demonstrated again and again in Missouri, as he directed the correction of evils and outlined
decent administrative policies for his military subordinates
there. However, Lincoln was far removed from the scene, and
most of his efforts were spent in remedying conditions caused
by initially faulty or weak governmental policies.

The absolute power of the Union military government between 1861 and 1865 was based on martial law. At the beginning of the Civil War the concept of the application of
martial law was poorly defined, and there had been few instances of its use in the United States to that time.[1] Actually,
martial law was not mentioned in the Constitution or statutes
of the nation, nor was much light thrown upon the subject
by the constitutions or laws of the states of the Union.[2] To
be sure, the Constitution did state positively that the privi-
lege of the writ of habeas corpus could not be suspended
except in case of rebellion or invasion when the public
safety would demand it. The Constitution did not, however,
mention by whose authority the vital writ might be suspended. Without the suspension of habeas corpus martial
law could not be effective, for martial law overrules and re-
places civil law and civil courts wherever applied. There
were, then, neither common nor statute sources concerning
the application of martial law available to the Union commanders of Missouri—beyond the fact that it lay implied in
their office, that it could exist only through suspension of the
writ of habeas corpus, and that that writ could be revoked
only when the public safety demanded it because of invasion
or rebellion.[3]

[1] Henry W. Halleck, *International Law; or Rules Regulating the Intercourse of States in Peace and War* (New York, 1861), 379.

[2] James G. Randall, *Constitutional Problems Under Lincoln* (New York,
London, 1926), 118-39.

[3] Halleck, *International Law*, 373.

The first military commander to apply martial law in Missouri was General Frémont. In August, 1861, Frémont issued a proclamation which stated, among a great many other things, that circumstances made it necessary for him "to assume the administrative power of the state," and that, in order to do this, he was declaring martial law over all Missouri.[4] Frémont explained that martial law was necessary because of the helplessness of the civil authorities and the pressure of "bands of murderers and marauders who infest nearly every county of the State." The general's proclamation was probably needed at the time. It also contained a provision for the continued function of civil government and law, and specified that the "ordinary tribunals of the country" and civil law and government were to be administered by civil authorities where peaceful conditions made it possible.[5]

This meant that Missouri would henceforth have a dual judicial and governmental system, subject to the decision of the Union commander of the department. In some places civil law and authority would be maintained; at others, martial law with its forms and soldier officials would operate. In either event the military could be supreme. Under certain Union commanders the extralegal provisional government of Missouri enjoyed power between 1861 and 1864; under others, as in the case of Frémont, its representatives spent most of their time in Washington trying to get the unsatisfactory general removed or his orders revoked. At any rate, General Frémont's act of martial law, with its dual provision for civil law, was followed and amplified by the various Union departmental commanders over Missouri until it was revoked by joint proclamation of General John Pope and Governor Thomas C. Fletcher in March, 1865.[6]

4 St. Louis *Republican*, August 31, 1861.
5 *O. R.*, Series 1, Vol. III, pp. 466-67.
6 *O. R.*, Series 1, Vol. XLVIII, Part 1, pp. 1115, 1203.

Typically, General Frémont seems not to have had prior approval from President Lincoln or his military superiors to exercise martial law in Missouri. His successor, old General Halleck, always meticulous about red tape, wrote General McClellan in November, 1861, that, although martial law had been in force for months, he could find no written authority from the President for it. Halleck felt that the need for martial law in Missouri was imperative, and informed McClellan that if the president was not willing to give him the authority to exercise it, he could relieve him. On November 1, 1861, President Lincoln authorized Halleck to suspend the writ of habeas corpus and to exercise martial law in his department where he deemed it necessary.[7]

Generals Schofield and Curtis continued martial law with all its implications under their commands, and it was not until the end of the year 1862 that questions concerning its necessity arose. Hearing of the abuse of civilians under its application, President Lincoln, on December 17, 1862, telegraphed General Curtis to ask if civil authority could not be introduced into Missouri "to any extent with advantage and safety." Curtis' reply on the same date was brief: "The peace of this State rests on military power. To relinquish this power would be dangerous. It would allow rebels to rule some sections and ruin the Union men who have joined the military power to put down the rebellion."[8] This was the end of the matter. For four years Missouri was under martial law, the Union military command superior to civil law and government. Many cruel and tyrannical acts were to be committed against the people by its authority.

In many parts of Missouri, however, martial law was the only law that could function. In the central and western part of the state guerrilla warfare gradually collapsed most civil

[7] *O. R.*, Series 1, Vol. VIII, 395, 401.

[8] *O. R.*, Series 1, Vol. XXII, Part 1, p. 839; see also pages 810-12, and Part 2, same volume, 357-58.

law and authority between 1861 and 1865. For example, on May 21, 1862, the *Kansas City Journal* stated that Quantrill's guerrillas had become so bold that the Jackson County sheriff had resigned his office, and the county coroner was unable to serve his processes because of threatened assassination. In January, 1863, Brigadier General Ben Loan wrote General Curtis about the conditions of law and order in the Central District, and mentioned the murder of Coleman Younger's father by one of his captains:

In several counties in the district no court of record of any kind have held a session for several terms past, say, for more than eighteen months. The records have been stolen, perhaps destroyed, and the civil officers driven from the country. Recently I had arrested a Captain Walley, who had murdered one Harry Younger, in Jackson County, for his money. The evidence of his guilt was so clear and conclusive that he confessed it. Preferring that he should be regularly tried and punished, I directed a court to be held in Independence for that purpose. The witnesses, soldiers in the Fifth Regiment Missouri State Militia, who were stationed at Harrisonville, in Cass County, were sent to attend court. When on their way they were bushwacked by a band under Bird Younger, a son of the murdered man, and the court was not held. No court has or can be held in Jackson, Johnson, Cass, Bates, Henry, or Vernon Counties. Last fall when I was at Lexington, with at least 1200 soldiers, 200 or 300 of whom were enrolled militia of the county, and with scouts out daily, I had a guard of 50 men, as a sheriff's posse, attacked and driven back by a force of some 200 rebels. It was impossible for the sheriff to serve a writ without a guard stronger than 50 men.[9]

Loan went on to say that it was "utterly false" that the machinery of government could be operated as in time of peace, because of the guerrillas. As the war progressed, conditions worsened over the entire state, and as late as July, 1864, Colonel T. A. Switzler, the provost marshal for the

[9] *O. R.*, Series 1, Vol. XXII, Part 2, pp. 78-82.

Central District, commenting on the need for martial law, wrote his superiors: "The civil law, the great palladium of liberty in Missouri, is now very weak. Whilst there is an almost universal desire for its restoration, yet the people are not in a condition to accept it unaided by the strong arm of the military power, as vouchsafing the protection necessary for their well-being."[10]

In most of central and western Missouri the Confederate guerrillas made martial law a necessity, the only law that could be maintained during the Civil War.

The administration of martial law by the Union military command required appropriate officers, military courts and commissions, and a large police and penal system. As there were no precedents for its application, these features developed and functioned according to the different ideas and temperaments of the successive departmental and district commanders. In the main, the Union officers of the districts of Missouri were fully occupied with the pressing and aggravating problem of combating guerrillas and guarding against Confederate invasion. However, if they were primarily concerned with tactical affairs, each one sooner or later came to realize that the real base of the partisan struggle in Missouri lay in the civil population. Every major Union commander not only had to manage his troops and fight guerrillas, but also had to govern and control the civil element which supported the partisans and made their activity possible. This dual responsibility, entailing the use of martial law, was not to the liking of many good field soldiers, especially those who had no political experience, ability, or aptitude. To many able Union cavalry officers it was a harassing responsibility. Most of them were courageous men, quite willing to command troops and meet an enemy in respectable open combat, but far too many of them were prone to leave the application of martial law and military government to local subordinates

10 *O. R.*, Series 1, Vol. XLI, Part 2, p. 88.

without many instructions or much supervision. Most of them could see the opportunity for recognition and promotion as the result of successful field leadership, but many would never realize the credit they would earn by sensitive civil administration and a sympathetic understanding of local problems.

Brigadier General John Pope was the first Union commander forced to grapple with the problem of local military government. In charge of the District of North Missouri in July and August, 1861, Pope abdicated his responsibility of securing peace and stability for the area by setting up his notorious Committees of Public Safety for every major community in his district. As has been noted, the general's committees were spectacular failures. Price's guerrillas sent railroad bridges and culverts up in smoke all over north Missouri, and, of course, the most conscientious committees were powerless to stop them. When mass retaliation against the towns and counties was ordered by Pope, insurrection and anarchy resulted. He then recommended even sterner disciplinary action so that those guilty of guerrilla activity or disloyalty toward the Union would be severely punished.

Unable to depend upon local law enforcement agencies and local courts, the Union command set up a system of military commissions which would act as tribunals. These were created under the provisions of Order Number One on January 1, 1862.[11] These commissions, composed of Union army officers, were to operate where civil courts could not be held or were untrustworthy, where civil offenses had become military offenses because of the war, and where trial by court-martial was not appropriate. Actually, military commissions were ordered by the same authority, constituted in the same manner, and conducted according to the same rules as courts-martial. "Old Brains" Halleck drew up Order Number One, which abounded with legal niceties and tech-

11 *O. R.*, Series 1, Vol. VIII, 476-78.

nicalities. Always intending to reserve final judgment to himself in all military matters, he directed that sentences of military commissions extending to loss of life, confiscation of property, or imprisonment of over thirty days were to be approved by the commanding general of the department.[12] There was one major weakness to this safeguard, and, of course, it was fatal. So many thousands of cases of "disloyalty" were discovered, so many men arrested, that the whole mechanism of commissions, trial, and review became hopelessly bogged down.

The system of military commissions established by General Halleck as the result of Pope's experiences in north Missouri in 1861 was exactly what the subordinate Union commanders believed they needed. Free of the statute limitations of both civil and military law, commissions were convened and put on permanent status all over the state. In January, 1862, a large number of Price's guerrilla bridge-burners were tried, sentenced to death, and the sentences approved by Halleck's headquarters.[13] Guerrillas were hard to catch, however, and as most were shot summarily when captured, the major efforts of the commissions soon were directed against those people whom it was believed sympathized with the Confederacy or encouraged insurrection. Literally thousands of men were arrested and imprisoned, charged with believing in rebellion, expressing disloyal sentiments, communicating with and aiding the enemy, or violating the numerous Union orders issued under martial law.[14] Sentences ranged from fines and confiscation of property to banishment, long-term imprisonment, and death. Many women, also, were arrested and jailed.

[12] O. R., Series 1, Vol. VIII, 834.
[13] St. Louis Republican, January 27, 1862.
[14] St. Louis Republican, 1862, 1863, 1864. Almost every edition in this period listed large numbers of persons received at St. Louis from military commissions.

With any flourishing court system there has to be an alert and aggressive police force. As there was no provision for police officers under martial law, the Union commanders established and utilized a system of local provost marshals to apprehend and arrest the guilty. Traditionally, and according to military law, a provost marshal of the United States army had concerned himself only with the police duties and law enforcement of the military establishment. Under martial law in Missouri the provost marshal of the department, with his subordinates, became the primary police officer of the state.

General Sam Curtis was the first commander of the Department of Missouri to publish an official directive concerning the provost marshal system and the duties connected with it. By General Order Twenty-three, dated December 1, 1862, Curtis directed that the provost marshal department in Missouri would be composed of one provost marshal general, district provost marshals, and as many deputies as might be needed. District provost marshals and their deputies were to be appointed by the provost marshal general upon the recommendation of the district military commander. A system of reporting was set up, and the order stated: "Officers of the provost-marshal's department, during the existence of civil war, are especially intrusted with the peace and quiet of their respective districts, counties, and sections; and to this end may cause the arrest and confinement of disloyal persons, subject to the instructions and orders of the department."[15]

Order Twenty-three also stated that district and deputy provost marshals were to dispose of minor offenses locally. Only serious cases were to be sent to St. Louis headquarters for disposition. Sworn written charges and all evidence were to accompany each prisoner sent in.

Curtis' order gave the Union provost marshals in Missouri

[15] *O. R.*, Series 1, Vol. XXII, Part 1, pp. 803-804.

complete authority to arrest and imprison citizens at their will, and they fell to their duties with gusto. Every town at which there was a military post soon had well-filled prison cells and stockades. By the late summer of 1862 the provost marshal general's office at St. Louis was swamped with prisoners under serious charges, and on September 4, 1862, the St. Louis *Republican* observed that the central office was examining thirty or forty cases daily. Hundreds of arrested men and women were being received each week, and, as minor cases were taken care of at the local level, many more were being held at the district offices and suboffices.[16] In a large number of Missouri communities the Union provost marshal, because of his unlimited power of arrest and imprisonment, became the most feared and despised man in the military government. Most of them were local men, recommended by the radical Union element of the area, and in far too many instances their arbitrary powers went to their heads. By the last of the year 1862 their abuses had become so notorious that the whole system came under the criticism of the United States War Department.

On December 24, 1862, no doubt as a Christmas present for the people of his department, Sam Curtis published a new order, Number Thirty-five, which gave the provost marshals in Missouri even greater powers.[17] When this order appeared in the newspapers, it was brought to the attention of President Lincoln, and on January 14, 1863, at his direction, Secretary of War Stanton wrote Curtis that the order must be suspended. To straighten the general out Stanton bluntly stated: ". . . all orders of provost-marshals in the State of Missouri respecting trade, commerce, or anything but the discipline and government of the troops in the

16 St. Louis *Republican*, August 5, 15, 16, 20, 27, September 4, 9, 11, 1862; *Daily K. C. Journal*, April 3, July 24, 1863; O. R., Series 1, Vol. XXXIV, Part 4, pp. 363-64, Vol. XIII, 132, 806-807.

17 O. R., Series 1, Vol. XXII, Part 1, pp. 868-71.

United States service be also suspended, and the provost-marshals be relieved from service in such capacity, excepting St. Louis."[18]

General Curtis, who believed in a severe Union policy in Missouri and who had allied himself with the Radical Republican element in the state, was outraged. Here in a single blow his police system was to be abolished. On the morning of January 15 he telegraphed Stanton, asking that he might confer by letter before executing the War Department order. Later during the day he wrote the Secretary of War the following buck-passing letter, obstinately defending a situation in his own command which he knew to be wrong:

The provost-marshal system is not of my planting or growth, but is now so old, deep-rooted, and wide-spread it cannot be summarily disposed of without danger of losses and disasters. It began in General Frémont's administration, by the appointment of Major McKinstry in this city, who was followed by Colonel McNeil and Captain Leighton; neither of them were properly in the United States service. From this it spread out through the whole department, and when I came in command Colonel Gantt was provost-marshal-general, and hundreds were elsewhere located; most of them not officers in the United States service, except by virtue of their appointment as provost-marshals. General Halleck had given the system a head by creating a provost-marshal-general and issued some orders devolving specific duties on these functionaries, and, by a kind of common understanding, provost-marshals took charge of prisoners, watched contraband trade, discovered and arrested spies, found out rebel camps, and pursued and arrested rebels in their neighborhoods. They operate with volunteers, militia, and police force, just as circumstances require, and in Southern Iowa and large districts of Missouri, where recruiting guerrilla agents strive to organize their bands, they are the only stationary permanent official sentinels, who keep me advised and guard the public safety. Public arms, prisoners, contraband property, and forfeited bonds are held by them

18 *O. R.*, Series 1, Vol. XXII, Part 2, p. 41.

and properly disposed of, and immediate discharge would create loss and confusion where everything is now quiet and secure. For instance, the provost-marshal at Glasgow has 30 or 40 prisoners.

. . . .

I regret that I am thus forced to defend a system I never did approve and have often condemned. I could find neither statute nor military law to rest it upon.[19]

With his letter Curtis enclosed one from the provost marshal general, Lieutenant Colonel F. A. Dick, who stated that if the system were done away with, it would be a serious blow to the Union cause in Missouri. He also fired a note off to Halleck, now general-in-chief, pleading for retention of the system.[20] Curtis' eloquent pleas were evidently accepted by Stanton, for the provost marshals continued to operate until the end of the war.

Under martial law, as it was loosely developed and put into operation, corruption, extortion, and injustice were bound to occur. When conscientious John Schofield resumed command of the department in 1863, he tried to straighten the situation out, and wrote Lincoln concerning provost marshals and members of military commissions whom he had arrested for "enormous frauds and extortions."[21] As late as April, 1865, General Clinton Fisk of the District of North Missouri informed departmental headquarters of a fantastic extortion ring conducted by the provost marshals in his command. Scheming provosts had caused fake charges to be brought against innocent men. These men were arrested and softened up in uncomfortable jails. They were allowed to see only a few shyster lawyers who would "arrange" a release after payment of exhorbitant sums of money. Fisk found that the lawyers and provost marshals

[19] O. R., Series 1, Vol. XXII, Part 2, p. 43.
[20] O. R., Series 1, Vol. XXII, Part 2, pp. 42-45, 48.
[21] O. R., Series 1, Vol. XXII, Part 2, pp. 482-84.

were then splitting the fees. The extortion ring was
crushed.[22]

Such was the mechanism by which the Union military
command held Missouri, controlled the disloyal, and put
down rebellion. This it did, but it had no pacifying effect
on the terrible conditions in the state between 1861 and
1865.

Venerable Edward Bates, Lincoln's United States Attorney General and a resident of Missouri for forty years, time
after time decried the illegality of military government and
martial law in his home state. When his protests were em-
phatic enough the President often ordered moderation, but
for the most part the military authorities had a free hand.
Describing the situation following his resignation from the
cabinet in 1864, Bates wrote bitterly:

I did not resign, however, until the affairs of the nation were
greatly altered for the better. My political chief had just passed
through the ordeal of a new election, and the Administration in
which I bore a part was then sanctioned by the nation. The success of our arms had turned a hope into a certainty, that the rebellion would be quelled; that the war would be brought to an
end; and that, with wisdom and virtue in the civil government,
law and order might be once more firmly established.

Such was then the prospect in the nation at large; and in this
State the outward appearances were no less cheering. Price's invasion (which ought never to have been allowed, and never could
have happened without gross dereliction on our part), was driven
back; there was no embodied enemy within the State, and no
enemy at all, but a few marauding outlaws, whose numbers are
estimated by General Pope, in his late letter to the Governor, at
only twenty for each county.

Such were the outward circumstances when I came home and
found, to my grief and shame, that, notwithstanding the absence

22 *O. R.*, Series 1, Vol. XLVIII, Part 2, pp. 35-36; *Daily K. C. Journal,* April
20, 1865.

of all enemies, except the few incapable of any serious mischief, unless by the sufferance of our military, the State was ruled only by the arbitrary will of a few men; that the law was trodden down, and too weak to give protection; that the spirit of the people was cowed by threats and violence; and that there was no longer any feeling of conscious security for life, liberty or property, nor any assured hope of stability in the Government or liberty by law, in the people.[23]

[23] Beale, Howard K. (ed.), *The Diary of Edward Bates, 1859-1866; Volume IV Of The Annual Report Of The American Historical Association For The Year 1930* (Washington, 1933), 571-612.

10

Control of the Populace

ARMED with the total power of martial law the Union military command in Missouri moved to eliminate opposition to its cause. It determined to control the entire population of the state, and as guerrilla resistance developed, its measures became progressively more drastic.

The most common device used by the Union provost marshals to control the civil population was a combination of loyalty oaths and performance bonds. Throughout the fall of 1861 and the winter of 1862 an increasingly large number of citizens of Missouri was required to swear and sign oaths of loyalty to the United States and to Hamilton Gamble's provisional government. By 1862 all officeholders, the electorate, and nearly every person in public service had been covered by such oaths. In the civil population the only persons at first required to take oaths and post bonds were men who had served in the State Guard or Confederate army, and who had applied for amnesty. However, as Quantrill, Porter, Hays, Poindexter, and their guerrillas ran wild through Missouri during the summer of 1862, the Union commanders began to require oaths and bonds of all people in their districts in a desperate attempt to keep down insurrection. As early as April, 1862, Bernard G. Farrar, departmental provost marshal general, advised the district commanders that all men suspected of "disloyalty" should be arrested and held in jail until they took oaths and put up bonds. Following Farrar's advice, General Egbert Brown, then in charge of the Southwest District, posted the following order:

I. It is therefore ordered that all citizens within the limits of the southwestern division of the District of Missouri shall at once appear before some properly qualified officer and take the oath of allegiance to the United States of America and to the Provisional Government of the State of Missouri, and receive a certificate thereof, unless they have already done so.

II. Every citizen who fails to obey the above order will be deprived of the ordinary privileges of loyal citizenship. He shall neither hold any office nor be permitted to vote. He shall not be allowed to serve as a juror or appear as a witness. . . . He shall not be permitted to pass at will on the public highway, but as a punishment for the apparent aid and countenance which he extends to the marauders who are preying upon the country he is declared to be a prisoner within the limits of his own premises.[1]

By August, 1863, every "disloyal" person in the troublesome Central District and the District of North Missouri was required to take the loyalty oath and post thousand-dollar bonds for the guarantee of such loyalty. It cannot now be determined how many thousands of Missourians were required to take the oath. In December, 1862, the unsavory provost of Palmyra, William "Beast" Strachan, boasted that he had administered it to "several thousand traitors," and had taken bonds for its observance to the amount of over a

[1] O. R., Series 1, Vol. XIII, 435, General Order Fifteen, dated June 16, 1862.

million dollars.[2] On April 23, 1863, the *Kansas City Journal* announced that Provost Marshal General Farrar held bonds of "traitors and secessionists" to the amazing sum of twenty-seven million dollars.

With the penalty for not taking the oath of allegiance arrest and imprisonment, apparently most men took it, hundreds with inner reservation because of its compulsory nature. As the guerrilla war flared on and off in 1862 and 1863 many men broke their word and risked the penalty of death. As has been indicated, the Union commanders were coldly severe with those persons who violated their oaths by taking up arms. Many were shot at the place and time they were captured.

The system of compulsory oaths and bonds made it difficult for numerous Missourians to live peacefully, since they were automatically labeled as potential traitors in their neighborhoods, and were fair game for the Union soldiery. Proscribed and subject to constant persecution and suspicion, some men joined the guerrillas; others left the state, and many were arrested on vague charges, or on no charges at all, and imprisoned without recourse to legal rights.

Out in the military districts of central and western Missouri whole communities were at times almost depopulated by the mass arrest of men and women suspected of disloyalty. It became Union policy by 1863 to place in confinement every person believed to be supporting or encouraging the guerrillas. For example, on November 14, 1862, General Ben Loan advised his headquarters that as a result of a scout in Lafayette and Jackson counties he had "left about 250 of the inhabitants in confinement and ordered others to be arrested."[3] On the nineteenth he wrote General Curtis about affairs in the Central District to this effect:

[2] *O. R.*, Series 1, Vol. XXII, Part 1, p. 862.
[3] *O. R.*, Series 1, Vol. XIII, 791-92.

It is much easier to catch a rat with your hands in a warehouse filled with a thousand flour barrels than it is to catch a band of guerrillas where every, or almost every, man, woman, and child are their spies, pickets, or couriers. There are some 200 here held as prisoners on the general charge of disloyalty. They are generally actively disloyal. The remainder of the disloyal inhabitants I propose to have brought in as rapidly as possible. In Jackson, Cass, Johnson, and Saline the same course will be pursued, until none but loyal men will be allowed to remain at large in the country.[4]

General Loan's policy of mass arrests was followed by General Brown in the Southwest District and elsewhere throughout the state.[5]

Female "rebels" were an especial source of irritation to the Union command, for no soldier, indeed no man, knows how to handle rebellious women. Tom Ewing lived to regret the day he had ever imprisoned a woman, and after having grappled with an unusually vocal group of secessionist girls, "Old Brains" Halleck sourly wrote:

Nearly all the secessionists of this State who have entered the rebel service have left their wives and daughters to the care of the Federal troops. There is scarcely a single instance where this confidence has been abused by us. But what return have these ladies made for this protection? In many cases they have acted as spies and informers for the enemy and have been most loud-mouthed in their abuse of our cause and most insulting in their conduct towards those who support it.[6]

As the guerrilla war progressed, the Union officers slowly lost the traditional respect for feminine prerogatives, and

[4] O. R., Series 1, Vol. XIII, 806-807.
[5] O. R., Series 1, Vol. XIII, 796-97; St. Louis Republican, August 20, September 1, 1862.
[6] O. R., Series 1, Vol. VIII, 657-58.

numerous Missouri women were imprisoned under various charges of disloyalty.[7]

Hasty and unrestricted arrest and imprisonment was, of course, accompanied by much injustice. Commenting on this, General Clinton Fisk, who was trying to clean out the corrupt provost marshals in the District of North Missouri in late 1864, wrote his district provost, Major R. A. De Bolt:

I have the honor to state that it has come to my knowledge that many persons have been arrested and imprisoned for a long time by some of your subordinates upon evidence insufficient to warrant the military authorities restraining citizens of their liberty. Great care should be exercised in the use of arbitrary power confided to provost-marshals, and we cannot be too cautious in receiving as truth the statements of apparently good men who seek through the military power the punishment of neighbors for alleged offenses, old grudges, local animosities, and private griefs, to frequently seek adjustment through the military arm of power, much to the scandal and prejudice of honesty and loyalty.[8]

With mass arrests the problem of military prisons in Missouri became acute. In the fall of 1861 the provost marshal general at St. Louis had seized the Gratiot Street medical college building of Dr. Joseph McDowell because of the doctor's outspoken support of the Confederacy, and converted it, along with "Lynch's slave pen" into a prison.[9] From the fall of 1861 until 1865 the Gratiot Street college was crammed with prisoners, the majority of them civilians. Conditions in the prison varied, according to the number of inmates, from extreme discomfort to sheer frightfulness during different periods of the war. On January 18, 1862, the

7 *Statesman*, September 2, 1864; *Daily K. C. Journal*, April 3, July 29, 1863; St. Louis *Republican*, August 19, 27, 1862; McLarty, "Lazear Letters," *loc. cit.*, No. 3, pp. 271-73.

8 *O. R.*, Series 1, Vol. XLVIII, Part 2, pp. 24-25.

9 William B. Hesseltine, "Military Prisons of St. Louis, 1861–1865," *Missouri Historical Review*, XXIII, No. 3 (April 1929), 381-82.

St. Louis *Republican* stated that the prison was filthy and unhealthy, the prisoners' fault, and that orders had been given to clean up the rooms and to provide doctor inmates with medicine so that the sick could be treated. The paper went on to say that twenty men, most of them from Johnson County, had been released on the seventeenth (after taking the loyalty oath and posting bond) to alleviate crowded conditions. On January 30 the *Republican* announced that the Alton, Illinois, military prison had been opened, and that henceforth Gratiot would be used primarily as a receiving prison.

Gratiot Street Prison had a capacity of about five hundred, but as fast as prisoners were sent to Alton, new ones were received from interior Missouri. Dreadful overcrowding was common since there was no control over the flow of captives. On November 5, 1862, there were 1,100 men and women confined there.[10] Sanitary conditions and prisoners' rations were atrocious and periodically the jail was swept with disease. Between November 1, 1864, and February 1, 1865, 881 cases of sickness were reported, and of these, 134 men died on the vile cold floors of the buildings. The mortality rate for prisoners during 1864 was almost fifty per cent. Horrified at the illness and death that stalked the place, Union Surgeon George Rex notified departmental headquarters in despair:

Notwithstanding repeated attention of the prison authorities has been called to this grave and prolific cause of disease, the evil [overcrowding] still continues unabated, and consequently no hopes of the decrease of the ratio of deaths.

. . . among these prisoners undergoing the confinement in these crowded and insufficiently ventilated quarters are many citizen prisoners, against whom the charges pending are of a very trivial character, or perhaps upon investigation by courts-martial no charges at all are sustained.[11]

[10] *Ibid.*, 381-86.
[11] *O. R.*, Series 2, Vol. VIII, 376-77.

Prison conditions elsewhere in the state were also gen- erally bad. In June, 1862, Egbert Brown wrote Schofield that his district prisoners at Springfield, awaiting military com- mission trial, were crowded into low and badly ventilated sheds, were living in filth, and that there was "much sick- ness."[12] Many Missourians were never to forget the condi- tions of summary arrest, farcical trials, or no trials at all by Union military commissions, and cruel imprisonment in the squalid, makeshift Union military prisons during the Civil War.

In addition to widespread imprisonment of the citizens of Missouri, the Union military command also banished many men and women from the state. On December 24, 1862, in his notorious Order Number Thirty-five, General Curtis directed his provost marshals to banish people, "though no specific act of disloyalty can be proven against them" should peace and safety require it.[13] This meant that potential trou- blemakers could be gotten rid of without the necessity of try- ing them before a military commission. In many cases banish- ment was made a commutation for imprisonment.[14] In No- vember, 1862, Ben Loan reported that he had paroled fifty "disloyal" men of Lafayette County on their promise to leave the state in ten days.[15] Commanding General Curtis com- plained that those banished from the department, "rebel wives and avowed secessionists," could not be sent into the Confederacy, for when they were sent East, they joined the Copperheads and made trouble.[16] Since the majority of people banished were likely to be the most prominent figures in their communities, the policy of banishment was subject to much criticism in Union circles. In December, 1862, General

12 *O. R.*, Series 1, Vol. XII, Part 1, pp. 868-69.
13 *O. R.*, Series 1, Vol. XIII, 455.
14 *O. R.*, Series 1, Vol. XXII, Part 2, pp. 42-43.
15 *O. R.*, Series 1, Vol. XIII, 791-92.
16 *O. R.*, Series 1, Vol. XXII, Part 1, p. 884; Part 2, p. 278-79.

Lewis Merrill of the Northeast District notified his provost marshal general that he was going to stop banishing men from his command "until I find that I am to be sustained, and that no influence, however strong, of personal friendship can recall the sentence of banishment. . . ."[17] President Lincoln was continually upset about the policy in Missouri. In January, 1863, he asked General Curtis to look into the case of Doctor Samuel B. McPheeters, the minister of the First Presbyterian Church of St. Louis, who had been ordered from the state because he had a "rebel wife, rebel relatives," and had sympathized with the rebellion in his sermons. Lincoln also informed the General that Representative James S. Rollins had asked him to allow the Reverend John M. Robinson, James L. Matthews, and James L. Stephens, all prominent citizens, to return to their homes in Boone County. Curtis cancelled the order concerning McPheeters, and told the President he would check on the Boone County men and write Representative Rollins, but "the cases must stand on their own merits, not his."[18] As has been indicated, Order Number Eleven which followed the attack on Lawrence in August, 1862, was a mass banishment of the rural population of almost four counties in western Missouri. This order uprooted and scattered several thousand people. The policy of banishment was maintained throughout the war by the Union command, especially against the relatives of guerrillas. As late as February, 1865, seven Clay County families were ordered to leave the state, one of them that of Frank and Jesse James.[19]

From the evidence available, the Union military government's most vigorous measure to control the civil population and to pay the costs of the guerrilla war was a vast system of

17 *O. R.*, Series 1, Vol. XXII, Part 1, p. 834.
18 *O. R.*, Series 1, Vol. XXII, Part 1, pp. 878-79; Part 2, pp. 6-7, 17-18, 42-43.
19 *Liberty Tribune,* February 5, 1865.

fines and assessments. In June, 1863, in a vain attempt to make guerrilla activity unprofitable, General Schofield issued an order that for every Union soldier or citizen killed by guerrillas five thousand dollars would be assessed and collected from the "disloyal" living in the neighborhood where the act was committed. In the case of the wounding of a soldier or citizen, from one thousand to five thousand dollars would be assessed, as well as the full value of all property destroyed or stolen as a result of the war. Money collected was to be paid to the widows and families of Union men killed or wounded, and to those who suffered property loss.[20] Schofield's life and property insurance plan fell through with a crash. So many Union men were shot, so much property destroyed, it was impossible for assessment officers to find enough "disloyal" people to pay the damages.

As a result of Quantrill's, Porter's, Hays's and Poindexter's guerrilla campaigns in the summer of 1862 the Union command set up assessment boards in every Missouri county affected. These boards had a dual function. They were to collect money to pay for the damages of the guerrilla war, and they were also to obtain funds to maintain the state militia which Schofield had called out in full strength. The Union assessment boards went to work with real energy, drawing up rolls of the "disloyal," estimating the property value and resources of those enrolled, and then collecting and disbursing the money.

On January 15, 1863, by Schofield's authority, General John McNeil ordered $300,000 collected in the district of North Missouri, and levied the following counties:

Adair	$ 3,000	Chariton	$24,600
Audrain	$21,600	Clark	$ 6,000
Boone	$32,000	Howard	$22,200
Callaway	$37,000	Knox	$ 3,300

20 *O. R.*, Series 1, Vol. XIII, 446-47.

Lewis	$ 7,500	Putnam	$ 2,100
Livingston	$ 7,500	Randolph	$11,700
Linn	$ 3,300	Ralls	$ 7,200
Lincoln	$ 5,700	Shelby	$ 5,400
Monroe	$38,700	Scotland	$ 3,300
Montgomery	$ 5,700	Schuyler	$ 2,700
Marion	$19,800	St. Charles	$ 6,000
Macon	$ 7,800	Sullivan	$ 2,100
Pike	$10,800	Warren	$ 3,300 [21]

McNeil told his assessing officers that the only "disloyal" persons in these counties to be spared were to be widows or orphans who had property of less value than five thousand dollars, "unless they have given aid and comfort to the guerrillas." [22] In the Central District Ben Loan also embarked on a heavy assessment program. Between September and November, 1862, these communities and counties in that area were known to have been fined:

Jefferson City	$ 5,000	Jackson County	$15,000
Boonville	$ 5,000	Cass County	$10,000
Lexington	$15,000	Johnson County	$10,000
Saline County	$15,000	Middleton Township,	
Dover	$ 4,000	Lafayette County	$ 6,000 [23]

In northwest Missouri General Dick Vaughan placed heavy assessments on his guerrilla counties. On December 19, 1862, Platte County was taxed $85,000, and the committee in wealthy Chariton County reported that between November 14 and December 16 it had levied assessments of $82,000, and collected and disbursed $34,231.38.[24] A great deal of money was changing hands at a high rate of speed.

[21] *O. R.*, Series 1, Vol. XXII, Part 2, pp. 47-48.
[22] *O. R.*, Series 1, Vol. XIII, 704-705.
[23] See *O. R.*, Series 1, Vol. XIII, 691, 693, 736-37, 800.
[24] *Liberty Tribune,* December 19, 1862; *O. R.*, Series 1, Vol. XXXIV, Part 2, pp. 657-58.

The Union assessment and disbursement system was shot through with graft and corruption. On August 28, 1862, General Schofield, needing money to fight the guerrilla war which was raging in central Missouri, assessed St. Louis $500,000 to help clothe and arm the militia. As the St. Louis assessment board went about its duties with cheerful vigor, howls of outrage arose. By the first part of December so much corruption was charged to the board that General Halleck investigated the situation and reported that its assessments were "arbitrary," were made more or less by the "accident of evidence offered," and that the "strict secrecy" accompanying its action did not help matters.[25]

Again President Lincoln had to step in. On December 10 he ordered assessments in St. Louis stopped, and requested departmental commander Sam Curtis to send him the facts about the matter with his recommendations. On December 31 Governor Gamble telegraphed the president that he had stopped assessments by state militia officers, and urged that they not be made by United States forces as "great distress is produced."[26] The Missouri congressional delegation on January 6, 1863, also presented Lincoln with a memorandum asking that assessments be ended.[27]

On January fifth President Lincoln, bedeviled by conflicting opinions, wrote General Curtis the following sensible letter:

I am having a good deal of trouble with Missouri matters, and I now set [sic] down to write you particularly about it. One class of friends believe in greater severity and another in greater leniency in regard to arrests, banishments, and assessments. As usual in such cases, each questions the other's motives. On the one hand it is insisted that Governor Gamble's Unionism, at most, is not better than a secondary spring of action; that hunkerism and a

25 *O. R.*, Series 1, Vol. XXII, Part 1, p. 830.
26 *O. R.*, Series 1, Vol. XXII, Part 1, pp. 826, 888.
27 *O. R.*, Series 1, Vol. XXII, Part 2, pp. 17-18.

wish for political advancement stand for Unionism with him. On the other hand, it is urged that arrests, banishments, and assessments are made more for private malice, revenge, and pecuniary interest than for the public good. This morning I was told by a gentleman, who I have no doubt believes what he says, that in one case of assessments for $10,000, the different persons who paid compared receipts, and found they had paid $30,000. If this be true, the inference is that the collecting agents pocketed the $20,000. And true or not in the instance, nothing but the sternest necessity can justify the making and maintaining of a system so liable to such abuses. Doubtless the necessity for the making of the system in Missouri did exist, and whether it continues for the maintenance of it is now a practical and very important question.[28]

The President then asked Curtis to meet with Governor Gamble, whom the general had little use for, to determine if the system was still desirable.

Lincoln, of course, made a great mistake if he believed that Sam Curtis was going to take his recommendations, or to concur in any way with Hamilton Gamble. On January 15 Curtis wrote the President, vigorously defending assessments. He stated, in part:

These assessments on persons for crimes committed in a neighborhood are considered a great restraint on rebels who have encouraged bands of rebels, and our friends fear that they will suffer if such restraints are taken off. I am implored not to remove them. I have earnest petitions and letters innumerable coming in, urging me to allow assessments to proceed. The county assessments are all made by local commanders, who claim that they understand their local difficulties better than I can.[29]

Judicious Abraham Lincoln was apparently not impressed with Curtis' rather vague arguments, for on January 20 Secretary of War Stanton wired Curtis that assessments must be

[28] *O. R.*, Series 1, Vol. XXII, Part 2, pp. 17-18.
[29] *O. R.*, Series 1, Vol. XXII, Part 2, pp. 42-43.

stopped until further notice.[30] By this time thousands of Missourians had been fined and their property seized and sold to obtain money.

The practice of confiscation of property had started in the winter of 1861 when several thousand persons had fled southwest Missouri before General Price's army. Many of these pitiful people arrived in St. Louis destitute. To help them, General Halleck directed by General Order Twenty-four, December 12, 1861, that they were to be quartered, clothed, and fed by the "charity of men known to be hostile to the Union." In addition, a "contribution" of $10,000 was levied, and provisions were made to sell the property of men who did not have the cash to pay their part of the levy.[31] "Old Brains" Halleck's assessment board did its work in such a thoroughly unsatisfactory fashion that a new committee was appointed in January, 1862, to revise the lists which indicated fines that were "disproportionate."[32] Many of the "disloyal" could not produce cash; therefore their furniture was seized and sold at public sales by the provost marshal. Household goods disposed of at these auctions proved real bargains, the St. Louis *Republican* reporting on February 4, 1862, that pianos worth $1,000 sold for $330, and instruments worth $500 to $600 were bid in at $240. The *Republican* added that a new "batch" of confiscated property was in the government warehouse and would be auctioned soon.

The official confiscation of private property continued throughout the military administrations of Generals Curtis and Schofield. John Schofield seems to have tried to be rational in his policy, but Curtis was so unrelenting, and used so little discretion that Schofield privately informed Lincoln that he had taken property "without any form of trial known

30 *O. R.*, Series 1, Vol. XXII, Part 2, p. 64.
31 *O. R.*, Series 1, Vol. VIII, 431-32.
32 St. Louis *Republican*, January 9, 1862.

to any law, either civil or military."[33] Much property was also simply stolen by the Union soldiery, who were, as a rule, ordered to live off the "disloyal" when in the field. Foraging was a grand opportunity for theft. Even the best-disciplined troops will loot, and the rough, underpaid Union cavalry became expert. Raid after raid was made on the property of the "disloyal," or those suspected of disloyalty. A common excuse was to search for arms, since by departmental orders no person thought to have secessionist views was allowed to keep a gun, caps, or powder.[34] In such searches personal and household goods were often stolen, and much private property was deliberately and wantonly damaged. To their great credit, the Union generals did their best to control looting. As early as November, 1861, General Halleck ordered stricter discipline for his troops and complained of the "numerous cases" of theft and destruction of property which indicated to him an "outrageous abuse" of military power.[35] In January, 1862, Schofield was forced to inform his subordinates by general order that "the practice of plundering and robbing peaceable citizens and of wantonly destroying private property has become so prevalent in some portion of this command as to require the most vigorous measures for its suppression."[36] Schofield added that any soldier caught looting would be arrested and placed in irons, and that officers who did not report violators would be considered criminals. Even unrelenting, flint-hearted General John McNeil informed his officers, "Your attention is again and for the last time called to the unauthorized taking of private property by officers and soldiers of this command," and ordered that this "gross outrage" must cease.[37]

[33] O. R., Series 1, Vol. XXII, Part 2, p. 483.
[34] O. R., Series 1, Vol. XXII, Part 1, pp. 868-71. By General Order Thirty-five, December 24, 1862, from Curtis' headquarters.
[35] O. R., Series 1, Vol. VIII, 380-81; Liberty Tribune, December 6, 1861.
[36] O. R., Series 1, Vol. VIII, 478.
[37] O. R., Series 1, Vol. XIII, 678.

So order after order against looting was posted, but their very frequency indicates that they were not very effective in correcting the evil. The unlawful acts of Kansas troops in Missouri, and the inability of the Union command to keep them out is already known.

Most of the Union cavalry on the border was also extremely careless with fire. Authorized to burn out the property of persons who harbored guerrillas, Union patrols were frequently guilty of plain arson. In September, 1862, General McNeil wrote of his "surprise and regret of [the] many instances in which houses have been burned" by the troops of his command in the field after the guerrilla Porter.[38] And, because of the nature of the warfare, and the savage and merciless attitude of extermination both sides took, many citizens were simply murdered by Union troops. Men were called to their doors at night by the militia and shot dead, or were taken from their homes and families and hung. A favorite trick of the Union cavalry was to trap civilians into admitting friendship for the Confederacy, or aiding and harboring guerrillas, and then executing them on the spot. An excellent example of this can be found in the cold-blooded murder of Allen McReynolds, a wealthy citizen of Saline County. Shot dead by a Union patrol seeking Quantrill's men, McReynolds' prominence in Missouri caused the Adjutant General of the United States army to demand an investigation of the case. The brutally brief explanation of Captain R. M. Box, and the almost nonchalant indorsement by General G. M. Dodge, who then commanded the Department of Missouri, indicate how lightly such matters were taken:

Col. JOHN F. PHILLIPS,
  Commanding District of Central Missouri:
COLONEL: I beg leave to submit the following statement connected with the killing of Allen McReynolds: I ordered Lieutenant

38 *O. R.*, Series 1, Vol. XIII, 678.

Crain with a portion of the command to proceed to Grand Pass Church, some six miles east of Waverly, and to remain there until joined by me. While there he sent two men of his command to the house of Allen McReynolds to get something to eat and to palm themselves off as bushwhackers, which they did successfully. While there McReynolds told them he was willing to feed them and aid them in any way he could, but declined to carry provisions to the brush for fear of being caught and killed by the Federals. He also informed them that they were unsafe where they were, as squadrons of Federal troops had left Warrensburg, Sedalia, and Marshall the day before to thoroughly scout the country thereabouts, and to then concentrate on Miami. He also advised them to proceed to one Tracy's for safety and security, it being an out-of-the-way place and where Federal scouts seldom traveled; that he (Tracy) had plenty of forage and would take pleasure in entertaining them. When the command were through feeding, Lieutenant Crain arrested McReynolds and brought him out to the command. Soon after I joined them; heard the evidence above given, which he (McReynolds) acknowledged, as also to the fact that Quantrill and band had stopped with him several times, and other bands of bushwhackers which he had never reported to the Federal authorities. On consultation with the squadron commanders (Captain Hamblin and Lieutenant Crain) it was decided to execute McReynolds, which was carried out under my orders.

Very respectfully, your obedient servant,

R. M. Box,
Captain Company H, Seventh Cavalry
Missouri State Militia.

Headquarters Department Of The Missouri,
Saint Louis, February 19, 1865

Respectfully forwarded to the Adjutant-General of the Army.

I gave this matter a thorough investigation at the time, and as it was clearly proven that McReynolds defiantly and openly assisted bushwhackers under a guise that deceived us, I took no action, though I do not approve of unlawful acts. This was done

by an officer, and such things sometimes tend to bad results. I have
given such orders as will prohibit any such action recurring. Hereafter men caught in arms will have no mercy shown them.

G. M. DODGE,
Major-General, Commanding.[39]

A dreary recitation of assassination serves no purpose, but
the murder of civilians by Union soldiers was so common
that the victims are listed by the dozens in almost every history of central and western Missouri.[40] Most of the newspapers
of the period found it hardly safe to comment on such vicious
acts, and, when they did, it was usually in a gloating manner
such as the article carried in the *Kansas City Journal* on April
7, 1863:

The military of this county are getting very careless of late. They
have been tormented and bothered so much that if they come
along where there are bushwhackers or rebel sympathizers the
soldiers get perfectly careless about the use of firearms and the
consequence is that a large number of these "Knights of the Bush"
have been killed "just that way," in fact there has been one or
two "Constitutional Union men" hurt right bad too. It can't be
helped, "accidents will happen."

To control business, trade, and travel in Missouri the
Union military government set up a rigid system of permits,
licenses, and passports. Early in 1862 General Halleck had his
provost marshal general issue a regulation concerning transportation and travel. This directive stated that all movement
of goods and individuals would be supervised by Union military and customhouse control. Boats operating on the Missouri rivers had to be licensed and inspected by the quarter-

<hr />

[39] *O. R.*, Series 1, Vol. XLVIII, Part 1, pp. 643-45.
[40] See Edwards, *Noted Guerrillas*, 186-88; *History of Howard and Chariton
Counties, Missouri* (St. Louis, 1883), 538-39; Ward Schrantz, *Jasper County in
the Civil War* (Carthage, Missouri, 1923), Appendix; *Liberty Tribune*, November 22, 1862; *California News*, September 17, 1864.

master of the Department of Missouri, and railroads and stage lines engaged in public service were required to have customhouse permits for all cargos. The baggage of travelers was inspected by customhouse officers, and provost marshal passes were required for persons moving about the state. By January, 1862, it was estimated that 85,000 such passes had been issued at St. Louis alone.[41]

In addition to general travel and passport regulations, the Union provost marshals instituted a permit system for persons engaged directly in trade and business in the military sub-districts. For example, General Ben Loan rigidly supervised all commerce and business in his guerrilla-tormented Central District. On November 16, 1862, he wrote General Curtis that when he assumed command of the area the "trade of the country" was under the control of rebels. To end this condition, and to restore trade to "loyal" men only, he published orders prohibiting the "transportation or removal" of livestock or goods in his district without permits from his provost marshal.[42] Loan stated that his orders were necessary to prevent disloyal men from buying stolen goods and livestock from guerrillas, and, in turn, selling them needed supplies. Ben Loan rigidly enforced his local orders in restraint of trade, and complaints were made to President Lincoln concerning their unfairness and the corruption that accompanied them. He was required to justify and explain his action, which he ably did by a letter report in January, 1863.[43] In April, 1863, by General Order Twenty-four, Loan directed that no "disloyal" man in his district would be allowed to raise crops, sell goods, or carry on business. The *Kansas City Journal,* commenting on this order on April 12, stated that

[41] St. Louis *Republican,* January 9, 14, 1862.
[42] *O. R.,* Series 1, Vol. XIII, 798-99; *O. R.,* Series 1, Vol. XXII, Part 1, p. 838, Part 2, pp. 78-79.
[43] *O. R.,* Series 1, Vol. XXII, Part 2, pp. 78-79.

it was being strictly enforced by Union troops in that area. Having trouble with the merchants of Lexington, which had a reputation as a rebel town, General Loan simply closed out all the business concerns there run by "men not friendly to the government" on May 4, 1863.[44]

The Union travel and trade restrictions also afforded grand opportunities for graft and bribery, and many provost marshals lined their pockets. President Lincoln was forced to intervene in this situation, too, as reports of vast corruption were brought to his attention. On October 5, 1863, he wrote Charles D. Drake, the leader of the Radical Republican faction in Missouri, who was demanding even sterner measures, concerning the permit system:

Agents to execute it, contrary to the great prayer, were led into great temptation. Some might, while others would not, resist that temptation. It was not possible to hold any to a very strict accountability, and those yielding to the temptation would sell permits and passes to those who would pay most and most readily for them, and would seize property and collect levies in the aptest way to fill their own pockets.[45]

The President sadly added: "Money being the object, the man having money, whether loyal or disloyal, would be a victim."

Opposition to the Union cause and the military government, either by utterance or through the press, was not tolerated in the Department of Missouri between 1861 and 1865. As soon as it assumed power, the military government closed down those papers which were openly secessionist and began to censor the remainder to insure their conformity in support of the Union.

In January, 1862, Provost Marshal General Farrar applied the first general censorship regulation to the press in Missouri

44 *O. R.*, Series 1, Vol. XXII, Part 1, p. 319.
45 *O. R.*, Series 1, Vol. XXII, Part 2, pp. 604-607.

at General Halleck's direction. Farrar ordered every newspaper, upon publication, to submit a copy to his office for inspection. Failure to do so would lead to suppression of the paper.[46] All newspaper editors were also required to take an "iron clad" oath of allegiance to the United States.[47] With these regulations to back them, the Union military government began to destroy or shut down those papers which it felt were not ardent in its support. In the summer of 1861 the St. Louis Morning Herald was suspended because of its secessionist expressions, the Lexington Expositor was raided by Kansas Jayhawkers and its press stolen, and the Express of the same town closed by military order.[48] The Platte City Sentinel was burned by Jennison, and when troops were sent to destroy the Argus in the same community, its editor loaded his type and press into a wagon, skipped town, and joined Price's army where he became the official printer of the Missouri Confederate government.[49] The St. Louis Missouri State Journal, the Cape Girardeau Eagle, and the Hannibal Evening News were shut down by Union troops, and when the editors of the Fayette Banner joined the Confederate forces their paper was seized, sold, and opened under a new name. The California News was ransacked by Union soldiers, and the Independence Border Star demolished by Kansans. During 1862 the Carrollton Democrat, the Franklin County Weekly Advertiser, the Shelby County Weekly, and the Columbia Standard were all suppressed. The editor of the Standard, Edmund J. Ellis, was banished and his press sold. Other papers, their names now lost, were "smashed" by Union troops at Boonville, Warrensburg, Troy, Osceola, Oregon, and Washington. The Macon

[46] William F. Swindler, "The Southern Press in Missouri, 1861-1864," The Missouri Historical Review, XXXV, No. 3 (April, 1941), 399.

[47] Liberty Tribune, July 11, 1862.

[48] St. Louis Republican, August 15, 1861; History of Lafayette County, Missouri (St. Louis, 1881), 272.

[49] Swindler, "The Southern Press in Missouri, 1861-1864," loc. cit.

Register was seized, its editor run off, and the paper published by soldiers.[50]

As might be suspected, the Union military government soon became as concerned with the control of the various publications representing the Union Democratic party, and the deviating factions of the Republican party, as it was in eliminating actual secessionist journals. Outstate newspapers of the "copperhead variety" were prohibited in the department at various times, among these the *Chicago Times,* the *Cincinnati Enquirer,* the *New York World,* the *Caucasian,* and *The Crisis.*[51] On September 17, 1863, General Schofield published General Order Ninety-six, which in part stated:

> Hereafter martial law will be rigidly enforced throughout this department against all persons who shall in any manner encourage mutiny, insubordination, or disorderly conduct, or endeavor to create disaffection among troops, and against all persons who shall publish or utter publicly words calculated to excite insurrection or lawless acts among the people, or who shall publish falsehoods or misrepresentations of facts calculated to embarrass or weaken the military authorities, or in any manner to interfere with them in the discharge of their duties. Any person guilty of the offenses above mentioned shall be punished by fine and imprisonment, at the discretion of a military commission, and any newspaper which shall contain publications in violation of this order will be suppressed.[52]

Schofield's order was not directed at secessionist orators or newspapers. It was a threat against the Radical Republican men of Missouri, who at the time were claiming that he and Governor Gamble were responsible for Quantrill's raid on Lawrence. It was especially aimed at the radical publications in St. Louis, the St. Louis *Democrat* and the German language

50 *Ibid.,* 398-400; *History of Howard and Chariton Counties, Missouri.*
51 *K. C. Journal,* June 23, July 10, 1863.
52 *O. R.,* Series 1, Vol. XXII, Part 2, p. 547.

Westliche Post. In July Schofield had arrested William McKee, editor of the *Democrat* for the unauthorized publication of a letter from President Lincoln. Lincoln asked Schofield to drop the charges against McKee, which he reluctantly did.[53]

Vocal support of the Confederacy or criticism of the Union led to arrest and fine or imprisonment. Great caution and circumspection of comment was required of the citizens of Missouri between 1861 and 1865. And again, the various Union military commanders from time to time arrested men who were perfectly loyal to the United States, but who differed over the policies of the military government and the civil government of Missouri and the United States. For example, Governor Gamble waked one morning in November, 1862, to find his Register of Lands, the eminently respectable Sample Orr, who had been the conservative Union candidate for governor in 1860, locked in jail by order of General Brown. Egbert Brown said that Orr had expressed what he felt to be "disloyal sentiments" in a speech at Jefferson City, and it took considerable effort on the Governor's part to get this prominent member of his administration out of the local military prison.[54] General Brown believed that he could smell a traitor even if the Union governor of Missouri could not.

All in all, the administrative and legal techniques used by the Union military government in Missouri between 1861 and 1865 enforced the state's allegiance to the United States. The great question is whether or not the occupation was absolutely required by conditions and the attitude of the majority of the people of the state. More important, did the devices of military government such as martial law, military commissions, arbitrary arrest and imprisonment, fines and assessments, the suppression of speech and press, and the revocation

53 *O. R.,* Series 1, Vol. XXII, Part 2, pp. 366, 373-74.
54 *O. R.,* Series 1, Vol. XIII, 806-807.

of other civil rights lead to pacification? In view of the fact that the guerrilla insurrection steadily increased in size and ferocity between 1861 and 1865, the answer can only be that they did not. Their application created and encouraged rebellion, more bloodshed, more bitterness, and less sympathy and understanding. The superior power of the military government, which was periodically antagonistic to the provisional civil government, prevented Governor Gamble from having a normal administration and made impossible many functions of civil law and order.

Actually, the military occupation and control of Missouri, and the resulting guerrilla war, led to a general collapse of efforts toward a moderate civil government by 1864. In that year Governor Gamble and the conservative wing of the provisional government fell before the assaults of the radical wing. In the election of November, 1864, by a carefully restricted electorate, the Radical Republicans carried the state and elected eight out of nine congressmen. Violently opposed by the radicals, Lincoln, however, won Missouri with the assistance of a large soldier vote. Under the direction of Governor Thomas C. Fletcher, and his mentor, Charles D. Drake, the radicals devised ousting ordinances which removed the judges of Missouri's supreme court and circuit courts, and then wrote a new constitution which allowed control of the electorate by the use of a loyalty test oath. Not until 1872, with the assistance of a liberal Republican party, did the Democrats regain control of the state. Once they did, Missouri remained predominantly Democratic for many years.

11

"Bloody Bill" Anderson
and George Todd

||||||||||||||||||||||||||||||||||||||||||||||||||||||||||||||||||||||||||||||

THE year 1864 dawned with very little military activity on the western border. After the stark horror of the summer and fall of 1863 the people of Kansas and the few remaining residents of western Missouri had devout hope that the new year would be free of savage and merciless partisan conflict. Colonel Dick Vaughan wrote General Egbert Brown that the spirit of the people of western Missouri was completely broken, and the *Kansas City Journal* spoke hopefully of peace and quiet on the frontier.[1] There seemed little reason to fear a regular Confederate invasion, for the dwindling, poorly led Confederate army had been pushed deep into Arkansas, and only small Union patrols were needed to hold the line across the Indian nations to the west. Surely it was

[1] *O. R.*, Series 1, Vol. XXII, Part 2, pp. 743-44; *Daily K. C. Journal*, April 8, 1864.

impossible, unthinkable in a logistic sense, that a major Confederate thrust could be mounted that would reach Kansas and Missouri in 1864. And, if the possibility of major invasion was remote, was it not logical that the dreaded guerrilla organizations might remain in far-off Texas, shunning the desolated border and the vengeance-ridden Union garrisons grimly stationed there?

Desperation, however, was the unaccountable element which was to blast all chances for peace on the border in 1864. The Confederate Trans-Mississippi, misdirected and isolated from her dying departmental sisters in the east, was to allow a final reckless raid north into Missouri. Aging Sterling Price, pursuing his fatal dream that thousands of recruits were only waiting his militant coming, was to lead a tattered, poorly armed army from Arkansas to the Missouri River in the fall of 1864. Far worse, from the civil point of view, Quantrill's raiders were also to return, brought back by the knowledge that they were considered pariahs and had no chance for compatible duty in the regular Confederate service. In co-operation, these two Confederate military elements were to strike Missouri its final and most tragic blow in the Civil War.

In the early spring of 1864 the Department of Missouri directed most of its energy toward the restoration of tranquility. Major General William S. Rosecrans had succeeded the controversial Schofield on January 30, and there were hopes that he would bring conciliation to the warring factions of the provisional government of the state. A failure after his blunders at Chickamauga the preceding fall, Rosecrans was a handsome, suave, intelligent man, far more successful as an administrator than as a fighting general. His choice as a military governor seemed excellent. On January 8 a new Department of Kansas had been created, and irritable old Sam Curtis had been given command of it. General Tom Ewing, despised because of Order Number Eleven, was transferred to the District of St. Louis, and his old District of the Border was abolished. Ravaged Jackson, Cass, and Bates counties, the area now a wilderness, were given to Egbert Brown and his Central District. Kansas troops, including Jennison's thieving Jayhawkers, were withdrawn from Missouri and were replaced by the cocky, hard-riding Second Colorado Cavalry under Colonel J. H. Ford. The Coloradoans were tough plainsmen. They did not hate Missourians, and they conducted themselves well on the field and in garrison.[2]

January and February, 1864, went by rather quietly, marked only by a few Kansas forays into Missouri. On January 22 General Brown informed departmental headquarters that Kansas cavalry was raiding in the western part of his Central District again, robbing the remaining citizens of slaves and other property of every description. Brown irritably stated: "If Kansas wants negroes I will send 500 women and children to the State in two days, as they are a great annoyance to me, and everybody wants them removed. But they do not want them; they want the property the negroes carry off and the opportunity of taking it by coming into the state."[3]

Of course, as Kansas troop depredations were renewed, mild guerrilla resistance began. Andrew Blunt, one of Quantrill's men, had remained in Missouri during the winter of 1863-1864. As spring returned, Blunt with some twenty companions began to skirmish about in the area and was vainly pursued by Union cavalry. On March 8 two of Blunt's men forced the Reverend Moses B. Arnold of Lafayette County to accompany them to the home of Judge Gray in Jackson County where the minister was required, at pistol point, to marry Miss Barbary Jane Gray to James W. Wilkenson, "the noted guerrilla, second in command to Blunt."[4] This audacity

[2] O. R., Series 1, Vol. XXXIV, Part 2, p. 49.
[3] O. R., Series 1, Vol. XXXIV, Part 2, p. 130.
[4] O. R., Series 1, Vol. XXXIV, Part 2, pp. 604-605.

goaded General Brown into action. He might tolerate Blunt's gang fighting with Kansans, but he saw no reason why he should allow the guerrillas to set up light housekeeping in his command. Union patrols were sent out from the various posts in the western portion of his district with orders to get Blunt. It is to be feared that Jim Wilkenson's marriage was not too peaceful, for on April 5 Egbert Brown wrote Robert Van Horn of Kansas City, "The guerrillas have been handled roughly by our troops; of Blunt's band of 20 that made their appearance about the 22d of February, 10 are under the sod, except the fellow Blunt, who has been left to rot, not being considered worthy of burial."[5]

There is no doubt that Brown believed that Andy Blunt's decomposing body would serve as a morbid warning to others who might have guerrilla yearnings.

William C. Quantrill and his only remaining lieutenant, George Todd, left the Trans-Mississippi Department in the second week of March, 1864. No one was sorry to see them go, and Bill Anderson and his company did not come with them on their long ride up to Missouri. Like evil animals their passage north was marked by fire, bloodshed, and alarm. Quantrill and Todd led about one hundred horsemen.

Throughout the Indian nations and up the Missouri-Kansas line the Union posts had watched the grass turn green and the growing season of the spring come on with apprehension and alertness. As whispers that Quantrill was going to come up again began to move along the border, the Union command put into effect a tactical plan of fortified garrisons, patrolling, and scouting that today would be called a hedgehog defense in depth. The details of the defense were simple to execute, but they held certain inherent dangers for the troops engaged.

In each military district small garrisons of cavalry were

[5] *O. R.*, Series 1, Vol. XXXIV, Part 3, p. 51.

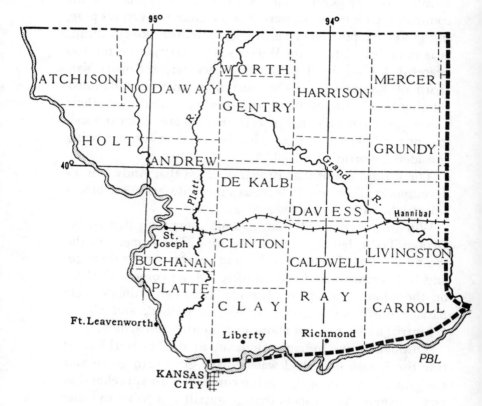

District of the Northwest

maintained in every principal town. The main garrison of a county was normally stationed at the county seat because of its central location and the presence of a courthouse and other substantial brick or stone buildings that could easily be sandbagged into forts. Experience had taught the Union captains that a few determined riflemen could hold a brick building against a large number of guerrillas who had no cannon. Heavy blockhouses were also erected at these posts and along the rail lines at bridge crossings.

From the small post cavalry patrols and scouts were sent out daily in all directions over the country, working from one station to another and back again. In this fashion the entire area was kept under observation, and if a guerrilla force was discovered, all nearby posts would be alerted, and additional cavalry called in to attack or pursue it. If the enemy party retreated, other posts along the line of retreat would be warned, and fresh troops could take up the pursuit. If the guerrillas scattered, it would be hard for them to regroup as the area would be saturated with Union patrols arriving from all directions. By these tactics the Union command hoped to hold its towns, discover any guerrilla force at an early moment, and run it to death.

The danger in the plan lay in two aspects. In the first place, local commanders were inclined to send out patrols which were either too large or too small. When large units were moved out, the post was vulnerable, and a poorly protected community invited attack. Small patrols, on the other hand, could be overrun and destroyed by more numerous guerrillas armed with their highly lethal revolvers. The second dangerous factor of the plan lay in the necessity for small posts to receive orders, rations, ammunition, and grain forage from headquarters and depots a considerable distance away. By the spring of 1864 western Missouri was so ravaged that it was necessary to haul in most of the rations and forage used by the

Union cavalry. General Brown informed his headquarters at St. Louis that spring that he was having to haul forage from thirty-five to fifty miles for half his command. As a consequence, many of his troopers had to be on continuous escort duty.[6] Such duty was burdensome, boring, and apt to be very dangerous. Regardless of these defects the Union commanders felt that they had perfected tactics that were the best answer to guerrilla warfare.

On April 21, 1864, the first information concerning Quantrill's march north was flashed up the border. On that date Colonel William A. Phillips, commanding the United States Army Indian Brigade at Fort Gibson in the Cherokee Nation, telegraphed General Curtis that the guerrillas had slipped through his lines at night, crossed the Arkansas River, and were moving north. On May 2 Southwest District headquarters at Springfield informed Rosecrans at Saint Louis that Quantrill had come through the Seneca Nation and was moving up the Arkansas state line. Its worst fears realized, the Union command in Missouri braced itself for the coming storm. On May 18, guessing as to where the guerrillas were ceased. Early that day Quantrill and his company passed boldly by the Union post at Carthage, the ruined county seat of Jasper County, and sent the commander there, Captain Philip Roher, an invitation to bring out his unit of the Seventh Missouri Cavalry and fight. Roher, intrenched among the burned houses and courthouse of the town which had been destroyed by guerrillas in 1862, declined the invitation.[7] With laughter and catcalls Quantrill's boys galloped on north, most of them wearing blue Union uniforms.

At dawn of May 20 they struck Lamar, the town which they had failed to take the preceding fall. The guerrillas charged

---

[6] *O. R.*, Series 1, Vol. XXXIV, Part 1, p. 996.

[7] *O. R.*, Series 1, Vol. XXXIV, Part 1, pp. 940-41; Britton, *The Civil War on the Border*, II, 354.

into what was left of the burned-out village, and this time their attack was a surprise. In the streets they found a small garrison of the Seventh Cavalry gathered around fires preparing breakfast. Orderly Sergeant Jefferson Cavender and nine other men of the Seventh managed to get into the brick courthouse, which had been burned to the first floor, where the muskets of the garrison were stored. This heroic little squad held off two fierce charges by over a hundred yelling guerrillas. The numerous muskets stacked in the foundation were each loaded with one heavy Minié ball and four buckshot, and in the hands of the desperate Cavender and his men created fearful damage to the Quantrill horsemen who swirled around the courthouse. The Union squad was invited to surrender several times, but remembering the fate of other garrisons, they decided to die fighting. Their determination and bristling resistance won the day for them. Quantrill and his men gave up the attack and limped on north taking thirty dead and wounded with them.[8]

The news that Quantrill was coming rang up the Missouri-Kansas line after the fighting at Lamar, and the Union military and civil population reacted in an almost frenzied fashion. Throughout western Missouri and eastern Kansas there came pleading requests and wild demands for troop reinforcements. All posts were on continuous alert, and patrols were out around the clock. General Brown left his headquarters at Warrensburg and announced that he would personally command "in the field."[9] As the hysteria spread across Kansas, the people of Emporia, almost a hundred miles west of the state line, held a mass meeting and implored General Curtis to send them troops because of the threat of guerrilla attack.

[8] *O. R.,* Series 1, Vol. XXXIV, Part 1, pp. 678, 941-42; Britton, *The Civil War on the Border,* II, 354-58.

[9] *O. R.,* Series 1, Vol. XXXIV, Part 3, pp. 385-87, 500-502, 622-23; *Daily K. C. Journal,* May 27, June 4, 5, 7, 12, 1864.

Every Kansas town felt itself marked as another Lawrence. Greatly alarmed, Curtis wrote Secretary of War Stanton suggesting the total mobilization of the Kansas militia. He informed Stanton that he was unable to move cavalry from the Kansas posts toward the guerrillas without creating "neighborhood terror and remonstrance." [10] Only the tough young men of the Second Colorado Cavalry found the situation pleasant. On April 29, 1864, the *Kansas City Journal* told its readers that the "Colorado boys" were asking for a chance at Quantrill.

The guerrilla column rode slowly northward, keeping within the Missouri border until it reached Cass County. There it disappeared as if swallowed by the earth until the morning of May 23. On that day Quantrill announced his presence by attacking a forage wagon escort on the headwaters of the Little Blue River. The Union cavalry escort was scattered, losing one man killed and one severely wounded. The forage wagon was emptied and burned, its mules shot in their traces. The guerrillas then cut the telegraph wire between Pleasant Hill and Warrensburg, stopping communication between General Brown and his troops in Cass County. On May 26 the mail escort between Pleasant Hill and Warrensburg was attacked, and the guerrillas captured all departmental orders and directives for several days past. By June 1 the escort of official mail was so hazardous south of the Missouri River, St. Louis headquarters directed that future communications were to be sent by the Hannibal and St. Joseph Railroad in north Missouri and then brought down to Kansas City.[11]

Egbert Brown went after Quantrill with all the troops at his immediate disposal and called on reinforcements. Four

---

[10] *O. R.*, Series 1, Vol. XXXIV, Part 3, p. 502.
[11] *Daily K. C. Journal*, May 27, June 1, 7, 15, 1864; *O. R.*, Series 1, Vol. XXXIV, Part 4, pp. 51-52.

companies of the Seventh Missouri Cavalry and six of the Fourth were ordered into the area.[12] Over three thousand blue-shirted soldiers were in the field. Brown had lost an arm in action earlier in the war, but his injury did not prevent his personally leading patrol after patrol. Throughout June there was continuous skirmishing, but the general complained that it was an "intangible war" in which Quantrill's men scattered when attacked only to form at some given point twenty miles away.[13] The Union cavalry was worn thin, its troopers and horses exhausted with continuous patrolling.

On June 11 General Brown found a new enemy on his hands. Bill Anderson, with glittering eye and fifty men, arrived in Johnson County, having made the long trip up the border from Texas unnoticed. On the morning of that day Anderson and his men, all dressed in blue uniforms, approached and suddenly fired into a fourteen-man squad of the First Missouri Cavalry led by Sergeant J. V. Parman, which was scouting between Holden and Kingsville. Only Parman and two of the men escaped alive. The guerrillas stripped the Union dead to obtain additional items of uniform.[14] On June 13 Anderson attacked a wagon escort of thirty men of the First Cavalry twelve miles south of Lexington. The Union force lost eight men killed, two ration wagons burned, and fifteen mules shot, but managed to fight its way back to its post. Simultaneously the Independence–Warrensburg stage was held up and telegraph wires in the entire area pulled down.[15]

With the central portions of the western Missouri River counties well ablaze with warfare, Quantrill and Anderson moved to the river and began attacking steamboats. General Brown had anticipated this and had ordered all boats plying

[12] *O. R.*, Series 1, Vol. XXXIV, Part 4, p. 53.
[13] *O. R.*, Series 1, Vol. XXXIV, Part 4, p. 221.
[14] *Daily K. C. Journal*, June 16, 1864; Britton, *The Civil War on the Border*, II, 372-73.
[15] *O. R.*, Series 1, Vol. XXXIV, Part 1, p. 996, Part 4, pp. 326-27.

between Jefferson City and Kansas City to protect their pilot-
houses and engine rooms with bulletproof works.[16] Brown had
excellent foresight, for on June 4 the *Prairie Rose,* William
Eads, master, was fired on near Waverly in Lafayette County.
The *Prairie Rose* turned and fled down-river, her pilothouse
riddled with revolver balls, but her pilot and engineers saved
by bulletproof bulkheads. General Curtis arrested the first
steward and the pantryman of the *Prairie Rose* when she finally arrived at Leavenworth, Kansas, charging them with
aiding the guerrillas by refusing to defend the boat and attempting to sabotage her by puncturing her oil can.[17]

Shooting at river boats must have been good sport, for on
June 5 the *Sunshine* was perforated at Wellington in Lafayette
County, and on June 26 the *West Wind* was attacked at Camden, Ray County. The *West Wind* was hailed by a single guerrilla who demanded her surrender. When she proceeded on
her way, she was fired on from the willows by forty or fifty
guerrillas. She had on board a cargo of powder which the partisans evidently needed badly.[18] By the end of June transportation had become so hazardous on the Missouri that it was
difficult to find pilots and crews who were willing to sign on
boats that had become floating shooting galleries. The Captain of the *James White* was forced to pay the premium rate
of a thousand dollars to a pilot for bringing his boat safely
from St. Louis to Leavenworth.[19]

Thoroughly exasperated by the new guerrilla war in his
Central District, General Brown requested the Department of
Missouri to take drastic measures. Reporting the situation on
June 14, he stated:

I have the honor to report that the depredations of guerrillas have
assumed a character that they demand the serious consideration of

16 *O. R.,* Series 1, Vol. XXXIV, Part 2, p. 327.
17 *O. R.,* Series 1, Vol. XXXIV, Part 4, pp. 237, 259.
18 *Statesman,* July 22, 1864; *O. R.,* Series 1, Vol. XXXIV, Part 4, p. 237.
19 *Daily K. C. Journal,* June 29, 1864.

the Government. They destroy the telegraph, rob the stages of mail and horses, plunder the resident population, and even the poor laborers that are employed in constructing the railroad, of property and money; they fire upon steamboats employed exclusively for commercial purposes. They assume the garb of our soldiers or of citizens as suits their convenience; they carry our flags; they murder their prisoners, even when wounded, and daily the citizens of the country are butchered for no cause, and unless the most severe retaliatory measures are resorted to they will soon depopulate the country. The Governor has in prison hundreds of their former associates who have been tried and sentenced to death for their crimes. They have forfeited their lives by every law, human and divine, and I respectfully but urgently recommend that the lives of these men be held as hostages for the good conduct of their friends in the brush.

The peace of the country, the safety of person and property of its citizens, and the blood of thousands of loyal citizens and brave soldiers who have been basely murdered by these demons demands that this measure of justice be executed on them. There is a sentiment fast growing in the country, and will soon manifest itself, that demands blood for blood, and unless it is appeased by stern justice to those who have been tried and condemned, will cause the death of hundreds of better men. It would be an economy of human life to adopt the cause I have recommended, and it is the only one through which the guerrillas can be reached.[20]

Following a long line of predecessors, Egbert Brown admitted that it was almost impossible for Union cavalry to stamp out the guerrillas.

On June 14, 1864, the *Kansas City Journal* re-examined the situation on the border, and compared the conditions that existed with those that had been so hopefully peaceful in the early spring. The paper observed editorially:

What is the condition of the truly loyal people of the border counties of Missouri south of the river? Simply one of seige. Outside of the military posts and their immediate vicinity, no man

[20] *O. R.*, Series 1, Vol. XXXIV, Part 4, pp. 363-64.

of known and open loyalty can safely live for a moment. The loyal people are collected in the scattered towns and military posts, while to all practical intents and purposes the rebels hold possession of the country.

On June 17 the *Journal* published a mournful article concerning the guerrillas under the headline "A Gloomy Prospect," which stated in part:

As soon as organized and mounted they [Quantrill's and Todd's guerrillas] will strike for higher game. They have shown their capacity for hazardous and unlooked-for enterprises. Their uniform success—unbroken as yet by a single failure, has emboldened them to make desperate ventures. If they are allowed to concentrate we look for an attack on some important post, either this city, Leavenworth, St. Joseph, Lawrence, or Topeka.

The publication went on to say that the bushwhacking question had again assumed such importance as to threaten the utter ruin of western Missouri and Kansas. Wildly apprehensive about Quantrill and Anderson, the people of Kansas City were called to a mass meeting on June 6 to discuss the protection of their town. The next day muskets were issued and every able-bodied man was ordered to take part in the defense of the community.[21]

General Rosecrans, alarmed over conditions in the western part of his department, decided to mount a major campaign against Quantrill and Anderson. In co-operation with General Curtis and the Department of Kansas, a giant expedition was planned against the guerrillas. The Kansas echelon of the force was composed of the Fifth, Eleventh, and Fifteenth Cavalry under the field command of Colonel Thomas Moonlight. This column left Aubry on June 16, crossed into Missouri, scouted the north fork of the Grand River valley, and then swept up to Pleasant Hill in Cass County. There it was

[21] *Daily K. C. Journal,* June 5, 7, 12, 1864.

joined by Colonel J. H. Ford with his Second Colorado, and the combined force fanned out and combed the heavy brush through Hickman Mills, Lone Jack, and the Sni River hills to the Missouri River. Although the expedition was kept secret in its formative stage, the guerrillas were apparently warned, for only a few small parties of them were ever seen fleeing eastward before the Union line toward Johnson County. The Union force marched and countermarched until June 20. It did not kill or capture a single guerrilla.[22]

The expedition by Moonlight and Ford caused Quantrill to divide his men into small groups as they moved to the east. He was never again to command them. George Todd, now insubordinate, took his place. At this time romance seems to have entered the life of strange William Quantrill. Finding his men scattered and no longer willing to obey his orders, he left the field of warfare for the field of love. For some time Quantrill had had a sweetheart in Jackson County, and he now took this girl, crossed the Missouri River into Howard County, and went into hiding with her. Very little is known about Quantrill's mistress, other than that she did exist. Many legends grew up about her. She was known as Kate Clarke. This was Bill Quantrill's middle name, but it was reported that her real name was Kate King. Fletcher Taylor, one of Quantrill's lieutenants, who later became a wealthy citizen of Joplin, stated that she was of low character and the proprietress of a house of ill fame in St. Louis following the guerrilla's death. Taylor, however, had reason to hate Quantrill and to blacken his memory. Other sources maintain that she was an honorable girl, and that she and Quantrill were married. At any rate, Quantrill took her with him when he left his men in June, 1864.[23]

22 *O. R.*, Series 1, Vol. XXXIV, Part 1, pp. 1018-24.
23 *The Kansas City Star,* May 23, 1926; Connelley, *Quantrill*, 442-43, 451 and footnote.

With the guerrillas scattered, General Brown took up the chase where Moonlight and Ford left off. In a most energetic fashion he harried the small bands now led by Richard Yeager, David Pool, Fletch Taylor, and Todd. Between June 10 and 19 he reported that he had put out sixty-two patrols and had had ten wild skirmishes. In this time he had lost twenty-three men killed or wounded and two wagons. His troopers had killed twenty-seven guerrillas including Dick Yeager. Brown's cavalry had marched a total of 3,810 miles in nine days; it had taken no prisoners.[24] The guerrillas continued to raid and attack, and their numbers were increasing.

A great deal of the failure of Egbert Brown's cavalry to exterminate the guerrillas in the spring of 1864 lay in the fact that most of the partisans were now dressed wholly or partially in blue Union uniforms. Early in April General Brown had informed departmental headquarters that nearly every guerrilla he killed was dressed in blue and that it was imperative that this should be known by all soldiers and civilians in the department.[25] On numerous occasions his scouting parties had approached what they thought were other Union patrols and had been fired into without warning. To combat this deceitful ruse the Union command was forced to set up an elaborate and burdensome system of signs, countersigns, and passwords for patrols to use when approaching each other in the field. Colored bands were also worn on hats and changed at specified intervals. As an example the following order was issued for troops in the Central District:

The following signals and pass words for July, 1864, will be transmitted by sub-district commanders to the commanding officer of each scout, detachment, or escort detailed from their respective commands, every precaution being taken to prevent their being known to unauthorized persons: During the daytime the

24 *O. R.*, Series 1, Vol. XXXIV, Part 1, pp. 995-99.
25 *O. R.*, Series 1, Vol. XXXIV, Part 3, p. 92.

commanding officer of a scout, detachment, or escort, upon observing the approach of a party or body of men, will ride a few
paces in advance of his command and raising his hat or cap, with
arm extended at full height, will lower it slowly and place it upon
his head. The commanding officer of the party thus challenged
will immediately answer the same by raising the hat or cap from
the head and extending the arm at full length horizontally, bringing the arm back slowly and replacing the hat or cap upon the
head. The signal to be given and answered, where the nature of
the ground will permit, before the parties have approached
nearer than from 300 to 350 yards.

At night the party who first discovers the approach of another,
when within challenging distance, will cry out loud and distinctly,
"Halt!" and the party thus challenged will immediately answer,
"Lyon," to be followed by a counter challenge of "Who comes
there?" to which the party last challenged will answer "Reno."
The failure of either party to answer promptly and correctly will
be the signal to commence firing. The badges to be worn during
the month of July will be as follows: On the odd days, as the 1st,
3d, 5th, 7th, &c., a red strip of cloth fastened around the hat or
cap, and on the even days of the month, as the 2d, 4th, 6th, 8th,
&c., a white strip will be worn in the same manner, the colors al-
ternating each day.

Special care will be taken to avoid mishaps through negligence
or the failure on the part of the men to change the badges as
herein directed.[26]

At best the Union challenges and badges were complicated,
and, in numerous instances, Bill Anderson and George Todd
learned them and used them themselves.[27] The civil population suffered the most, however, from the confusion. No person, regardless of his sympathies, could any longer be certain
whether he was meeting or conversing with legitimate Union
soldiers or masquerading guerrillas. A good many men were

26 *O. R.*, Series 1, Vol. XXXIV, Part 4, p. 550.
27 *Daily K. C. Journal,* May 25, 1864; *O. R.*, Series 1, Vol. XLI, Part 2, pp.
840-41.

pistoled down when they guessed wrong. The partisans obtained their uniforms from the bodies of the soldiers they killed, and prisoners were forced to strip before being shot. Naked or nearly naked corpses littered the woods and fields of Missouri during the summer and fall of 1864.

Early July saw the guerrilla war growing in intensity. Conditions on the Missouri River became so bad that General Rosecrans forbade steamboats to go above Jefferson City without armed crews sufficient to defend them. On July 13 General Brown stopped all river traffic "until further notice," because of guerrilla attacks. A company of the Fourth Cavalry was on the *Post Boy* with orders to cruise the Missouri to destroy flatboats and skiffs, and to watch for guerrillas crossing.[28] As General Brown applied heavier and heavier pressure against the partisans in the middle of his district, they moved west into Jackson County. On July 6 George Todd and his men ambushed a patrol of the Second Colorado, dispersed it, and killed its captain and seven men. He also worked over the stage and mail lines with such success that General Brown had to inform Colonel Ford that his command could no longer furnish escorts for the lines except in "extreme cases." The mail agent for Jackson County notified Brown that unless escorts were provided for his stages, he would stop them. On July 14 Brown ordered the lines between Independence and Kansas City shut down.[29]

In the middle of July Colonel Ford was forced to take his Colorado Cavalry across the river into Ray County to put down disturbances. Todd and his guerrillas had the impudence to move to the outskirts of Independence and openly threaten the weak garrison Ford had left there. When the Coloradoans thundered back across the Missouri no enemy was to be found. General Brown intensified his campaign. Be-

28 *O. R.*, Series 1, Vol. XLI, Part 1, p. 55; Part 2, pp. 128, 177.
29 *O. R.*, Series 1, Vol. XLI, Part 1, pp. 49-50; Part 2, pp. 62-63, 189, 246.

tween July 1 and July 20 he sent out over a hundred patrols, fought the guerrillas twenty-eight times, and killed nearly a hundred of them. In the same period he lost forty-two men killed and two seriously wounded. His cavalry had marched a total of 10,000 miles.[30] Brown's men took no prisoners, but for each partisan they exterminated two more seemed to spring up and go in the bush.

Toward the latter part of July, 1864, headquarters, Department of Missouri, began to suspect that the Confederate Trans-Mississippi Military Department was again encouraging and directing the guerrilla insurrection which was rapidly spreading. On July 22 Rosecrans wrote Secretary Stanton that there was every indication of an uprising in north Missouri, and that a number of Confederate officers had been sent into the area to co-ordinate the insurrection with a major raid from Arkansas.[31] Rosecrans' opinion was verified by Brigadier General Clinton Fisk, commanding the District of North Missouri, who later stated that at least seventy Confederate officers had come into his district to direct operations and to gather recruits, while the guerrillas provided diversion by laying a path of blood across the area.[32]

The *Kansas City Journal* also coldly blamed the insurrection in western Missouri on the Confederacy. In an editorial on June 26, 1864, the paper stated:

Quantrell [*sic*] is a regularly commissioned officer of the Confederacy. His murderous raid on Lawrence was openly defended by the rebel papers in Richmond, and there is no doubt that his operations and those of his companions are under the general direction and control of the Confederate government. They are rebel forces employed, sanctioned, and kept up by the rebel government. The regular forces of the rebellion were long since expelled from

30 *O. R.*, Series 1, Vol. XLI, Part 2, pp. 62-63, 246, 290-92.
31 *O. R.*, Series 1, Vol. XLI, Part 2, p. 332.
32 *O. R.*, Series 1, Vol. XLI, Part 1, pp. 418-20.

the State. The rebel lines are hundreds of miles from our border. There was never a more atrocious system of arson, robbery, and murder, set on foot anywhere than the Confederate authorities have inaugurated and sustained in Missouri.

General Rosecrans, however, was unable to believe that the ferocious guerrilla organizations active in his department could really be under the recognition or direction of General Price. Here Rosecrans overestimated his enemy. He did not know the desperate straits of the Trans-Mississippi Department, how in its dying gasp some of its officers would use any weapon at hand to strike at the Union foe. The general wanted to know who he was fighting, so early in August he sent Brigadier General Edwin W. Price, the captured and paroled son of Sterling Price, into the central part of the state to contact the guerrilla leaders Clifton Holtzclaw, Caleb Perkins, John Thrailkill, and Bill Anderson to ascertain under what authority they were acting. On August 12, 1864, the *Columbia Statesman* under the headline "Interesting Question—Are Missouri Guerrillas Commissioned Rebels," stated that if Rosecrans found that the partisans were commissioned by the Confederacy, he planned on retaliating against Confederate prisoners. Edwin Price disappeared into the woods of Howard County, and in a few days dutifully reported that Holtzclaw had been commissioned by his father to recruit in Howard and Perkins in Boone County.[33]

The last weeks of August and the first weeks of September, 1864, saw the guerrillas north and south of the Missouri River in continuous violent attack against Union forces. In Johnson County George Todd and his boys swept through the populace murdering in cold blood discharged Union soldiers, Union civilians, and all men of German ancestry.[34]

[33] *O. R.*, Series 1, Vol. XLI, Part 3, p. 488; St. Louis *Democrat*, October 3, 1864.
[34] *O. R.*, Series 1, Vol. XLI, Part 1, p. 739.

In Lafayette County Fletch Taylor led a company in desperate fighting for a few weeks until his left arm was shattered by a Union Minié ball. Taylor's men "forced" Doctors Murphy and Regan of Wellington to go with them into the woods where an emergency amputation was performed on the youthful guerrilla lieutenant. The Second Colorado, hot on the trail, found a blood-stained spot, bandages, and a pillow, but Taylor, a great friend of the James brothers, managed to escape and survived his wound. As it was forbidden to treat guerrillas, Doctor Murphy was arrested, but was able to clear himself.[35] Waggish David Pool, another little bearded lieutenant of Todd's, harassed the road between Warrensburg and Lexington and openly boasted that he controlled the stages and telegraph on it.[36]

During the first ten days of July terrible Bill Anderson also operated in Lafayette and Saline counties, flaunted his company at the door of the Union post at Lexington, and corresponded with its officers and the newspapers there. Bloody Bill was, as usual, wild with rage at General Brown, Colonel James McFerran, who commanded at Lexington, and the local press. Anderson was angry with the newspapers because they had urged all men to take up arms against him. He was mad at McFerran because he felt that the colonel was a bluff and a liar. Always sensitive over the fate of his sisters, he hated General Brown because he had just convened a military commission that sentenced Miss Anna Fickle of Warrensburg to three years confinement in the Alton military prison. Miss Fickle had attempted to aid a prisoner escape from the provost prison at Lexington.[37]

Bill Anderson's letters are worth reproducing, for they are the only known genuine examples of his writing. Literate,

35 *O. R.*, Series 1, Vol. XLI, Part 1, pp. 739, 766.
36 *O. R.*, Series 1, Vol. XLI, Part 1, pp. 255-56.
37 *Statesman*, July 1, 1864.

savage, almost incoherent with ire in parts, they reflect the guerrilla's unstable mind, and they are especially interesting in that the one directed to the newspapers denies he ever had any connection with the Confederacy:

To the editors of the two papers in Lexington, to the citizens and the community at large, General Brown, and Colonel McFerran and his petty hirelings, such as Captain Burris, the friend of Anderson:

MR. EDITORS:

In reading both your papers I see you urge the policy of the citizens taking up arms to defend their persons and property. You are only asking them to sign their death warrants. Do you not know, sirs, that you have some of Missouri's proudest, best, and noblest sons to cope with? Sirs, ask the people of Missouri, who are acquainted with me, if Anderson ever robbed them or mistreated them in any manner. All those that speak the truth will say never. Then what protection do they want? It is from thieves, not such men as I profess to have under my command. My command can give them more protection than all the Federals in the State against such enemies. There are thieves and robbers in the community, but they do not belong to any organized band; they do not fight for principles; they are for self-interest; they are just as afraid of me as they are of Federals. I will help the citizens rid the country of them. They are not friends of mine. I have used all that language can do to stop their thefts; I will now see what I can do by force. But listen to me, fellow-citizens; do not obey this last order. Do not take up arms if you value your lives and property. It is not in my power to save your lives if you do. If you proclaim to be in arms against the guerrillas I will kill you. I will hunt you down like wolves and murder you. You cannot escape. It will not be Federals after you. Your arms will be no protection to you. Twenty-five of my men can whip all that can get together. It will not be militia such as McFerran's, but regulars that have been in the field for three years, that are armed with from two to four pistols and Sharps rifles. I commenced at the first of this war to fight for my country, not to steal from it. I have chosen guerrilla warfare to revenge myself for wrongs that I could not honorably avenge otherwise. I lived in Kansas when this war commenced. Because I would not fight the people of Missouri, my native State, the Yankees sought my life, but failed to get me. Revenged themselves by murdering my father, destroying all my property, and have since that time murdered one of my sisters and kept the other two in jail twelve months. But I have fully glutted my vengeance. I have killed many. I am a guerrilla. I have never belonged to the Confederate Army, nor do my men. A good many of them are from Kansas. I have tried to war with the Federals honorably, but for retaliation I have done things, and am fearful will have to do that [sic] I would shrink from if possible to avoid. I have tried to teach the people of Missouri that I am their friend, but if you think that I am wrong, then it is your duty to fight. Take up arms against me and you are Federals. Your doctrine is an absurdity and I will kill you for being fools. Beware, men, before you make this fearful leap. I feel for you. You are in a critical situation. But remember there is a Southern army headed by the best men in the nation. Many of their homes are in Missouri, and they will have the State or die in the attempt. You that sacrifice your principles for fear of losing your property will, I fear, forfeit your right to a citizenship in Missouri. Young men, leave your mothers and fight for your principles. Let the Federals know that Missouri's sons will not be trampled on. I have no time to say anything more to you. Be careful how you act, for my eyes are upon you.

Colonel McFERRAN:

I have seen your official report to General Brown of two fights that have taken place in Johnson and La Fayette Counties with your men. You have been wrongfully informed, or you have wilfully misrepresented the matter to your superior officer. I had the honor, sir, of being in command at both of those engagements. To enlighten you on the subject and to warn you against making future exaggerations I will say to you in the future to let me know in time, and when I fight your men I will make the proper report. As to the skirmish I had with your men in Johnson, I started to Kingsville with fifty men to take the place, but before I arrived there I discovered a scout, fourteen or fifteen of your men, on the prairie some half a mile distant to my left. I immediately gave chase. They fled. There were not over eight of my men ever got near them. They did not surrender or I would not have killed them, for I understood that Company M were Southern men; they sent me that word. I ordered them to halt and surrender. I was astonished to see them refuse after sending me such word. One of their lieutenants even planned the assassination of General Brown and the taking of his headquarters, but I refused to commit so foul a deed. But they refused a surrender and I had them to kill. I regret having to kill such good Southern men, but they are fit for no service but yours, for they were very cowardly. Myself and two men killed nine of them when there were no other men in sight of us. They are such poor shots it is strange you don't have them practice more. Send them out and I will train them for you. After that I came down near Burris' camp with twenty-five regulars, all told, belonging to the Kansas First, some of my first men. I understood that Burris was anxious to give me a thrashing. Not wishing to lose more than twenty-five men at one time, I thought I would try him with the aforesaid number, but while I was waiting for him to come out from camp, that I might devour him or be devoured, forty-eight of your men coming from Lexington with three wagons had the audacity to fire on my pickets, and very imprudently asked me to come out of the bush and fight them. I obeyed reluctantly. They dismounted and formed on a hill. I formed under their fire under the hill and charged. They fled and I pursued. You know the rest. If you do not, I can inform you; we killed ten on the ground and wounded as many more. Had all of my men done their duty we would have killed thirty of them. Farewell, friend.

To Burris:

Burris, I love you; come and see me. Good-by, boy; don't get discouraged. I glory in your spunk, but damn your judgment.

General Brown:

General: I have not the honor of being acquainted with you, but from what I have heard of you I would take you to be a man of too much honor as to stoop so low as to incarcerate women for the deeds of men, but I see that you have done so in some cases. I do not like the idea of warring with women and children, but if you do not release all the women you have arrested in La Fayette County, I will hold the Union ladies in the county as hostages for them. I will tie them by the neck in the brush and starve them until they are released, if you do not release them. The ladies of Warrensburg must have Miss Fickle released. I hold them responsible for her speedy and safe return. General, do not think that I am jesting with you. I will have to resort to abusing your ladies if you do not quit imprisoning ours. As to the prisoner Ervin you have in Lexington, I have never seen nor heard of him until I learned that such a man was sentenced to be shot. I suppose that he is a Southern man or such a sentence would not have been passed. I hold the citizens of Lexington responsible for his life. The troops in Lexington are no protection to the town, only in the square. If he is killed, I will kill twenty times his number in Lexington. I am perfectly able to do so at any time.

Yours, respectfully,

W. ANDERSON
Commanding Kansas First Guerrillas.

(Editors will please publish this and other papers copy.)

These three letters of Anderson's were delivered, and Egbert Brown forwarded them to General Rosecrans, "as a curiosity and specimen of a guerrilla chief's correspondence."[38]

On Tuesday, July 11, Anderson with some twenty-odd men uniformed in blue crossed the Missouri River near Wakenda in Carroll County. Provided with lists of Union men, most of whom were enrolled in a local state militia company, the guerrillas diabolically murdered nine men that day. Several of the victims, presuming that they were speaking with Union cavalry, stated that they were or had been in the militia, and were shot dead where they stood. One man cursed Anderson, however, and grinning little Archie Clement threw him to the ground and cut his throat with a Bowie knife. Another of

[38] *O. R.*, Series 1, Vol. XLI, Part 2, pp. 75-77.

the murdered men, Solomon Baum, was a known secessionist. Believing he was talking to Union troops, he stoutly maintained his loyalty until a rope was put around his neck. Realizing his error, he cried out his true feelings, but Anderson brutally cut off his life with the remark, "Oh, string him up; God damn his little soul, he's a Dutchman anyway."[39]

Roaring westward through Chariton County, Anderson raided his old home at Huntsville, the county seat of Randolph County, on July 15. Here he killed one man and robbed the merchants and a bank of around $45,000. Thirty-five men were with him now, all dressed in blue.[40] Several of his boys must have noticed how easily the bank gave in. On July 17 the guerrillas charged into Rocheport on the Missouri River in western Boone County. While there they rioted around and entertained many friendly inhabitants by attacking the steamboat *War Eagle.* Bloody Bill called the little community "my capital," and Union reports of the week announced that the Perche Creek hills of Boone County were "swarming with guerrillas."[41] All central Missouri was terrified. On July 23, with his band now grown to a hundred riders, Anderson struck the North Missouri Railroad at Renick and Allen in Randolph County. The depot at Renick was burned and telegraph wire pulled down for some miles, but the guerrillas were held off at Allen by thirty militiamen and the arrival of a train loaded with a company of the Seventeenth Illinois Cavalry down from Macon. Bloody Bill fell back east on the Huntsville road, and on the morning of the twenty-fourth ambushed the Seventeenth and the militia and dispersed them. Two of the Illinois cavalrymen who were killed were scalped. Fastened to the collar of one was this message: "You

[39] *History of Carroll County, Missouri* (St. Louis, 1881), 343-44, 351, reports this crime and gives the men's names; *O. R.,* Series 1, Vol. XLI, Part 1, p. 55, Part 2, p. 38.

[40] *Statesman,* July 22, 1864; *O. R.,* Series 1, Vol. XLI, Part 2, pp. 209, 216-17.

[41] *O. R.,* Series 1, Vol. XLI, Part 2, p. 235; *Statesman,* July 22, 1864.

come to hunt bush whackers. Now you are skelpt. Clemyent Skept you. Wm. Anderson." [42] Obviously, Bill did not write this note, but it expressed his sentiments perfectly. After the fight at Renick the guerrillas raced north through Monroe County, and into Shelby County. Here they burned the 150-foot span over Salt River on the Hannibal and St. Joseph Railroad. Depots at Lakenan and Shelbina were also sent up in flames. The destruction of the Salt River bridge was serious, as trains had to be sent to transfer troops east and west at the broken span. [43] By July 31 Anderson and his men were back in Carroll County moving westward. Again there was a carnival of blood and arson. Houses were burned, home guard units were ambushed, men were shot, scalped, and stripped. The guerrillas raced across Carroll and suddenly disappeared in Ray. [44]

[42] *Statesman*, August 5, 1864.
[43] *O. R.*, Series 1, Vol. XLI, Part 2, p. 423.
[44] *History of Carroll County, Missouri*, 348-51.

12

The Last Campaign

|||||||||||||||||||||||||||||||||||||||||||||||||||||||||||||||||||||||||||||||||||||||||||||||||||||||||||||||||

A NDERSON'S slashing July raid across central Missouri had taken General Rosecrans by surprise. Its success was due largely to the fact that he had ordered Union troop concentrations further west, and the guerrillas had slipped in behind them. Rosecrans suspected that the Confederacy again had plans for a major invasion into his department. The guerrillas were increasing rapidly in numbers; new bands were springing up in central Missouri, and there were constant rumors that a powerful Confederate secret society was preparing a revolution against the Union military government.

All of Rosecrans' suspicions had some grounds. The Confederate Trans-Mississippi Department was planning an invasion of Missouri, and intended to utilize the guerrillas. There was also a secret organization of a sort anxious to assist in the enterprise. For three years the Union military authorities in Missouri, Illinois, Kentucky, Indiana, and Ohio had been aware that a secret society, known as the Knights of the Golden Circle existed in those states for the purpose of aiding the Confederacy. Organized at Cincinnati, Ohio, in 1854 by George W. L. Bickley, the Knights had as their purpose until 1860 the seizure of Mexico and the creation of a new nation subject to the United States.[1] The Knights had an elaborate ritual, various degrees, passwords, "castles," and much more of the mumbo-jumbo that Americans of the nineteenth century loved. The organization was very popular in the South, and when war came, it was a natural vehicle for subversion in those states bordering the Confederacy.

The Knights of the Golden Circle had a number of goals in their wartime mission, but primarily they attempted to find volunteers for the Confederate armies and to encourage resistance to the Union draft. In general, they desired to sabotage the United States wherever and however possible. In their plans they were joined by Copperheads of every faltering degree of loyalty. The Confederacy supported the Knights as best it could, and spent large sums of money on the Sons of Liberty, its sister organization, which planned in a vague way to organize an armed Northwestern Confederacy, and to free Southern soldiers held in Union prison camps.[2]

The Knights of the Golden Circle were never more than a weak menace in Missouri. The firm Union military occupation of the state in 1861 made serious subversion almost impossible, and, as was the case wherever they existed, most of the Knights seem to have been men anxious to foment revolution, but highly unwilling to take up arms. In 1861 the Missouri Knights were being closely watched, and for this reason a new society named the Corps de Belgique was created by a secessionist who was employed as the Belgian consul at St.

1 George F. Milton, *Abraham Lincoln and the Fifth Column* (New York, 1942), 67-69.
2 Wood Gray, *The Hidden Civil War* (New York, 1942), 167-69.

Louis.[3] In 1863 Phineas C. Wright, a St. Louis lawyer who had been active in the Corps, started a new society, called the Order of American Knights, which in Missouri, Illinois, and Indiana took over the members and ambitions of the Golden Circle and Sons of Liberty. The O.A.K. had five mystical degrees, and was also devoted to a Northwestern Confederacy to be allied with the South. By the summer of 1864 it was believed that secret "councils" had been set up all over north Missouri with memberships of between ten and sixty thousand men. The "Grand Commander" of the Missouri organization in 1864 was Charles L. Hunt.[4]

General Rosecrans moved swiftly to destroy the O.A.K. during the spring and summer. Provost Marshal Colonel John Sanderson was especially assigned to investigate the organization, and in a short time his agents had infiltrated most of the St. Louis and outstate councils. Sanderson and his men made the most of a pretty benign situation, sent Rosecrans wildly exaggerated and alarming reports, and soon had the General convinced that north Missouri was rotten with treason.[5] However, when Hunt and twenty-odd other leaders were suddenly arrested and clapped into Gratiot Street Prison, the whole organization was found to be a shell. With the arrest of a few out-state leaders, the movement collapsed and was of no further assistance either to Sterling Price or his guerrillas.

Rosecrans' fears of a major Confederate invasion of his department had much better foundation than did the various secret subversive organizations. In mid-July the officials of the Confederate State of Missouri and the commanders of the Trans-Mississippi completed final plans for a heavy fall raid into Missouri. Ageing Sterling Price was to command the invading force, his objective to capture St. Louis and the entire

[3] Milton, *Abraham Lincoln and the Fifth Column,* 72.
[4] *Ibid.,* 192-94, 253.
[5] *Ibid.,* 290.

state if possible.[6] Major John N. Edwards, who, as General Jo Shelby's adjutant was in a position to know, stated that when Price was chosen to command, he sent word for the guerrilla leaders to hold a council for the purpose of planning diversionary measures. As Price pushed up from Arkansas, the partisans were to turn north Missouri into a battleground in order to draw Union troops away from St. Louis. Captain John Chestnut was selected by the general as a courier to go north to meet with the guerrillas.[7] In the light of what actually occurred, Edwards' remarks are quite accurate. On August 9 Rosecrans was advised by Colonel James H. Ford from Independence that one of his scouts had located all of the guerrilla leaders, Quantrill, Todd, Anderson, and Thrailkill, with from three to five hundred men, in the Sniabar Creek timber, twelve miles north of Chapel Hill in Lafayette County. Ford's scout, T. C. Kelsey, stated that the guerrillas had held a council of war and then had broken up again. He believed that they were waiting for General Shelby to come up from Arkansas at which time they would make a big raid on Kansas.[8] General Clinton Fisk, District of North Missouri, was also advised by an informer that 1,300 guerrillas had been ordered into his district to prevent Union troop concentrations, destroy the Hannibal and St. Joseph and North Missouri railroads, and to co-operate with a grand Confederate recruiting expedition from Arkansas.[9]

In compliance with Price's orders (or request), the guerillas began to move north of the Missouri River. Bill Anderson and his gang were the first to go into action. During the week of August 5 they raided in Clay County, taking money, arms, and the best horses they could obtain from Union citizens.[10]

[6] Kirkpatrick, "Missouri, the Twelfth Confederate State," 244-46.
[7] Edwards, *Noted Guerrillas*, 283.
[8] *O. R.*, Series 1, Vol. XLI, Part 1, pp. 232-33, Part 2, p. 623.
[9] *O. R.*, Series 1, Vol. XLI, Part 3, p. 395.
[10] *Liberty Tribune*, August 12, 1864.

Moving eastward to Fredericksburg, Ray County, on August 12, Anderson pounced on a patrol of the Fifty-first Missouri Cavalry led by Captain Patten Colley, out of Richmond. The patrol was scattered, and Colley and four men were killed. Anderson was reported racing eastward with seventy men in his command.[11] On August 13 Bloody Bill was in Carroll County, pursued by all the Union militia in the area. Throughout the following two days he engaged in rear guard skirmishing with the militia cavalry, killing eight or more of them. He finally caused them to give up the chase because of exhaustion at Grand River on the Chariton County line, and then passed unopposed through Chariton and Howard counties, where during the week of August 20 he joined Clifton Holtzclaw and his men in the wild Perche Creek hills of northern Boone County. Holtzclaw and a Captain Thomas Todd had a Confederate recruiting camp at Dripping Springs in the hills.[12]

For several days Anderson dashed about Howard County, and then staged an attack on the steamboat *Omaha,* twelve miles below Glasgow. The *Omaha* was not captured, but her captain was so alarmed that he refused to leave port unless the gunboat *Fannie Ogden* accompanied him as guard at his wood lot stops. During the week Union patrols, out after the guerrillas, found that Anderson had discovered and was utilizing their identifying signals and pass words, ruining them for further use in the sub-district.[13] Throughout the week of August 24 there was hot skirmishing between guerrillas and Union cavalry which had been hastily ordered into Boone and Howard counties. In his report for the period, General Clinton Fisk coldly informed Department of Missouri Headquarters: "My dispatches of to-day [August 24] from the bush-

---

11 *O. R.,* Series 1, Vol. XLI, Part 1, pp. 251-52.
12 *O. R.,* Series 1, Vol. XLI, Part 2, pp. 824-25; *Statesman,* August 19, 1864.
13 *O. R.,* Series 1, Vol. XLI, Part 2, pp. 840-41.

whack hunters report forty-one guerrillas mustered out by
our boys in the brush in the lower counties. . . . we are doing
all we can with the means in our hands to exterminate the
murdering fiends."[14] Fisk's patrols were reporting the guerrillas that they killed as hunters would their strings of game.

On August 28 Anderson and Holtzclaw struck back by ambushing a forty-man patrol of the Fourth Missouri Cavalry
from Boonville. Led by Captain Joseph Parke, the Union
squadron had come down to Rocheport where the troopers
spent several hours announcing their intention of running
Anderson to earth. As the cavalry marched out of town, it was
fired upon from the wooded bluff east of Moniteau Creek,
and then literally run over by howling guerrillas. Parke's men
rode off in all directions, and the captain reported that he had
seven dead, three men wounded, and three missing. Four of
the dead were barbarically scalped, one was hanged and
scalped, and three had their throats cut.[15] Central Missouri
shuddered. Over at Columbia, fifteen miles east, the home of
the University of Missouri, the citizens' home guard unit, the
Tigers, was called to active duty, and stationed in the barricaded courthouse, university building, and in a stout blockhouse built in the middle of Broadway at Eighth Street. Remembering Anderson's visit to the bank at Huntsville the
preceding month, R. B. Price, a nephew of Sterling, secretly
removed the gold assets of his Boone County National Bank
and buried it under fence posts where it remained until the
end of the war.[16]

On the thirtieth Bloody Bill poured his wild crew into
Rocheport, robbed all the Union stores in town, and drank
the saloons dry. Taking over the Jefferson City penitentiary

14 *O. R.*, Series 1, Vol. XLI, Part 2, p. 839.

15 *O. R.*, Series 1, Vol. XLI, Part 1, pp. 299-300.

16 This was related to the writer by R. B. Price II, the grandson of banker
Price, and now president of the Boone County National Bank at Columbia,
Mo.

steam tug *Buffington,* which was unfortunately docked there, the guerrillas stoked up its boilers, and yelling and hooting, churned up and down the Missouri, outrageously pleased at having a private navy. The captain and pilot of the *Buffington* objected and were shot dead.[17]

Bill and his boys stayed in and around Rocheport for a week. On September 5 they amused themselves by ambushing the steamboat *Yellowstone* as she came in to dock. The *Yellowstone* backed away and escaped downstream, the guerrillas shooting into her again and again. Seeing the *Mars* coming upriver, two of Anderson's boys foolhardily set out in a skiff and demanded her surrender. Guards on the *Mars* fired on them, and one of the guerrillas was mortally wounded. The boat retreated to Jefferson City. All traffic on the Missouri River stopped.[18] September 7 saw the guerrillas on the North Missouri Railroad in northern Boone County tearing down telegraph lines and holding up a train from which they took four carloads of Union cavalry mounts.[19]

George Todd and John Thrailkill with 130 men moved north of the Missouri River just below Dover in Lafayette County at dawn of September 19. They threatened Carrollton, the county seat of Carroll County, and then went on east into Chariton County, riding over forty miles in a day and a night. On September 20 they roared into Keytesville, the county seat of Chariton County, and surrounded a Union garrison of thirty-five militiamen ensconced in the fortified brick courthouse. Thrailkill went in with a white flag, stated that he was a Confederate major acting under orders from General Price, and demanded that the garrison surrender. It promptly and shamefully did. The courthouse was burned, and Keytesville was looted, although in many instances Thrail-

[17] *O. R.*, Series 1, Vol. XLI, Part 2, p. 959, Part 3, pp. 9, 310; *Statesman,* September 2, 1864.

[18] *Statesman,* September 9, 1864.

[19] *O. R.*, Series 1, Vol. XLI, Part 1, p. 745.

kill forced his men to return money taken. Robert Carman, the county sheriff, and William Young, a prominent Union man, were marched out of town and shot. Seven of the militiamen joined Thrailkill's company, indicating that they had been drafted into the wrong army. George Todd at this time informed Lieutenant Anthony Pleyer, who surrendered the Union post and was later court-martialed, that he was not a Confederate officer, "but that he was a bushwhacker . . . and intended to follow bushwhacking as long as he lived." As a result of the capture of Keytesville, the "disloyal" citizens of Chariton County were promptly fined $50,000, with $10,000 going to Young's heirs, $5,000 to Carman's, and $35,000 to build a new courthouse.[20]

In the meanwhile Bill Anderson and his men were active in Howard County. By September 13 stages had been robbed, and all mails stopped between the military posts at Fayette, Franklin, and Renick. Major Austin King, commanding the Union garrison at Fayette, reported that his patrols had been skirmishing with Anderson for several days and had managed to kill six guerrillas. Twelve revolvers had been taken from the bodies of Anderson's men. One of the dead had decorated the bridle of his horse with human scalps.[21]

By the middle of September it was known that Todd, Thrailkill, and Anderson had joined forces in Boone County. On the twenty-third they struck a savage blow by wiping out a twelve-wagon military train ten miles northeast of Rocheport. The train, escorted by Captain James W. McFadden and thirty-five troopers of the Third Missouri Cavalry, was on its way from Rocheport to Sturgeon. At sunset McFadden was met by Captain James Roberts and a patrol of twenty-five additional men of the Third Missouri. The parties had just come together and were discussing the quietness of the

20 O. R., Series 1, Vol. XLI, Part 1, pp. 424-29.
21 O. R., Series 1, Vol. XLI, Part 3, p. 194.

day when they were suddenly charged by some three hundred guerrillas. The Union cavalry fled in disorder, and Anderson's men captured eighteen thousand rounds of ammunition, a wagonload of uniforms, and a thousand rations. Twelve Union cavalrymen and three Negro teamsters were killed. The bodies of the Negroes were put in a wagon and burned. That evening, Brigadier General J. B. Douglass, who had just arrived by boat at Rocheport with five hundred men, went north after Anderson, but could not locate him. Major Reeves Leonard with a company of the Ninth Missouri Cavalry came down to the scene from Fayette. He encountered only six guerrillas, of whom he killed five. Thirty revolvers were found on their horses and bodies.[22] While Leonard was moving toward General Douglass, the guerrillas neatly circled him, and at dawn of the next day were on the outskirts of Fayette, the county seat of Howard County, a community of nearly a thousand people.

As Anderson and Todd rested in the hills south of Fayette, they were joined by their old captain, William Quantrill, who evidently had found the events of the past few days more exciting than his mistress. The three men sat down and discussed the possibility of raiding the town. Anderson and Todd were of the opinion that the Union post had been drained of men; Quantrill, who had had some sad experiences with fortified brick courthouses, believed that the village should be avoided. Heated words were exchanged concerning the courage and intelligence of the three leaders, but Bill Anderson prevailed, and an attack was decided upon. The guerrillas formed in a column in the timber south of town, and at a trot proceeded up Church Street west of the city cemetery. As they reached the edge of the sleeping town, they broke into a gallop, and with their fierce Rebel yells charged

[22] *O. R.,* Series 1, Vol. XLI, Part 1, pp. 432-33; *Statesman,* September 23, 1864; St. Louis *Democrat,* September 23, 1864.

into the courthouse square. Here they were met by a volley of Minié balls from some thirty troopers of the Ninth Cavalry barricaded in the courthouse and in a heavy railroad-tie blockhouse on the hill where Central College is presently located. The guerrillas had again stuck their heads into a hornets' nest. Commanded by Lieutenants Joseph M. Street and Thomas H. Smith, the Union troopers picked them off as they circled around the courthouse, firing their pistols futilely at brick walls. Bill Anderson led one wild dash at the blockhouse, his black curls streaming out from under a large plumed hat, but the guerrillas had no way of entering it. Frank James afterwards said, "It was like charging a stone wall only this stone wall belched forth lead," and added: "The worst scared I ever was during the war was in the Fayette fight."[23] In a few minutes it was all over. The guerrillas pulled north out of town, leaving thirteen dead behind, and holding in their saddles some thirty wounded companions.[24] They went slowly up the Roanoke Road, leaving their wounded to be hidden by sympathetic farmers. At dusk Quantrill and a few men parted with Anderson and Todd in disgust. That night Todd and Thrailkill and their company also left Bloody Bill.

The next morning Todd and Thrailkill with some 250 men surrounded Huntsville in Randolph County and demanded the surrender of the Union post there. The garrison was commanded by Lieutenant Colonel A. F. Denny, and that officer, secure behind the brick walls of the county courthouse, stoutly informed the partisans that if they wanted him they could come in and get him.[25] With the fiasco at Fayette fresh in his mind, Todd moved south and east to Renick

23 *The Columbia Missouri Herald*, September 24, 1897, carried an interview with James concerning the fight.
24 Connelley, *Quantrill*, 452-53; McCorkle, *Three Years With Quantrill*, 110-12; *O. R.*, Series 1, Vol. XLI, Part 1, pp. 415-16, 440.
25 *O. R.*, Series 1, Vol. XLI, Part 3, p. 397.

where he vented his rage by pulling down miles of telegraph wire along the North Missouri Railroad. By September 26 he had disappeared into Boone County.

Following the Fayette fight Anderson took his men on north and east into Audrain County. News of the direction of his march reached Paris, the county seat of Monroe County, on the morning of September 26, and Major A. V. E. Johnson of the Thirty-ninth Missouri Infantry, mounted 158 of his riflemen and moved south to intercept the guerrillas. Anderson and his company ran into Johnson's scouts about noon, and turning away, retreated rapidly south, crossing the rails of the North Missouri a little east of Centralia in Boone County as darkness fell. Here they learned that Todd and Thrailkill were camped on the farm of one Singleton, four miles south of Centralia. They pushed on to the camp and joined their friends. Two hundred and twenty-five guerrillas sat around the fires on the prairie at Singleton's that night. The main topic of conversation was that on September 19 Sterling Price, with twelve thousand Confederates, had entered Missouri near Doniphan in the southeastern part of the state and was heading toward St. Louis. The great invasion was on; the guerrillas must be even more active.

September 27, 1864, dawned clear and cool. Bill Anderson arose from his blanket at Singleton's, and restless and impatient for news, mounted thirty of his men and rode into Centralia to get St. Louis newspapers. At his right hand trotted little Archie Clement, his flat eyes blinking, his perpetual smile a grimace. Bloody Bill found Centralia sleeping, and he waked the hamlet of one hundred people with pistol shots and yells. For three hours his boys sauntered around the village, terrorizing the inhabitants, demanding and getting breakfast, and looting the depot, stores, and houses of pro-Union men. Several guerrillas got drunk, and in their excitement set the depot on fire. At midmorning the Columbia

stage rolled in, and its passengers were hauled off and glee-
fully robbed. One of them was United States Representative
James S. Rollins, on his way to a political meeting. Rollins, a
pistol under his nose, did some magnificent impromptu acting, passing himself off as a local farmer and an ardent sup-
porter of the Confederate States of America. He finally managed to slip away to hiding in the attic of Sneed's Hotel. One
of the guerrillas rifled his valise and put on a shirt which bore
the elegant initials of the congressman. About noon the west-
bound North Missouri train from St. Charles whistled in the
distance, and Anderson's men piled ties on the track and hid
to await its arrival. The engineer, James Clark, saw the smoking depot but did not reverse his engine because there was a
gravel train behind him. As the cars pulled up to the depot
the guerrillas surrounded them, fired their pistols into the
windows, and as the passengers dismounted, they robbed
them. Twenty-five unarmed Union soldiers were on board,
and these were lined up and marched down the platform by
Archie Clement with a guard of fifteen men.

In a few minutes Bloody Bill rode his horse in front of the
Union captives and began to question them. Finding out that
most of them were on furlough, the guerrilla told them that
his men needed their uniforms and ordered them to strip.
The miserable prisoners did as they were directed, and soon
stood naked or in long underdrawers under the guerrilla
guns. Anderson then asked if any were officers or noncommis-
sioned officers. There was a long moment of hesitation, and
then one man, Thomas Goodman, stepped forth, and although believing that he would be instantly shot, admitted
that he was a sergeant of Missouri Engineers. Anderson care-
lessly ordered Goodman out of the line, and turning to Clement, told him to "muster out" the soldiers. Little Archie, a
Colt revolver in each hand, grinned at his master, turned
and fired point blank at the soldiers. The rest of the guard

also began shooting. The Union soldiers died with amaze-
ment marked on their faces. One of them bounded out of the
line, wounded, knocked down a guerrilla, and having no
other refuge, crawled under the wooden station dock. It was
set on fire, and when the man was forced by the flames to
crawl out, he was pistoled. The North Missouri train was
then set ablaze, and without engineer or passenger was started
west toward Sturgeon, five miles away. The engine whistle
was tied down, causing the boiler to empty a short distance
from town. The burning cars sent a column of oily black
smoke into the clear noon air, which was observed for miles.
Anderson mounted his men at once, and they rode back down
to Singleton's, shouting and singing. During the morning they
had discovered a case of boots, and each rider had several pair
hung over his horse's neck, filled with whiskey from a large
keg they were unable to carry off. Sergeant Tom Goodman
was taken along, his feet tied under a horse. Goodman
escaped from the guerrillas three nights later while they
were crossing the Missouri River.[26]

Major Johnson and his mounted Union infantry from Paris
marched into Centralia at four o'clock that afternoon. He
found the town in a state of shock, the women and children
screaming and crying, the men standing around white-faced
with disbelief. Learning that only thirty men had been with
Anderson, Johnson divided his command, leaving half of it
under Captain Adam Theis to restore order in town. Then,
in spite of warning that there were many guerrillas in the
neighborhood, he took the rest of his force out of Centralia
south on Anderson's trail. A mile from Centralia he saw ten
horsemen to his front who retreated rapidly before him, as

---

[26] For accounts of the Centralia "massacre" see: *O. R.*, Series 1, Vol. XLI,
Part 1, pp. 440-41, 443, 448, 521-22; St. Louis *Democrat*, September 28, 30,
1864; *Statesman*, September 30, 1864; *Columbia, Missouri Herald*, September
24, 1897.

they had been ordered to do by Todd and Anderson. Johnson pressed rapidly after them and into an ambush. Nearing the Singleton farm, the Union force topped a gentle rise in the prairie and saw, to what must have been their complete horror, a line of two hundred dismounted guerrillas standing silently to their horses at the foot of a sloping hill. Major Johnson was a brave officer. He knew many of his men were recruits, all had been trained to fight on foot as infantry, and and he saw that he could not retreat. He calmly dismounted his company, sent his horses back where they were held, and formed a twenty-yard line of battle.

The guerrillas were astounded. One of Todd's men, John Koger, suddenly said in a voice that could be heard up and down their line, "The fools are going to fight us on foot," and then added, "God help 'em." George Todd roared for the guerrillas to mount, and led by screaming Bill Anderson, they charged up the hill at the Union infantry. Johnson's men fired one volley with their single-shot Enfield muskets. That volley, downhill, was high, and only three of the partisans were hit. "Hank" Williams, one of Anderson's men, pitched from his horse, dead, and Frank Shepherd, shot through the head, dashed his brains and blood over the leg of Frank James, who rode next to him.[27] Richard Kenney was fatally wounded. In the next minute the guerrillas, their terrible revolvers popping, had ridden into the terrified Union infantry, through it, and had scattered its horses. Frank James stated that some of the soldiers were desperately biting cartridges, attempting to reload; some were trying to fix bayonets; others simply threw down their rifles and looked up dazed. In a few minutes most were dead, shot through the head. Major Johnson, courageously firing his pistol, went down before the guns of seventeen-year-old Jesse James. The

27 *Columbia, Missouri Herald*, September 24, 1897, according to Frank James.

guerrillas roared back into Centralia and rode over Theis's men. Captain Theis got to his horse, and with a few troopers raced west to the blockhouse at Sturgeon. He and only eighteen others reached there safely. Frank James, mounted on his horse "Little George," and Archie Clement followed Theis under the rifles of the Union post in their excitement. In little more than an hour the Thirty-ninth Missouri Infantry had lost 114 men and two officers killed, two men wounded, and six men missing. The guerrillas rode back to Singleton's, killing all the wounded they could locate. Joking little David Pool counted the dead at Singleton's by jumping from one body to another, crowing, "If they are dead I can't hurt them, I cannot count 'em good without stepping on 'em. When I get my foot on one this way I know I've got him."[28] Major Johnson and many of his men were stripped, and it was reported at the time that their bodies were mutilated. This atrocity story was not so.[29]

The almost complete destruction of Johnson's command panicked the entire area. It was several days after the massacre and fight at Centralia before federal cavalry in the area began to feel out cautiously after the guerrillas. By that time Anderson, Todd, and Thrailkill had separated and faded into hiding in Howard County.

On October 3, 1864, a band of guerrillas robbed and burned two trains on the Hannibal and St. Joseph Railroad at Hunnewell in Shelby County, and on the fifth, because of this attack, Isaac H. Sturgeon, the president of the North Missouri, sent General Rosecrans the following letter:

SIR: Since the murdering of the unarmed soldiers on our train on Tuesday a week ago and the burning of our cars we have not

[28] *Columbia, Missouri Herald,* September 24, 1897.

[29] For accounts of the fight at Singleton's and Centralia, see: *O. R.,* Series 1, Vol. XLI, Part 1, pp. 440-41, Part 3, pp. 488, 491, 521, 522, 693; Britton, *The Civil War on the Border,* II, 385-86; *Statesman,* September 30, 1864; St. Louis *Democrat,* September 28, 30, 1864.

felt that we could with any safety go beyond Saint Charles with
our trains, and the destruction of trains on the Hannibal and St.
Joseph Railroad confirms us in the propriety of not attempting
to run trains until the road is guarded by a sufficient military
force. In the multitude of matters that you have to think of, I
feel you will not deem it out of place on my part to make suggestions, even if what I suggest is of no value or has been thought
of by you. Three thousand cavalry distributed along our line of
road and west of the Hannibal and St. Joseph road, patrolling
the road, ever on the march backward and forward, taking sections of fifty miles for 300 or 400, and scouring the country each
side, armed with plenty of heavy revolvers as well as the musket,
as the guerrilla bands are, would soon enable us in safety to run
our trains. If we have not horses press them and mount our infantry, and let our men live as the guerrillas do, off the country,
giving vouchers to the loyal and none to rebel sympathizers. At
Wellsville, Mexico, Centralia, or Sturgeon, and at Macon there
should be garrisons of infantry, with log-houses or some fortifica-
tion, so as to defend against a superior force. At Perruque [sic]
bridge a guard should be kept till all trouble is over; also the
bridges just north and south of Mexico should be guarded. We
are anxious to move our trains as soon as you can make it safe
to do so. I know that you will give us protection as soon as circumstances will admit of it.[30]

Anderson, Todd, and their men had accomplished a good
part of their military mission. North Missouri was under a
reign of terror, and rail transportation was paralyzed in the
face of General Price's advance up through the state.

If the guerrilla campaign along the Missouri River was a
success in August and September, Price's invasion was not
doing at all well. On September 27 his army had suffered a
bloody rebuff at Pilot Knob in Iron County where General
Tom Ewing and a small force in Fort Davidson held off two
thirds of the Confederate force for twenty-four hours and

30 *O. R.*, Series 1, Vol. XLI, Part 3, p. 634.

then managed to escape. Losing his nerve, "Old Pap" Price
turned west from St. Louis, which he could easily have taken,
and straggled toward Jefferson City. On October 2 he was in
front of the state capital, but did not attack the inferior Union
force holding fortified positions around the town. Gathering
his ragged cavalry together he moved on up the Missouri
River to Boonville on the ninth. He was now being pressed
from the east by General Alfred Pleasonton with cavalry
from Jefferson City. On his left flank Union troops under
General A. J. Smith were beginning to close in, and at his
right lay the almost impassable river. Ahead of him to the
west forces from Missouri and Kansas were gathering under
Generals Curtis, Blunt, and the unsavory Doc Jennison. Sterling Price's position was becoming serious, and instead of acting vigorously the old man rode in an ambulance or lay on a
carpet drinking toddies.[31] Again the Union trap was closing
on him.

[31] Monaghan, *Civil War on the Western Border*, 320-25.

13

The Final Struggle

‖‖‖

O N October 11, 1864, Bill Anderson, William C. Quantrill, and George Todd met General Sterling Price at Boonville. Price welcomed the "distinguished partisan leaders" who, in the words of Captain T. J. Mackey of the general's staff, "were the terror of the enemy in that section and accustomed to operating on railroads."[1] General Price had a choice at this time. He could either denounce the guerrillas and send them out of his lines, or he could be blind to their methods and utilize them. Assessing his poor military position, he determined to use them, and in his own words later officially stated:

Captain Anderson, who reported to me that day with a company of about 100 men, was immediately sent to destroy the North Missouri Railroad. At the same time Quantrill was sent with the men under his command to destroy the Hannibal and

[1] *O. R.*, Series 1, Vol. XLI, Part 1, p. 718. In testimony at a court of inquiry concerning Price's disastrous campaign which was held at Shreveport, Louisiana, in April, 1865.

Saint Joseph Railroad, to prevent the enemy, if possible, from throwing their forces in my front from Saint Louis. These officers I was informed afterwards did effect some damage to the roads, but none of any material damage, and totally failed in the main object proposed, which was to destroy the large railroad bridge that was in the end of Saint Charles County.[2]

The general then issued the following terse order which was later found on Bill Anderson's body:

SPECIAL ORDER)   HEADQUARTERS ARMY OF MISSOURI
                                      Boonville, October 11, 1864

Captain Anderson with his command, will at once proceed to the north side of the Missouri River and permanently destroy the North Missouri Railroad, going as far east as practicable. He will report his operations at least every two days.

By order of Major-General Price:

MACLEAN,
Lieutenant-Colonel and Assistant Adjutant General[3]

With Anderson and Quantrill assigned, George Todd and his new men were sent south of Boonville to cut the Pacific Railroad. Sterling Price's use of Anderson, Quantrill, and Todd in his campaign of 1864 raised a storm of criticism in the Missouri newspapers. The *Liberty Tribune* stated editorially:

There seems no longer to be any doubt that General Sterling Price has given full countenance and indorsement to the scoundrelly and murderous operations of Anderson, Quantrell, [*sic*] Reeves, and other guerrilla chieftains in this State. It is reliably reported that when the rebel commander was at Booneville [*sic*] the villain Bill Anderson presented "Old Pap" with a pair of costly silver-mounted pistols, and that in his speech in response, the recipient complimented Anderson, saying that if he had fifty thousand such men he would hold the state permanently.[4]

2 *O. R.*, Series 1, Vol. XLI, Part 1, p. 632.
3 *O. R.*, Series 1, Vol. XLI, Part 4, p. 354.
4 *Liberty Tribune*, November 4, 1864; St. Louis *Democrat*, October 28, 1864.

Expediency was likely the only motive which moved General Price to employ the guerrillas. He was so hard-pressed that he was almost forced to welcome any fighting men who would kill the Union force that was relentlessly surrounding him. The guerrillas were great killers, and William Quantrill, Bill Anderson, and George Todd all died in action against a Union foe.

Neither Anderson nor Quantrill paid much attention to their Boonville orders. Anderson and his men were put across the river by ferry, and the guerrilla did send a party east along the Boone's Lick road which leads into the North Missouri Railroad. On October 14 some eighty of his men fell on Danville, the county seat of Montgomery County, killed five militiamen, several civilians, and burned and robbed most of the stores and houses in the community. They announced that they were Anderson's men, and then went on east to loot New Florence and High Hill, burning the railroad depots in those towns.[5] The guerrillas were scattered by militia the next day.

Bill Anderson was not present at the Danville raid. Both he and Quantrill were at Glasgow with General Jo Shelby when he captured that Howard County river town on October 14. The guerrilla leaders again showed their basically outlaw natures following the Confederate victory at Glasgow. Quantrill sent two of his men to the home of pro-Union banker W. F. Dunnica, and that unhappy man was forced to open the safe of his counting house and hand over $21,000 to the guerrilla. Bloody Bill entertained himself by going to the home of Benjamin Lewis, the wealthiest citizen of the town, and by the use of threats and a beating obtained $5,000 in gold and notes from his victim.[6]

Following the capture of Glasgow, Quantrill again faded

5 O. R., Series 1, Vol. XLI, Part 1, p. 888; Part 3, p. 893.

6 O. R., Series 1, Vol. XLI, Part 1, p. 431; St. Louis Democrat, October 21, November 14, 1864; History of Howard and Chariton Counties, Missouri, 289.

into obscurity, and made no move north toward the Hannibal and St. Joseph Railroad. Anderson took his men on west along the Missouri River, keeping pace with Price's army, which was fighting continuous rear guard action with Pleasonton's Union cavalry on the other side of the stream. George Todd and his men were successful in stopping rail transportation on the Pacific road, burning the bridge, depot, water tanks, and houses at Otterville in Cooper County.[7] He and his company were then assigned to Jo Shelby's cavalry division and rode as scouts for that hard-fighting elite unit. They were in every advance guard skirmish as Price lunged westward toward Independence and the Kansas line.

On October 21 Shelby's division reached the Little Blue River just east of Independence, and found its old enemy, the Kansas militia, commanded by Generals Blunt, Jennison, and Moonlight, holding the crossings. The Confederates pushed the Kansans back and into Independence where fierce block-to-block fighting took place. As the outnumbered Union troops retreated, George Todd and his scouts followed them closely. Two and one half miles northeast of town the guerrilla leader reined in his horse on a little rise and rose in his stirrups to watch the enemy. At that moment a Spencer carbine ball fired by a Union sniper smashed into his neck, and he crashed from his mount. His men came to him quickly and found him suffocating in his blood, paralyzed and unable to ride. They carried him into town to the house of a Mrs. Burns where he was placed on a bed while attempts were made to dress his wound. He lived only an hour. George Todd was buried by his men that night in the Independence Cemetery. He had died fighting, the only suitable way for death to come to him.[8]

---

[7] O. R., Series 1, Vol. XLI, Part 3, p. 741.

[8] O. R., Series 1, Vol. XLI, Part 4, pp. 194, 206; Connelley, *Quantrill,* 454-55; Edwards, *Noted Guerrillas,* 321.

Old General Sam Curtis, who commanded all of the Union forces on the Confederate western front, took time in the middle of desperate battle on October 22 to send his wife the following communication: "It is certain that among the rebels killed yesterday the notorious Todd, one of the murderers of our son, was one among many who were killed."[9] Curtis had never forgotten Baxter Springs. David Pool took over Todd's company, and they moved on west with Price, who was defeated the next day at the battle of Westport. When Price's shattered army started its long and hopeless retreat toward Arkansas, Todd's men went with it.

The sands were now running out for Bill Anderson. Through the middle of October he moved westward through Chariton and Carroll counties, murdering Union men and burning houses. Little Archie Clement was at his diabolical work again with his ready knife and pistols. At one place the guerrillas forced a hapless German named Eisenhour to guide them. When they were done with his services, Archie shot him, cut his head off, and placed it in the hands of the corpse on its chest.[10]

The last week of October saw Anderson and his men in the lower part of Ray County, isolated in north Missouri as Price's defeated Confederates marched toward Arkansas. On October 26, 1864, Bloody Bill fought his last battle. His death came at the hands of the Missouri State Militia. On the morning of the twenty-sixth, as the result of information given by a country woman, the guerrilla and his men were located in camp near Albany, one mile north of Orrick in southwest Ray County. A Union force, commanded by Majors Samuel P. Cox and John Grimes, and composed of 150 men of the Fifty-first and Thirty-third Missouri Infantry from Ray,

9 *O. R.*, Series 1, Vol. XLI, Part 4, p. 190.

10 *History of Carroll County, Missouri*, 362-63; St. Louis *Democrat*, October 30, 1864.

Daviess, and Caldwell counties, was sent down from Richmond into the area.[11]

Anderson and his men had no suspicion that there were any enemy troops in the neighborhood. When the guerrilla arose on the twenty-sixth, he and a few of his boys rode to the nearby house of W. R. Blythe and demanded breakfast. While it was being prepared, Bill, always vain and jaunty, washed his face and hands, combed his long curls, and looking in a mirror, bowed and remarked, "Good morning, Captain Anderson, how are you this morning?" And then, grinning, he answered his question, "Damn well, thank you."[12]

About noon Major Cox reached the neighborhood and found exactly where the guerrillas were bivouacked. As there was only one road leading into the area, he posted half his men under Major Grimes in ambush along it, and drew up the rest in a battle line across it. The day was crisp and cool, and the dense Missouri woods were quiet except for the slowly falling leaves. A little after noon the Union troops heard the beat of many hoofs up the road and broken words and laughter coming toward them. Cox's soldiers in the road and in the ambush cocked their heavy Enfield rifles and silently waited. Suddenly, around a curve dashed Bill Anderson, followed by about seventy riders. The guerrilla leader saw the Union infantry drawn across the road and pulled his horse up to a halt. Then, he drew his revolver, and with a shrill yell charged. It was to be Centralia again.

The cheering guerrilla column, closely packed in the road, galloped into the ambush. Grimes and his men rose as one, and from the woods at point-blank range poured a volley of Minié balls and buckshot into them. At the same moment Cox and his men fired at Anderson and the head of the column. When the smoke cleared, the lane was filled with threshing horses and dead and dying guerrillas. Only Bill Anderson

---

[11] O. R., Series 1, Vol. XLI, Part 1, p. 442.
[12] Pigg, "Bloody Bill, Noted Guerrilla of the Civil War," loc. cit., 18.

continued the charge; the rest of his men dashed into the woods. The partisan leader spurred on toward Cox and his men in the road, the Union infantry now shooting at him with revolvers. Anderson reached the blazing blue clad line, broke through it, and then, throwing his arms in the air, he toppled backwards off his horse. Cox's men cautiously approached the figure in the road, their guns covering him. It was Anderson, dead, two balls through the back of his head, a pistol clutched in each of his fists. He had died as he had lived, violently, seeking no quarter.[13]

The body of the handsome guerrilla was put in a wagon, and Cox and his jubilant men, only four of them wounded, rode back to Richmond. The corpse was put on public display at the courthouse, and all night long by flickering torch and candle it was viewed by almost every person in the little community. When the sun rose "Doctor Kice," the town photographer, washed the pallid face of Bill Anderson, propped the body up, and took pictures of it "to supply the people with his likeness." Major Cox had the guerrilla buried, without services, in an unmarked grave in the Richmond cemetery. He provided only a "decent" coffin.[14]

Anderson's horse and the articles found on his body aroused great public interest. The bridle of his mount was braided with a human scalp. There were six revolvers in his saddle holsters and his belt. In the dead guerrilla's pockets were found pictures of himself and his wife, letters she had written from Texas, a lock of her hair, $600 in gold and Union greenbacks, a little Confederate flag with the words, "Presented to W. L. Anderson by his friend F. M. R.," and the orders General Price had given him at Boonville.[15]

---

[13] *O. R.*, Series 1, Vol. XLI, Part 1, p. 442; Britton, *The Civil War on the Border*, II, 544-45.

[14] *Liberty Tribune*, November 11, 1864.

[15] *Liberty Tribune*, November 4, 1864; *O. R.*, Series 1, Vol. XLI, Part 4, p. 334.

The Union military command in Missouri could not have been more pleased over Bloody Bill Anderson's demise. Major Cox became a military hero, was promoted, and he and his men were specially cited in a departmental general order. In this order General Rosecrans directed that Anderson's watch and pistols were to be kept by the officers of the victorious militia, and the money found on him was to be divided among the men.[16]

William L. Anderson's frightful military record during the Civil War on the border can only speak for itself. When he died, the Confederacy lost an insanely effective warrior, a man who was never accused of cowardice in the face of an enemy. All things considered, perhaps he understood in his rage-filled mind far better than others placed high in the embattled South the necessary cruel and remorseless ingredients required for a successful rebellion.

Anderson's leaderless men chose nineteen-year-old Archie Clement as their new captain, but the wild spirit that had directed them was gone. Archie's plain viciousness could not replace it. The unit split up; a number of the boys led by Clement slipped through the Union lines and made their way down to their old winter haunts in Texas.

December, 1864, saw the last Confederate hopes in Missouri crushed. William C. Quantrill, in hiding since the capture of Glasgow, decided to leave the state. In the middle of December he gathered together thirty-three of his old boys who had hidden out in Jackson County, and this party, dressed in Union blue, passed across Missouri and entered Kentucky late in January, 1865. During that spring Quantrill and his men roamed aimlessly about in the north central part of the state, committing crimes and skirmishing in a minor fashion with the Union militia. Bill called himself Captain "Clarke."[17] He was used up as a leader, and must

16 *O. R.*, Series 1, Vol. XLI, Part 1, p. 317.
17 Connelley, *Quantrill*, 460-61.

have known that most men spoke his name with disgust and horror.

On May 10, 1865, Quantrill and his little gang were camped in a barn lot on the farm of James H. Wakefield in the southern part of Spencer County. Here he was surprised and attacked by a Union ranger party commanded by Captain Edward Terrill. Quantrill and his men scrambled wildly for their horses, and, while running, the guerrilla leader was hit in the back by a pistol ball that entered his body at his left shoulder blade and smashed downward into his spine. Bill Quantrill dropped into the manure and mud of the horse lot, fatally wounded and completely paralyzed below the arms. On May 12 Captain Terrill loaded the wounded guerrilla into a wagon and hauled his prize to the hospital of the military prison at Louisville. Here Quantrill lingered in miserable pain until he died following an operation on June 6, 1865. The Louisville *Daily Democrat* and *Journal* took only passing notice of his death. While he lay in the hospital he was nursed by a priest, and before he gasped out his last breath, he made a full confession and was baptized in the Roman Catholic faith. He was buried in the old Portland Catholic Cemetery at Louisville, but in 1887 his mother had his bones brought back to Ohio. The man she paid to remove the body stole some of the skeleton, and years later parts of it turned up in the hands of a Kansas collector.[18]

So Quantrill died. A singular man, a truly able cavalry leader, yet with such major defects of character as to render him continuously defeated in what might have been a distinguished military career. His name, along with Anderson's and Todd's, is in most instances now better remembered than any other of the many captains, North and South, who took part in the terrible Civil War on the western border.

[18] Connelley, *Quantrill*, 35-36, 477-80.

14

Surrender

━━

THE early spring of 1865 found the eastern Confederacy staggering, its morale crushed by Sherman's great raid through its heartland and Lee's increasing inability to hold the northern lines around Richmond. In Missouri and Arkansas all hopes for ultimate Confederate victory had guttered out with Sterling Price's rout in the fall of '64, and the armies of the Trans-Mississippi Department were disintegrating through desertion and lack of supplies. Effective guerrilla operations along the border had ceased with the death of Anderson and Todd, and most of the partisans had sulked down to Texas or had gone to Louisiana with Price. In April, 1865, the end came. General Lee surrendered his army in Virginia and Joe Johnston surrendered in North Carolina. Kirby Smith turned the Trans-Mississippi Department over to the Union forces, after some delay, on May 25.

Only a few guerrillas had remained in Missouri through the winter of 1864–1865, and these, with no hope of being

232

considered as Confederate partisans, degenerated into bands
of outlaws. On March 29, 1865, the *Kansas City Journal*,
under the headline "Bushwhacking Played Out," announced
that Union Colonel Chester Harding, who now commanded
the Central District, was making plans to exterminate or
drive out the few remaining guerrillas. In April the Columbia
Statesman stated that most of the bushwhackers were leaving
central Missouri, and advised its readers to adopt the following policy toward them: "Let the sight of a guerrilla be the
signal to shoot him. If he comes to your house shoot him;
if you meet him in the road shoot him down; in short resolve
that those devils shall no longer rob, insult and outrage you,
and hold in jeopardy your property and very existence."[1]

On May 15, 1865, the citizens of Liberty held a mass meeting and passed a resolution asking the county court to offer a
thousand-dollar reward for the apprehension and delivery,
dead or alive, of "the few marauders and thieves" who were
still operating as guerrillas in Clay County.[2] Martial law had
been ended by joint proclamation of Governor Thomas Fletcher and General Pope in March, and civil courts were again
beginning to hold their terms. The exhausted people of
ruined Missouri felt that the war was over and that all further hostility was futile and should cease. The savage fires of
four years of guerrilla warfare had burned out both civil resistance and the desire for further punitive measures by the
Union military command. All parties felt only sullen fatigue.

Colonel Harding and his cavalry pursued the guerrillas
remaining in western and central Missouri throughout the
spring, killing them when they came across them. On May 1
he reported to departmental headquarters that in the past
three months he had shot only thirty-four bushwhackers, and
that conditions were generally quiet. He believed, however,

1 *Daily K. C. Journal*, April 13, 1865, citing the *Statesman*.
2 *Liberty Tribune*, May 19, 1865.

that with the dissolution of the western Confederate armies his district would receive "the worst elements of the disbanding . . . rebels," and asked that a policy be established whereby repentant Southern soldiers might become prisoners of war.[3] A kindly, decent officer, Chester Harding knew that peace was coming and that somehow returning Confederates would have to be accepted and accommodated under that peace. He was very sick of war.

On the morning of May 7, 1865, the tranquility of Harding's Central District came to a surprising and shocking end. At 2:00 A.M. forty guerrillas charged into the village of Holden in western Johnson County, robbed two stores, and killed a man. An hour later 110 horsemen roared into Kingsville, five miles west, sacked the town, killed eight men, wounded two, and burned five houses. Little Archie Clement was back from Texas and had paid his home town his first call in the state.[4] Seemingly from nowhere a major partisan force had again sprung into existence.

Down at St. Louis, Major General Grenville M. Dodge, who now commanded the Department of Missouri, could hardlly believe the reports from Holden and Kingsville. Dodge, too, thought the war was over, and was anxious to start on his plans for a transcontinental railroad. He acted swiftly against the guerrillas. All of the Central District Militia Cavalry was called to duty and put in the field, and a regiment of infantry was placed on the cars of the Missouri Pacific at Jefferson City and sent to Warrensburg. Six companies of cavalry were sent into the area from Henry County.[5]

The *Kansas City Journal* was outraged over the raids on the Johnson County towns. On May 11, 1865, it angrily informed its readers: "These guerrillas in addition to being

[3] *O. R.*, Series 1, Vol. XLVIII, Part 2, p. 286.

[4] *O. R.*, Series 1, Vol. XLVIII, Part 2, pp. 342, 352, 353; *Daily K. C. Journal,* May 10, 1865.

[5] *O. R.*, Series 1, Vol. XLVIII, Part 2, pp. 342, 352-53.

thieves and robbers and murderers are rebels," and added
that their immediate suppression was an "essential part of the
closing up of the war." The *Journal* also accused the Union
military of having known of the presence and progress of the
guerrillas from the time they had crossed the Arkansas River
in the Indian nations. This accusation was not true, as General Dodge admitted that the first knowledge his department
had of them came with this appearance at Holden. However,
the Department of Kansas had warning of their coming. On
May 5 Colonel Charles W. Blair, commanding Fort Scott, had
informed the Union post at Mound City that a large band of
guerrillas was moving north in Missouri about twenty-five
miles east of the Kansas line. This information was apparently
not relayed on to Missouri. On the evening of May 8 the guerrilla party was reported by Union scouts to be moving north
toward Lexington, and, in a flurry of warning telegrams to
his posts, General Dodge complained that "they are just as
well posted about my plans as I am."[6] Throughout western
Missouri the question was, Who are these men; who leads
them? On the morning of May 9 this was answered by Major
B. K. Davis, commanding the post at Lexington. Davis informed Colonel Harding at Warrensburg that his scouts had
obtained the following information the night before. The
guerrillas were members of Bill Anderson's old gang. They
were just up from Texas. They were being led by Archie
Clement, David Pool, and Jim Anderson, Bill's brother. They
had told people of the neighborhood south of Lexington that
they had known nothing of General Johnston's surrender in
North Carolina, and many of them refused to believe that Lee
had quit fighting. More important, Major Davis reported, "a
large portion of them are anxious to give themselves up if
they can be treated as prisoners of war."[7]

6 *O. R.*, Series 1, Vol. XLVIII, Part 2, pp. 325, 352-55.
7 *O. R.*, Series 1, Vol. XLVIII, Part 2, pp. 370-71.

Colonel Harding had been advised by the Department of Missouri on May 7 as to the position to take concerning the surrender of guerrillas at that time. At that time General Dodge wrote him: "You can say to all such who lay down their arms and surrender and obey the laws that the military law will not take any further action against them, but that we cannot protect them against the civil law should it deem best to take cognizance of their cases." [8]

Harding passed this word on to Davis at Lexington, and this lenient policy was followed generally by the Union commanders throughout the department.

On the morning of May 11 little Archie Clement sent Major Davis the following impudent note under a flag of truce: "This is to notify you that I will give you until Friday morning, May 12, 1865, to surrender the town of Lexington. If you surrender we will treat you and all taken as prisoners of war. If we have to take it by storm we will burn the town and kill the soldiers. We have the force and are determined to have it." [9]

Archie was obviously not ready to end the war, and it is certain that he had little belief that he would ever receive amnesty for his deeds either from the military or the civil authorities. David Pool was another person, however. His record had been fairly clean, and he entered into conversations with Davis concerning surrender. On May 16 the Lexington post commander advised Harding that:

David Pool professes to be in the Sni Hills collecting his men in order to give them up. Pool's first lieutenant is south of here doing the same thing, and I have every assurance that he will give himself up as soon as he gets his men together, whom he and Pool assert were disbanded to meet on the 20th instant. I am almost certain that Clement with five or six men, was on the river

[8] O. R., Series 1, Vol. XLVIII, Part 2, pp. 341-42.
[9] O. R., Series 1, Vol. XLVIII, Part 2, pp. 408-409.

yesterday, between here and Berlin, prospecting for crossing the river. . . . His letter sent in is dated May 14, and proposed with five men to meet an equal party at the Mound, on Warrensburg road, on the 17th instant, to learn particulars of terms. &c.[10]

On May 21, 1865, the great news was flashed across the entire state of Missouri. David Pool with eighty-five of Anderson's and Todd's guerrillas had surrendered to Colonel Harding at Lexington. The act was performed in a strictly military manner. At noon of the twenty-first Pool sent a rider bearing a large white flag into Lexington to advise the post of his presence. Colonel Harding then rode out with an escort a mile and a half from town and led the guerrillas into Lexington and down the streets to the provost marshal's office. In the shadow of the county courthouse, its stately columns clipped by cannon balls from the battle of four years before, Pool raised his hand and the riders came to a halt. For the first time the ragged partisans were being treated as enemy soldiers. Now they tried to act like soldiers. At a command they dismounted as a company and stood to horse. Pool rasped out another order, and in a body his men stepped two paces forward and laid down their rifles. Next, heavy pistol belts were unstrapped and placed on top of the carbines. Silently they filed before the provost marshal; each man raised his hand and took an oath of allegiance to the United States and received a parole certificate. They then returned to their horses, and Colonel Harding told them to return home and live in peace. Only a few of the boys had any home to go back to; most of their families were scattered far over the west.

That night Chester Harding jubilantly telegraphed General Dodge at St. Louis, "Bushwhacking is stopped."[11] Dur-

10 *O. R.*, Series 1, Vol. XLVIII, Part 2, p. 470.

11 *O. R.*, Series 1, Vol. XLVIII, Part 2, p. 545; *Liberty Tribune*, May 26, 1865. If published at the time, the Lexington newspapers of the period are not available.

ing the next few days many other guerrillas rode in, put down their guns, and took the oath. But Archie Clement, Jim Anderson, and a few others did not. They knew that there could never be any peace for them, and about June 1 they crossed the Missouri and moved down to Howard County.

David Pool, the guerrilla comedian, became a sort of celebrity with the Union officers of the Lexington post. After his parole he was sent out into the district with a cavalry escort to urge other guerrillas to give themselves up, living evidence that it was safe to do so. Up and down the Central District the partisans came out of the woods and surrendered at Pool's urging. On May 31 Colonel Harding reported:

For the information of the commanding general I have the honor to report that no hostile shot has been fired in this district since Sunday, three weeks ago. Over 200 bushwhackers have accepted the terms offered them at Lexington. Small parties have come here and at other places. The citizens who do not help us are vexed at the course pursued. They think we should meet these fellows in the brush and kill them, or else violate our plighted faith when they are in our power. We have been very anxious to find them in the brush. No one can judge of the difficulties attending the attempt until he tries to do so. It took Dave Pool nearly a week to collect his small band of forty. The men were lying by twos and threes in the brush from the Sni Hills to the mouth of the La Mine. It is the same with other gangs; they live with their friends in the country, and are plowing or planting as we pass by. Pool has been out with Lieutenant Saltzman, acting assistant adjutant general, and has showed him some of the tricks of the bushwhackers, among others is that of spreading their blankets across the road and marching their horses on the blankets to prevent a trail being made. Pool is doing good work. The Governor promises him full pardon if he keeps on as he has now started. Some of the surrendered men are abusing their privileges. I have notified the bushwhackers that the mercy extended to them is unparalleled, and that we expect them to keep the same good faith which we show them. If they step over the line of their obligations they will be arrested and shot without trial. It is useless to depend upon civil authorities here; the very men who are most fierce in their denunciations of the military arm for protecting rebels are the men who dare not go before a justice of the peace or a grand jury to testify against the culprits. Farmers are returning to their farms. No one need be afraid to travel alone north of this point.[12]

On May 23 the *Kansas City Journal* announced cheerfully: "In Missouri the war of the roses and bushes is virtually over. In a short time the bushwhackers will be gone over and amen done for." However, a week later, the same publication sourly stated: "Thirty bushwhackers surrendered at Lexington last week. If they are really bushwhackers they should be decently treated, decently tried, decently convicted and decently hung."[13]

Elsewhere in north Missouri the surrender of the guerrillas did not go off so smoothly. Over in Clay County, where Frank and Jesse James were to return home, Oliver Shepherd, later an outlaw, asked the Union post at Liberty for terms that would allow him and six others of Quantrill's old boys to keep their side arms in order to protect themselves. Advised that they must turn in their pistols, Shepherd and his men gave themselves up and took the loyalty oath. As soon as they put down their revolvers, two of them were promptly arrested by the civil authorities, one for murder, one for stealing a horse.[14]

Down in Howard County, Archie Clement and Jim Anderson again tried to arrange terms for themselves and six other men with them. On June 2 they approached Colonel A. F. Denny, commanding the post at Glasgow, who advised them that they would have to surrender unconditionally. Clement

12 *O. R.*, Series 1, Vol. XLVIII, Part 2, pp. 705-706.
13 *Daily K. C. Journal*, May 27, 1865.
14 *Liberty Tribune*, May 20, June 29, 1865.

and Anderson procrastinated and did not come in. They delayed matters to such an extent that Denny was ordered not to parley further with them, but to catch them and kill them.[15] The Union command was itching to get its hands on little Archie. He and Anderson slipped back into Texas, where the latter had his throat cut on the state capitol lawn at Austin.

The last of the boys who had gone to Kentucky with Quantrill surrendered at Samuel's Depot in that state on July 26, 1865. They were allowed to take the oath of allegiance and go their way.[16] One of them was Frank James. His brother Jesse had been shot through the lung early in the spring, and it is believed he was being nursed by his mother, who had been driven temporarily out of Clay County to Rulo, Nebraska.

In this manner most of the guerrillas were given the chance to put down their arms in 1865, granted truly generous terms, in view of their bloody record, by the Union military authorities. Would these young men be able to patch up their lives, return to their home communities, find ways of making a living, and develop into normal citizens? Could they live in peace? Most had known nothing but war since childhood.

Of the several hundred guerrillas who survived the war and surrendered in 1865, a majority seem to have either followed peaceful pursuits or to have left Missouri. A considerable number of these wild young men, however, either could not, or would not, lead orderly lives. They became troublemakers, gunmen, and ultimately outlaws.

To a very great extent postwar conditions in Missouri were against the ex-guerrillas, as indeed they were against the beaten regular Confederate soldiers who straggled back and attempted to make a normal living. From 1865 until 1872 the state was controlled by the Radical Republicans, who en-

---

[15] *O. R.*, Series 1, Vol. XLVIII, Part 2, pp. 737-38, 785, 848, 872.
[16] Connelley, *Quantrill*, 479.

forced a severe reconstruction policy. The Confederate soldier, regular or irregular, returned to a community where he
was disfranchised and without many other civil rights, a community in which he felt that the government, the laws, and
the courts were hostile to him because of the cause he had
served. The ex-Confederate was usually without funds or
property, and in the ruined economy of Missouri it was difficult for him to make a new start. For the men who had ridden
with Anderson, Quantrill, or Todd, there was an additional
threat. Possibly the civil law might try them for their wartime deeds, and the state was full of Union men who had
suffered at their hands and now might seek revenge. And for
many of the young guerrillas farming must have seemed very
hard and very unexciting.

Between 1865 and 1870 there was a great wave of lawlessness and violence in central and western Missouri. Much of it
was very partisan, either directed at the ex-Confederate or
created by him. Conditions became so bad in the old Central
Military District that troops were sent back into the area in
October, 1866, and in December, Governor Fletcher called
twenty-four militia cavalry companies and ten infantry companies back to duty and stationed them in Lafayette and Jackson counties. The governor stated that the troops would remain there until the normal processes of law could be executed.[17]

In this troubled area, their original home, some of the
guerrillas began to turn up in the news again. At Lexington
the presence of "Captain" David Pool was unsettling to the
community. The ex-guerrilla always went about heavily
armed, and his place of business (no one was certain what his
business was), was usually in the saloons of the town.[18] From

[17] Lexington, Missouri *Missouri Valley Register*, October 11, December 13,
1866; the Lexington *Weekly Caucasian*, December 26, 1866.
[18] *Missouri Valley Register*, October 25, December 27, 1866, January 24,
1867.

time to time he was visited by hard-faced young men who would drink with him for a few days and then ride on. To make matters worse, Archie Clement came back to Lafayette County from Texas in the summer of 1866, and although a reward was offered for him, no one seemed very interested in trying to collect it. He spent his time visiting old comrades, especially Dave Pool. They made a great couple: Pool with his ready jokes, and Clement with his perpetual smile. It was more than the Union men of Lexington could stand.

Little Archie was a marked man, but of course his life could end only in a bizarre fashion. In December, 1866, under a new state act, all men over eighteen were required to register for possible muster into the Missouri State Militia. There was a twenty-dollar fine for all who did not. Pool and Clement must have seen the joke at once. Imagine their being members of the militia at some future date! At any rate, Clement sent word to the military authorities at Lexington that he would like to come in and enroll, providing that the soldiers would not bother him while he was in town. David Pool was called for and sent out to inform Clement that he would not be molested.

On the morning of December 13, 1866, twenty-six men dashed into Lexington in military formation. At the head of the party rode Archie Clement, armed to the teeth, and at the rear of it, Dave Pool. The men dismounted at the City Hotel, repaired to the bar for a few rounds of drinks, and then enjoyed a good dinner. They then proceeded stiffly to the state militia office at the courthouse, carefully eyeing everyone on the street. They were enrolled and advised to leave town.

After performing their civic duty, the ex-guerrillas rode out of Lexington, but in a few minutes Clement and another man returned. Archie went back to the City Hotel bar and took up where he had left off that morning. Hearing that the guerrilla was still in town, Major Bacon Montgomery, who commanded the state militia company on duty at Lexington, sent three of his soldiers to the City Hotel to arrest Archie. When the troopers entered the barroom and confronted the little guerrilla, he pulled his revolvers, and in a blast of rapid shots and bursting bottles, fled through the side door of the saloon. Vaulting to his horse, he galloped up Franklin Street past the courthouse, all men in the block taking cover. He must have smiled at the windows of Major Montgomery's office in the courthouse, and it was his last smile. From every window of the side of the building hidden riflemen fired down at him. His mount slowed to a walk, and a short distance down the block Archie Clement pitched face first from his saddle. When by-standers reached the boy he was dead, shot through the body in numerous places.[19] Little Archie had never surrendered.

During 1866 and 1867 an unusual type of crime, daylight bank robberies, exploded all over western Missouri. In February, 1866, the Clay County Savings Bank at Liberty was held up by ten or twelve men who took $60,000, and, in shooting up the town, killed a William Jewell College student.[20] The officers of the bank believed ex-guerrillas from Jackson County were responsible, and, of eight men said to have been recognized, five, Oliver Shepherd, Bud and Donnie Pence, Frank Gregg, and Jim Wilkerson (Wilkinson), were known to have ridden with Quantrill, Anderson, or Todd.[21] On October 30 the Alexander Mitchell Bank at Lexington was robbed by four unidentified men, who were leisurely pursued, the *Missouri Valley Register* reported, by a posse led by, of all persons, David Pool.[22] Collusion of the most friendly type was hinted at.

19 *Missouri Valley Register,* December 20, 1866.

20 Settle, "The Development of the Jesse James Legend," 38-39.

21 *Liberty Tribune,* February 16, 1866; *Daily K. C. Journal,* February 16, 1866.

22 *Missouri Valley Register,* October 25, December 27, 1866, January 24, 1867.

Bank holdups came natural to the ex-guerrillas. They had found out during the war the handsome amount of cash such institutions kept on hand, and how easily it could be gathered up at pistol point and conveniently carried away. On May 22, 1867, the Hughes and Wasson Bank at Richmond was robbed by twelve or fourteen men, and in the gunplay which took place three citizens were killed, including Mayor John B. Shaw. Of the nine men for whom warrants were issued for this affair, six were identified as ex-guerrillas. They were Dick Burns, Payne Jones, Ike Flannery, Andy McGuire, Tom Little, and Allen Parmer, the latter a brother-in-law of Frank and Jesse James. Tom Little and Andy McGuire were arrested and lynched by angry mobs at Richmond and Warrensburg before coming to trial.[23]

And so it went. Ex-guerrilla George Shepherd was jailed for holding up a bank at Russellville, Kentucky, on March 20, 1868. Frank and Jesse James were suspected of robbing one at Gallatin on December 7, 1869, and although protesting innocence, they turned outlaw by resisting arrest. They stated that they would be lynched if they were jailed. Coleman Younger and Clell Miller were suspected of the holdup of a Missouri Pacific train at Otterville in 1876, and as bank after bank and numerous trains fell to robbers, Missouri gained the national name of "The Outlaw State." Finally it came to be generally believed that the "James-Younger gang" was responsible for most of these robberies, and that the members of that rather extensive organization were all ex-Civil War guerrillas.[24]

Bank robbery was a dangerous business, however, and by the first years of the eighties many of the outlaws had been killed or imprisoned, among them Cole and Jim Younger, who were captured after a holdup at Northfield, Minnesota,

23 Settle, "The Development of the Jesse James Legend," 46-48.
24 Ibid., 42, 51-52, 179-82.

in 1876. The assassination of Jesse James on April 3, 1882, at St. Joseph, and the surrender of Frank James to Missouri's Governor Thomas Crittenden the following October, saw the end of the "James gang." The "boys" of Quantrill, Anderson, and Todd were now nearing middle age. Soon they would have only dim recollections of their wild days in the great Civil War.

For many years the ex-guerrillas seem to have had no desire to take part in a reunion such as veterans of both the Union and Confederate armies were so prone to organize and attend. At first it was not safe for them to gather in a group, and later a great many of their number, for various reasons, were in hiding and on the run. It was not until 1889 that they began to toy with the idea of holding their own private reunion. Judge A. J. Liddel of Independence and Kansas City seems to have been the principal organizer, and for a few years the gatherings were small enough to be held in his law office.[25] By 1905, however, an association had been perfected, and annual two-day meetings were held each August in Jackson County.

Quantrill's men conducted their reunions with great style, and every effort was extended toward making them comfortable and convivial. On their eleventh annual conclave which opened at Independence on August 20, 1909, the boys "hired" an entire building, and held a short business meeting which saw the election of Ben Morrow as "Captain," Levi Potts as "Lieutenant," and Warren Welch as "Secretary." The next day thirty-two of a total membership of seventy-nine men "still living" had registered, and the Independence press announced rather sadly that neither Frank James nor Coleman Younger were present.[26]

The men of Quantrill, Anderson, and Todd met again at Independence in August, 1910. Each delegate wore an elegant

25 Independence, Missouri *Independence Examiner*, August 20, 1909.
26 *Independence Examiner*, August 21, 1909.

medallion engraved with the portrait of William C. Quantrill hung on a very appropriate red ribbon. The reunion was highlighted by Cole Younger, a figure of considerable note in carnival and wild west show circles since his release from the Minnesota Penitentiary. Cole gave a little talk entitled "On What Life Has Taught Me," which was well received by the "boys."[27] What tales these old gray-headed men must have passed around! Memories of Bill Quantrill and his horse, Charlie, whom he had taken at Independence from Buel's quartermaster; how gamely Bloody Bill and Todd had died; how shamefully Jesse and Little Archie had been assassinated. And wasn't it grand that old Jim Lane had blown his own brains out, and that that damned Jennison had been finally court-martialed by the Union service in '65.[28] And what about Ewing and his fiendish Order Number Eleven? Hadn't George Bingham taken care of him in Ohio with his painting, ruining him with the Democratic party there when he ran for the United States Senate! And so on . . . "the militia, the Jayhawkers, Ford's Colorado boys, Blunt, right out of his buggy at Baxter Springs, Cole finally arranging funeral services for Bill at Richmond. . . ."

This was about all that was left. Old age and respectability had caught up with the scourges of the border. In a few years only a few men remained of those who had followed Quantrill, Anderson, and Todd. To the end they kept a certain notoriety, for they had been brave and bold and viciously dangerous. They had been natural fighters, and they had actually served the Confederate States of America better than they knew.

[27] *Independence Examiner,* August 19, 1910.
[28] Connelley, *Kansas,* Vol. 11, 894-95; Monaghan, *Civil War on the Western Border,* 351.

Selected Bibliography

GOVERNMENT PUBLICATIONS

UNITED STATES

U. S. War Department. *The War of the Rebellion: A Compilation Of The Official Records Of The Union and the Confederate Armies.* 130 vols. Washington, D. C., 1880-1902.

Report of The Special Committee Appointed To Investigate The Troubles in Kansas, With The Views Of The Minority of Said Committee (34th Cong., 1st sess.; House Report No. 200.) Washington, D. C., 1856.

U. S. War Department, Record and Pension Office. *Organization and Status of Missouri Troops, Union and Confederate, In Service During the Civil War.* Washington, D. C., 1902.

Population Of The United States In 1860; Compiled From The Original Returns Of The Eighth Census, Under The Direction Of The Secretary Of The Interior. Washington, D. C., 1864.

STATE OF MISSOURI

Journal of the House of Representatives of the State of Missouri at the First Session of the Twenty-First General Assembly. Jefferson City, 1861.

Journal of the Senate of Missouri at the First Session of the Twenty-First General Assembly. Jefferson City, 1861.

Laws of the State of Missouri, Passed at the Regular Session of the 21st Gen-

eral Assembly, Begun and Held at the City of Jefferson, on Monday, December 31, 1860. Jefferson City, 1861.

Journal And Proceedings Of The Missouri State Convention, Held At Jefferson City And St. Louis, March, 1861. St. Louis, 1861.

Journal of the Missouri State Convention Held at Jefferson City, July, 1861. St. Louis, 1861.

Journal of the Missouri State Convention Held at the City of Saint Louis, October, 1861. St. Louis, 1861.

Journal of the Missouri State Convention Held in Jefferson City, June, 1862. St. Louis, 1862.

Proceedings of the Missouri State Convention, Held at Jefferson City, July, A. D. 1861. St. Louis, 1861.

Proceedings of the Missouri State Convention Held at the City of St. Louis, October, A. D. 1861. St. Louis, 1861.

Proceedings of the Missouri State Convention Held in Jefferson City, June, 1863. St. Louis, 1863.

Manuscript Material

Branson Diary. Unpublished diary covering the years 1861 and 1862, written by W. W. Branson, a member of the First Regiment of the Iowa Volunteers, while on duty in Missouri. University of Missouri Western Manuscripts Collection, Columbia, Missouri.

Broadhead Papers. Letters and papers of J. O. Broadhead between the years 1802 and 1903. Missouri Historical Society Library, St. Louis, Missouri.

Gamble Papers. Letters and papers of Governor Hamilton R. Gamble written during his life. Missouri Historical Society Library, St. Louis, Missouri.

Gregg Manuscript. Unpublished 125-page manuscript written in longhand by William H. Gregg, a leading member of Quantrill's guerrillas. Manuscripts collection of the State Historical Society of Missouri, Columbia, Missouri. This manuscript was written from memory in the early 1900's.

Reynolds Papers. Letters and papers of Thomas C. Reynolds between the years 1815 and 1890. Missouri Historical Society Library, St. Louis, Missouri.

Reynolds Manuscript Collection. Numbered letter books of Thomas C. Reynolds containing letters and other documents written during his term as governor. Library of Congress, Washington, D. C.

　　Book no. 4463, December 27, 1862, to December 23, 1863.

　　Book no. 4464, December 24, 1863, to February 21, 1865.

James S. Rollins Manuscript Collection, State Historical Society of Missouri, Columbia, Missouri. Letters and papers of Representative J. S. Rollins written during his life.

Newspapers

(The newspapers listed below are in the State Historical Society of Missouri Library, Columbia, Missouri.)

Weekly California News, California, Missouri, 1860; January–November, 1861; January–November, 1863; January–May, 1865.
Columbia, Missouri Herald, Columbia, Missouri, September 24, 1897.
Columbia, Missouri Statesman (weekly), Columbia, Missouri, 1860–1866.
Columbia Daily Tribune, Columbia, Missouri, December 24, 1945.
The Independence Examiner (weekly), Independence, Missouri, August, 1909; August, 1910.
Kansas City Enquirer and Star (weekly), Kansas City, Missouri, December, 1860.
Western Journal of Commerce (weekly), Kansas City, Missouri, January–December 27, 1860; 1861, incomplete; 1862, incomplete; 1863, incomplete; 1864, incomplete; 1865, incomplete.
The Daily Kansas City Western Journal of Commerce, Kansas City, Missouri. January–December, 1860; January–August 21, 1861; March 18–December, 1862; 1863; 1864; January–June 30, 1865; July 4–December, 1865.
Lexington Weekly Union, Lexington, Missouri, January, February, April, July, 1865, incomplete.
The Weekly Caucasian, Lexington, Missouri, April–December, 1866.
Missouri Valley Register (weekly), Lexington, Missouri, January 4–April 19, 1866.
The Liberty Tribune (weekly), Liberty, Missouri, 1860; 1861; 1862; 1863; 1864; 1865. The name of this paper was changed from *Liberty Weekly Tribune* on August 17, 1860, to *The Liberty Tribune*.
Tri-Weekly Missouri Democrat, St. Louis, Missouri, February 26–December 31, 1861; 1862; 1863; January–June; September–December, 1864.
Tri-Weekly Missouri Republican, St. Louis, Missouri, April 28–December 29, 1860; 1862; 1863; 1864.

Magazine Articles

BLANTON, B. F. "A True Story Of The Border Wars," *Missouri Historical Review*, XVII, No. 1 (October, 1922).
FITZSIMMONS, MARGARET L. "Missouri Railroads During the Civil War and Reconstruction," *Missouri Historical Review*, XXXV, No. 2 (January, 1941).
HARLOW, RALPH V. "The Rise and Fall of the Kansas Aid Movements," *American Historical Review*, XLI, No. 1 (October, 1925).
HERKLOTZ, HILDEGARDE R. "Jayhawkers in Missouri, 1858-1863," *Missouri Historical Review*, XVII, No. 3 (April, 1923).
HESSELTINE, WILLIAM B. "Military Prisons of St. Louis, 1861–1865," *Missouri Historical Review*, XXIII, No. 3 (April, 1929).
ISLEY, W. H. "The Sharps Rifle Episode in Kansas History," *American Historical Review*, XII, No. 3 (April, 1907).
LEWIS, LLOYD D. "Propaganda and the Missouri Kansas War," *Missouri Historical Review*, XXXIV, No. 1 (October, 1939).
LYNCH, WILLIAM O. "Population Movements in Relation to the Struggle for Kansas," *Indiana University Studies*, XII (1925).

McLarty, Vivian K. (ed.). "The Civil War Letters of Colonel Bazel F. Lazear," *Missouri Historical Review*, XLIV, No. 3 (April, 1950), and No. 4 (July, 1950), and XLV, No. 1 (October, 1950).

Magers, Roy V. "The Raid on the Parkville Industrial Luminary," *Missouri Historical Review*, XXX, No. 1 (October, 1935).

Malin, James C. "The Pro-Slavery Background of the Kansas Struggle," *Mississippi Valley Historical Review*, X, No. 3 (December, 1923).

Pigg, Elmer L. "Bloody Bill, Noted Guerrilla of the Civil War," *The Trail Guide*. Kansas City, 1956.

Quaife, M. M. (ed.). "Bleeding Kansas and the Pottawatomie Murders," *Mississippi Valley Historical Review*, VI, No. 4 (March, 1920).

Shoemaker, Floyd C. "The Story of the Civil War in Northeast Missouri," *Missouri Historical Review*, VII, No. 3 (April, 1913).

Smith, William E. "The Blairs and Fremont," *Missouri Historical Review*, XXIII, No. 2 (January, 1929).

Snyder, J. B. "Battle of Osawatomie," *Missouri Historical Review*, VII, No. 2 (January, 1912).

Swindler, William F. "The Southern Press in Missouri, 1861–1864," *Missouri Historical Review*, XXXV, No. 3 (April, 1941).

Viles, Jonas (ed.). "Documents Illustrating the Troubles on the Border, 1858," *Missouri Historical Review*, I, Nos. 3, 4; II, No. 1 (April, October, 1907).

Unpublished Theses and Dissertations

Kirkpatrick, Arthur R. "Missouri's Secessionist Government 1861-1865," (unpublished Master of Arts thesis, University of Missouri, 1949).

———. "Missouri, The Twelfth Confederate State." Unpublished doctoral dissertation, University of Missouri, 1955.

Parrish, William E. "The Provisional Government of Missouri 1861-1865." Unpublished Master's thesis, University of Missouri, 1953.

Pruitt, William M. "The More Definitely Pro-Southern Group In Missouri Between August, 1860, and March, 1861." Unpublished Master's thesis, University of Missouri, 1932.

Settle, William A. "The Development of the Jesse James Legend." Unpublished doctoral dissertation, University of Missouri, 1945.

Books

Anderson, Galusha. *Border City During the Civil War*. Boston, 1908.

Beale, Howard K. (ed.). *The Diary of Edward Bates, 1859-1866. (The Annual Report of the American Historical Association for the Year 1930*, Vol. IV.) Washington, D. C., 1933.

Britton, Wiley. *The Civil War on the Border*. 2 vols. New York, London, 1891.

Carr, Lucien. *Missouri, A Bone of Contention*. Boston and New York, 1888.

CONARD, HOWARD L. (ed.). *Encyclopedia of the History of Missouri.* 6 vols. St. Louis, 1901.

CONNELLEY, WILLIAM E. (ed.). *Collections of the Kansas State Historical Society, 1913-1914.* Topeka, 1915.

————. *Quantrill and the Border Wars.* Cedar Rapids, Iowa. 1910.

————. *A Standard History of Kansas and Kansans.* 2 vols. Chicago, 1918.

CUTLER, WILLIAM G. (ed.). *History of the State of Kansas.* Chicago, 1883.

DAVIDSON, ALEXANDER, and STUVÉ, BERNARD. *Complete History of Illinois.* Springfield, 1874.

EDWARDS, JOHN N. *Noted Guerrillas, or The Warfare of the Border.* St. Louis, 1877.

GLENN, ALLEN. *History of Cass County, Missouri.* Topeka, Kansas, 1917.

GRAY, WOOD. *The Hidden Civil War.* New York, 1942.

HALLECK, HENRY W. *International Law; Or, Rules Regulating the Intercourse of States in Peace and War.* New York, 1861.

History of Carroll County, Missouri. St. Louis, 1881.

The History of Cass and Bates Counties, Missouri. St. Joseph, Missouri, 1883.

History of Clay and Platte Counties, Missouri. St. Louis, 1885.

The History of Henry and St. Clair Counties, Missouri. St. Joseph, Missouri, 1883.

History of Howard and Chariton Counties, Missouri. St. Louis, 1883.

History of Howard and Cooper Counties, Missouri. St. Louis, 1883.

The History of Jackson County, Missouri. Kansas City, Missouri, 1881.

History of Lafayette County, Missouri. St. Louis, 1881.

History of Ray County, Missouri. St. Louis, 1881.

History of Saline County, Missouri. St. Louis, 1881.

History of Vernon County, Missouri. St. Louis, 1887.

HYDE, WILLIAM, and CONARD, HOWARD L. (eds.). *Encyclopedia of the History of St. Louis.* 4 vols. New York, Louisville, St. Louis, 1899.

LEOPARD, BUEL, and SHOEMAKER, FLOYD C. (eds.). *Messages and Proclamations of the Governors of the State of Missouri.* 16 vols. to date. Columbia, Missouri, 1922-1951.

LIEBER, FRANCIS. *Guerrilla Parties, Considered with Reference to the Laws and Usages of War.* New York, 1862.

McCORKLE, JOHN. *Three Years with Quantrill—A True Story.* Armstrong, Missouri, n.d.

McELROY, JOHN. *The Struggle for Missouri.* Washington, D.C., 1909.

MALIN, JAMES C. *The Nebraska Question, 1852-1854.* Lawrence, Kansas, 1953.

————. *John Brown and the Legend of Fifty Six.* Philadelphia, 1942.

MILLER, GEORGE. *Missouri's Memorable Decade, 1860-1870.* Columbia, Missouri, 1898.

MILTON, GEORGE F. *Abraham Lincoln and the Fifth Column.* New York, 1942.

MONAGHAN, JAY. *Civil War on the Western Border, 1854–1865.* Boston, Toronto, 1955.

MORGAN, MANIE. *The New Stars: Life and Labor in Old Missouri,* arranged by Jennie A. Morgan and edited by Louis Filler. Yellow Springs, Ohio, 1949.

O'FLAHERTY, DANIEL. *General Jo Shelby, Undefeated Rebel.* Chapel Hill, North Carolina, 1954.

PECKHAM, JAMES. *Gen. Nathaniel Lyon and Missouri in 1861.* New York, 1866.

RANDALL, JAMES G. *Constitutional Problems Under Lincoln.* New York, London, 1926.

ROMBAUER, ROBERT J. *The Union Cause in St. Louis in 1861.* St. Louis, 1909.

RYLE, WALTER H. *Missouri: Union or Secession.* Nashville, 1931.

SCHOFIELD, JOHN M. *Forty-six Years in the Army.* New York, 1897.

SCHRANTZ, WARD L. *Jasper County in the Civil War.* Carthage, Missouri, 1923.

SHALER, NATHANIEL S. *Kentucky, A Pioneer Commonwealth.* Boston, 1888.

SHOEMAKER, FLOYD C. *Missouri and Missourians; Land of Contrasts and People of Achievements.* 5 vols. Chicago, 1943.

SMITH, EDWARD C. *The Borderland in the Civil War.* New York, 1927.

SNEAD, THOMAS L. *The Fight for Missouri from the Election of Lincoln to the Death of Lyon.* New York, 1888.

SPRING, LEVERETT W. *Kansas, The Prelude to the War for the Union.* Boston, 1885.

STEVENS, WALTER B. *Centennial History of Missouri (The Central State), One Hundred Years in the Union, 1820-1921.* 3 vols. St. Louis, Chicago, 1921.

STEPHENSON, WENDELL H. *The Political Career of General James H. Lane.* Topeka, 1930.

TREXLER, HARRISON A. *Slavery in Missouri, 1804-1865.* Baltimore, 1914.

VILES, JONAS. *A History of Missouri for High Schools.* Columbia, Missouri, 1944.

VIOLETTE, EUGENE M. *A History of Missouri.* New York, 1918.

WEBB, WILLIAM L. *The Centennial History of Independence, Missouri.* Place of publication not indicated, 1927.

YOUNGER, COLEMAN. *The Story of Cole Younger by Himself.* Chicago, 1903.

Appendix

KNOWN MEMBERS OF QUANTRILL'S, ANDERSON'S AND TODD'S GUERRILLAS

NAME	*ORGANIZATION*	*REMARKS*
Agen, ————	Anderson	Killed 1864
Akers, Sylvester	Quantrill	Survived war
Anderson, James (Jim)	Anderson	Survived war
Anderson, William (Bill)	Anderson	Killed 1864
Archie, Hugh	Todd	
Archie, William	Todd	
Atchison, Bes	Todd	
Baker, John	Todd	Killed 1865
Baker, Valentine	Anderson	Killed 1864
Barbie, Johnson	Anderson	
Barnhill, John	Quantrill	Survived war
Bassham, Ike	Quantrill	
Bassham, Solomon	Quantrill	Survived war
Bassham, William	Quantrill, Todd	Survived war
Beard, Frank	Quantrill	Killed 1863
Beard, William	Quantrill	Killed 1863
Bell, Thomas	Anderson	

NAME	ORGANIZATION	REMARKS
Berry, Ike	Anderson	Survived war
Berry, Richard	Anderson	Survived war
Bishop, Jack	Quantrill	
Bisset, James	Anderson	Killed 1864
Blackmore, William	Anderson	
Bledsoe, J. L.	Quantrill	Killed 1863
Bledsoe, William	Quantrill	Killed 1863
Blunt, Andrew	Quantrill	Killed 1864
Blythe, Theodore	Quantrill	Killed 1863
Bowles, Jeptha	Anderson	Killed 1864
Brinker, John	Quantrill	
Brooks, Samuel	Anderson	
Broomfield, Benjamin	Quantrill	Killed 1863
Brown, Harvey	Anderson	Killed 1864
Buford, Henry	Anderson	Killed 1864
Burns, Richard	Quantrill	Survived war
Burton, Peter	Quantrill	Killed 1862
Campbell, Andrew	Anderson	
Campbell, Doc	Quantrill	
Carr, William	Quantrill	
Carroll, Dolf	Anderson	Killed 1864
Castle, Theodore	Anderson	Killed 1865
Chatman, John	Anderson	Killed 1865
Chiles, Jim Crow	Anderson	Survived war
Chiles, Joel	Quantrill	Killed 1864
Chiles, Kit	Quantrill	
Chiles, Richard	Quantrill	Killed 1865
Chiles, William	Quantrill	
Clayton, George	Quantrill	
Clayton, James	Anderson	
Clement, Archie	Anderson	Survived war
Clement, Henry	Anderson	
Constable, Sam	Quantrill	
Corley, Dock	Anderson	
Corum, Alfred	Todd	
Corum, James	Anderson	
Coward, Henry	Todd	
Cravens, Robert	Anderson	Killed 1864
Crawford, Riley	Quantrill, Todd	Killed 1864
Creek, Abner	Anderson	
Creek, Creth	Anderson	
Creek, Sid	Quantrill	
Crew, Pate	Anderson	

NAME	*ORGANIZATION*	*REMARKS*
Cunningham, Albert (Ab)	Quantrill	Killed 1862
Cummings, Jim	Anderson	Survived war
Daily, George	Anderson	
Davenport, William	Quantrill	
Davis, Jo	Todd	Killed 1864
Debenhorst, Paul	Anderson	Killed 1864
DeHart, E. P.	Todd	
Devers, Arthur	Todd	Killed 1864
Devers, James	Todd	Killed 1864
Donohoe, James	Quantrill	Killed 1862
Ellington, Richard	Anderson	
Emery, Jeff	Anderson	
Esters, Joshua	Anderson	Killed 1865
Estes, ————	Quantrill	
Evans, James	Quantrill	
Farley, Peter	Anderson	Killed 1864
Fickell, Joseph	Quantrill	
Finnegan, Samuel	Anderson	Killed 1864
Fisher, John	Anderson	
Flannery, Ike	Quantrill	Survived war
Flannery, Si	Todd	
Freeman, Will	Quantrill	Killed 1862
Fugitt, Press	Quantrill	Killed 1865
Fulton, Thomas	Anderson	Killed 1864
Garrett, ————	Quantrill	Killed 1864
Gaw, William	Quantrill	
George, Gabriel	Quantrill	Killed 1862
George, Hicks	Quantrill	
George, Hiram	Quantrill	
Gibson, James	Quantrill	
Gilchrist, Joseph	Quantrill	Killed 1862
Glasscock, Richard	Quantrill	Killed 1865
Gordon, Cy or Si	Quantrill	Killed 1864
Graham, Jack	Quantrill	
Graym, Frank	Anderson	
Greenwood, William	Quantrill	
Gregg, Frank	Quantrill	Survived war
Gregg, William H.	Quantrill	Survived war
Grindstaff, William	Anderson	
Groomer, Garrett	Anderson	Killed 1864
Grosvenor, ————	Anderson	Killed 1864
Guess, Hiram	Anderson	
Hall, George	Quantrill	

NAME	ORGANIZATION	REMARKS
Hall, Isaac	Quantrill	
Hall, Joseph	Quantrill	
Hall, Robert	Quantrill	
Hall, Thomas	Quantrill	
Hallar, Ab	Quantrill	Killed 1863
Hallar, William	Quantrill	Killed 1862
Halley, ————	Quantrill	
Hamet, Jesse	Anderson	Drowned 1864
Hampton, John	Quantrill	Killed 1862
Hardin, Joseph	Quantrill	Killed 1862
Harris, John	Quantrill	
Harris, Thomas	Quantrill	
Harrison, Ki	Quantrill	
Hart, Joe	Quantrill	Killed 1864
Hays, John	Quantrill	
Hays, Perry	Quantrill	Killed 1863
Hays, Upton	Quantrill	Killed 1862
Hays, William	Quantrill	
Helms, Polk	Anderson	
Helton, David	Quantrill	
Henaburg, William	Anderson	
Hendricks, James	Quantrill	
Hill, Tom	Quantrill	Survived war
Hill, Tuck	Quantrill	
Hill, Woot	Quantrill	
Hinds, James	Quantrill	
Hink, Edward	Quantrill	Killed 1864
Hinton, Otho	Quantrill	Killed 1862
Hockensmith, Clark	Quantrill	Killed 1865
Hockensmith, Henry	Quantrill	
Holt, Joseph	Anderson	Killed 1864
Holtzclaw, Clifton	Anderson	
Hope, John	Todd	
Hotie, Richard	Quantrill	
House, John	Todd	
Hoy, Perry	Quantrill	Killed 1862
Hudspeth, Babe	Quantrill	Survived war
Hudspeth, Robert	Quantrill	
Hudspeth, Rufus	Quantrill	
Huffaker, Moses	Anderson	
Hulse, William	Quantrill	
Jackson, John	Quantrill	Killed 1864
James, Frank	Quantrill	Survived war

NAME	*ORGANIZATION*	*REMARKS*
James, Jesse	Anderson	Survived war
James, William	Anderson	
Jarrette, John	Quantrill	Survived war
Jenkins, Snowy	Anderson	Killed 1864
Jessup, Sam	Quantrill	Killed 1863
Jobson, Presley	Todd	Killed 1864
Jobson, Smith	Todd	Killed 1864
Johnson, Oliver	Quantrill	Killed 1864
Johnson, Richard	Todd	
Johnson, Socrates	Anderson	Killed 1864
Jones, Payne	Quantrill	Survived war
Kelly, James	Quantrill	
Kennedy, David	Quantrill	
Kennedy, Sterling	Quantrill	
Kerr, Nathan	Quantrill	
Key, Foster	Quantrill	Killed 1865
King, Silas	Anderson	Died 1864
Kinney, Richard	Quantrill	Killed 1864
Koger, Edward	Quantrill	Killed 1862
Koger, John W.	Quantrill	
Lee, Albert	Quantrill	
Lee, Joseph	Quantrill	
Lester, Frank	Anderson	
Lewis, Bart	Todd	
Liddel, A. J.	Quantrill	Survived war
Lilly, James	Quantrill	
Lisle, Marston	Anderson	Killed 1864
Litten, Ling	Anderson	
Little, James	Quantrill	Killed 1865
Little, John	Quantrill	Killed 1862
Little, Thomas	Quantrill	Survived war
Long, Peyton	Quantrill	Killed 1864
Lotspeach, William	Quantrill	Killed 1863
Luckett, ————	Anderson	Killed 1864
Maddox, George	Quantrill	
Maddox, Richard	Quantrill	Survived war
Magruder, Rezin	Anderson	Killed 1864
Majors, Newt	Quantrill	
Marshall, Edward	Quantrill	
Marshall, James	Quantrill	
Martinez, Leon	Anderson	Killed 1864
Masterson, Hiram	Todd	Killed 1864
Mattox, M. T.	Quantrill	Survived war

NAME	ORGANIZATION	REMARKS
Maupin, John	Quantrill	
Maupin, Thomas	Quantrill	Killed 1865
Maxwell, Ambrose	Quantrill	
Maxwell, Thomas	Anderson	
McAninch, Henry	Quantrill	
McBurgis, ———	Quantrill	
McCorkle, Job	Quantrill	
McCorkle, John	Quantrill	Survived war
McCorkle, Joshua	Quantrill	
McGuire, Andy	Quantrill	Survived war
McGuire, William	Quantrill	Killed 1864
McIlvaine, John	Anderson	
McMacane, Sandy	Anderson	Killed 1864
McMurty, Lee	Quantrill	
McMurty, ———	Todd	Killed 1864
Mead, Jacob	Todd	
Miller, Clell	Anderson	Survived war
Moody, Jasper	Anderson	Killed 1864
Morris, James	Quantrill	Killed 1863
Morrow, Ben	Quantrill	Survived war
Morrow, George	Quantrill	
Morton, Wade	Quantrill	
Murray, Plunk	Anderson	
Nagle, Patrick	Quantrill	Killed 1863
Ney, Foss	Quantrill	Killed 1865
Nicholson, Arch	Anderson	
Nicholson, Joseph	Anderson	
Noland, Edward	Quantrill	
Noland, Henry	Quantrill	Killed 1865
Noland, William	Quantrill	Killed 1865
O'Donnell, Pat	Quantrill	
Ogden, Henry	Quantrill	
Oliphant, Newton	Anderson	Killed 1864
Parmer, Allen	Quantrill	Survived war
Parr, Buster	Anderson	
Parr, Mike	Quantrill	
Patterson, Henry	Anderson	Killed 1864
Pence, Bud	Quantrill	Survived war
Pence, Donnie	Quantrill	Survived war
Perry, Joab	Quantrill	Survived war
Peyton, ———	Anderson	Killed 1864
Phillips, Edward	Anderson	
Pool, David	Todd	Survived war

NAME	*ORGANIZATION*	*REMARKS*
Pool, John	Quantrill	
Porter, Henry	Quantrill	Survived war
Potts, Levi	Todd	Survived war
Pringle, John	Anderson	Killed 1864
Privin, Hence	Quantrill	
Privin, Lafe	Todd	
Quantrill, William	Quantrill	Killed 1865
Rains, John	Anderson	
Reed, James	Quantrill	
Rennick, Chat	Todd	Killed 1865
Reynolds, William	Anderson	
Rice, Ben	Quantrill	
Ridings, William	Anderson	Killed 1864
Robinson, George	Quantrill	Executed 1865
Robinson, Gooly	Anderson	Killed 1864
Robinson, William	Anderson	
Rodes, Jasper	Quantrill	
Rollen, ————	Quantrill	Killed 1862
Rollen, ————	Quantrill	Killed 1862
Ross, John	Quantrill	Survived war
Runnels, William	Quantrill	
Rupe, Dock	Anderson	Killed 1864
Rupe, John	Anderson	
Saunders, Charles	Quantrill	Killed 1864
Schull, Boon	Quantrill	Killed 1863
Scott, Al	Quantrill	
Scott, Fernando	Quantrill	Killed 1863
Shepherd, Frank	Quantrill	Killed 1864
Shepherd, George	Quantrill	Survived war
Shepherd, Martin	Quantrill	Killed 1862
Shepherd, Oliver	Quantrill	Survived war
Shores, Stephen	Quantrill	
Simonds, ————	Anderson	Killed 1864
Simmons, Young	Quantrill	Killed 1862
Skaggs, Larkin	Quantrill	Killed 1863
Smith, Perry	Todd	Killed 1864
Smoot, Archibald	Todd	Killed 1864
Sorrels, Thomas	Todd	Killed 1864
Southerland, Zack	Anderson	
Stewart, Charles	Anderson	
Stewart, William	Anderson	
Stone, William	Anderson	Survived war
Storey, Bud	Todd	

NAME	ORGANIZATION	REMARKS
Strother, William	Quantrill	Killed 1863
Stuart, William	Anderson	Killed 1864
Swisby, Oscar	Anderson	Killed 1864
Talcott, Parker	Anderson	Killed 1864
Talley, George	Quantrill	Killed 1862
Talley, Thomas	Quantrill	
Tarkington, William	Anderson	Killed 1864
Taylor, Charles F.	Quantrill	Survived war
Thompson, James	Quantrill	Killed 1863
Thompson, Oliver	Todd	Killed 1864
Thrailkill, John	Todd	Survived war
Tigue, Nat	Anderson	
Todd, George	Quantrill	Killed 1864
Todd, Robert	Anderson	Killed 1864
Todd, Thomas	Anderson	
Toler, ———	Quantrill	
Tolliver, Anson	Anderson	Killed 1864
Tomlinson, Clarence	Anderson	Killed 1864
Toothman, William	Quantrill	Killed 1864
Traber, Zach	Quantrill	
Trow, Harrison	Quantrill	Survived war
Tucker, James	Quantrill	
Tucker, William	Quantrill	
Tuckett, Thomas	Anderson	Killed 1864
Vandiver, Louis	Anderson	Survived war
Vaughan, Joe	Quantrill	
Vaughn, Dan	Quantrill	Survived war
Venable, Randolph	Quantrill	Survived war
Wade, David	Anderson	
Wade, Newman	Anderson	Killed 1864
Wade, Sam	Anderson	Killed 1864
Walker, Andrew	Quantrill	Survived war
Ward, Robert	Quantrill	Killed 1863
Warren, John	Anderson	
Wayman, F. Luther	Quantrill	
Wayman, Matt	Todd	
Webb, Charles	Todd	Survived war
Webb, George	Quantrill	
Webb, Pres	Quantrill	
Webster, John	Quantrill	
Webster, Noah	Quantrill	Killed 1863
Welby, James	Todd	
Welch, Warren	Quantrill	Survived war

NAME	ORGANIZATION	REMARKS
West, Richard	Anderson	
Whitsett, Sim	Quantrill	
Wigginton, George	Quantrill	
Wilcox, Lawrence	Anderson	
Wilkenson, James	Quantrill	
Will, Jack	Anderson	
Williams, Dan	Quantrill	Killed 1862
Williams, Henry	Todd	Killed 1864
Williams, Jack	Todd	
Williams, Jim	Quantrill	
Wilson, John	Anderson	Killed 1864
Winchester, William	Anderson	Killed 1864
Wood, Bennett	Quantrill	
Wood, Hop	Quantrill	Killed 1862
Woodruff, Silas	Quantrill	Killed 1863
Woodward, William	Quantrill	
Wyatt, Al	Todd	Killed 1863
Wyatt, Cave	Quantrill	
Yager, Richard	Quantrill	Killed 1864
Young, Joseph	Quantrill	
Younger, Coleman	Quantrill	Survived war
Younger, James	Todd	Survived war

INDEX

Index

Adair County, Mo., 87, 165
Adams, Charles W., 109
Albany, Mo., 227
Allen, Mo., 204
Allsman, Andrew, 89, 90
Alton, Ill., 13
Alton Prison, 162
Alward, William, 82
Anderson, Jennie, 118
Anderson, Jim, 137, 235, 238-40
Anderson, Josephine, 118
Anderson, Mary, 118
Anderson, William C., 4, 53, 62, 118-19, 121, 127, 141, 183, 189, 192, 195, 198-206, 209-10, 213-16, 223-25; origin of, 137-38; and Centralia massacre, 217-21; death of, 227-29
Ankeny, William H., 73
Arkansas, 15, 186

Arkansas River, 186
"Army of the West," 18
Arnold, Moses B., 182
Assessments, 165-69
Aubry, Kan., 63, 122, 192
Audrain County, Mo., 165, 216
Austin, Tex., 240
Auxvasse Creek, 86

Baird, Major A., 48
Ball, Charles, 56
Banzhaff, Charles, 65
Barton County, Mo., 106
Bates, Edward, 49, 155-56
Bates County, Mo., 40, 106, 126, 147
Baum, Solomon, 204
Baxter Springs, Kan., 128, 131, 134, 227
Bee, H. P., 111, 140
Berlin, Mo., 236

Bickley, W. L., 207
Big Creek, Mo., 73, 104
Big Hill, Mo., 102
Bingham, George Caleb, 43, 44, 45, 46, 49, 118, 126, 246
Blackwater Creek, 121
Blair, Charles W., 235
Blair, Frank P., 12, 13, 14
Blue River, 64, 65, 75
Blue Springs, Mo., 56, 58, 59
Blunt, Andrew, 182-83
Blunt, James G., 98, 99, 115, 134, 222, 226; Baxter Springs massacre, 128-30
Blythe, W. R., 228
Bonham, Tex., 136, 139, 141
Boone County, Mo., 24, 86, 88, 164-65, 204, 210, 212, 216
Boone County National Bank, 211
Boone's Lick Road, 225
Boonville, Mo., 15, 166, 222-23, 225
Box, R. M., 171-72
Breckinridge-Democrats, 11
Bredett, Eliphalet, 71
Breeden, Martin, 106
Britton, Wiley, 31, 32
Brooks, John W., 35
Brown, Egbert B., 68, 81, 126, 158, 160, 163, 178, 180-81, 183, 186-89, 190-91, 194, 196-97, 199, 200-202
Brown, John, 9
Brown's Spring, 86
Buel, James T., 70, 93, 94, 95, 246
Buffington, steamboat, 212
Burns, Dick, 244
Burris, John T., 98, 100-102, 200, 202
Butler, Mo., 106

Caldwell, H. C., 83
Caldwell County, Mo., 228
Callaway County, Mo., 86, 165
Camden, Mo., 190
Camp, Bragg, Ark., 131

Canadian River, 131
Canal Dover, Ohio, 54
Cane Hill, Ark., 110
Canton, Mo., 87
Cape Girardeau, Mo., 22, 37
Carman, Robert, 213
Carney, Thomas, 125
Carroll County, Mo., 203, 205, 210, 212, 227
Carrollton, Mo., 212
Carthage, Mo., 15, 127, 186
Cass County, Mo., 43, 50, 63, 68, 69, 72, 73, 104, 115, 126, 147, 160, 166, 188, 192
Catherwood, E. C., 93, 105
Cavender, Jefferson, 187
Central College, 215
Centralia, Mo., 24, 216-20
Chapel Hill, Mo., 209
Chariton County, Mo., 90, 165-66, 204, 210, 212-13, 227
Chariton River, 24, 88
Cherokee Nation, 186
Chestnut, John, 209
Chiles, Richard, 103
Chilhowee, Mo., 23
Christian, Ben, 139
Cincinnati, Ohio, 207
City Hotel, Lexington, Mo., 242
Clark, James, 217
Clark, Samuel C., 67
Clark County Mo., 165
Clarke, George W., 9
Clarke, Kate, 193
Clay County, Mo., 30, 47, 62, 64, 164, 209, 239
Clay County Savings Bank, 243
Clement, Archie, 62, 138-39, 141, 203, 205, 216-18, 220, 227, 230, 234-36, 238-39; death of, 242-43
Clinton, Mo., 23, 72, 98
Clopper, John Y., 82
Cobb, Alvin, 86, 87, 108
Cochran, Captain, 70

Cockrell, J. Vard, 79, 93, 108
Coffee, John T., 79, 93, 97, 98, 100
Colbert's Ferry, 131
Collamore, mayor of Lawrence, Kan.,
124
Colley, Patton, 210
Colt revolvers, 104
Columbia, Mo., 211, 216
Columbia Tigers, 211
Columbus, Mo., 63
Committees of Public Safety, 34, 149
Confederate Partisan Ranger Act, 77,
78
Connelley, William, 110
Cooper, Douglas H., 131
Cooper County, Mo., 226
Copeland, Lieutenant, 101
Copperheads, 207
Corps de Belgique, 207
Council Grove, Kan., 137
Cowert, Charles, 100
Cox, Samuel P., 227-30
Crawford, Jeptha, 61
Crawford, Riley, 61, 62
Crittenden, Thomas, 245
Cross Hollows, Ark., 106, 110
Curtis, H. Z., 129
Curtis, Samuel R., 27, 109, 112-13,
146-47, 151-54, 159, 163-64, 167-69,
174, 181, 186-88, 190, 192, 222, 227;
assumes command of Department
of Missouri, 108

Danville, Mo., 225
David, Daniel H., 102, 103
Daviess County, Mo., 228
Davis, B. K., 235-36
Davis, Jefferson, 13, 16, 77, 90, 111
Dayton, Mo., 63
Dean, John, 56
De Bolt, R. A., 161
Democratic party, 11
Denny, A. F., 215, 239-40
Department of Kansas, 21, 97, 98, 108

Department of the West, Union, 17,
18
Des Arc, Ark., 29
Dick, F. A., 154
District of Arkansas, 76
District of the Border, 113-15
District of the Frontier, 113-15, 129
District of the Indian Territory,
C.S.A., 134
District of Texas, 134
Dodge, Grenville M., 171, 173,
234-37
Doniphan, Mo., 216
Douglass, J. B., 214
Douglas, Stephen A., 11
Dover, Mo., 166, 212
Drake, Charles D., 175, 179
Dripping Springs, Mo., 210
Dunnica, W. F., 225

Eads, William, 190
Eastern emigrant societies, 8
Edwards, John N., 110, 140, 209
Eldridge Hotel, Lawrence, Kan., 123
Ellis, Edmund J., 176
Emilie, steamboat, 88
Ewing, Thomas, 160, 181; commands
District of the Border, 115;
banishment policy, 117-18; Order
Number Eleven, 125-26

Fannie Ogden, steamboat, 127, 210
Farrar, Bernard G., 158-59, 175-76
Fayette, Mo., 213-15
Fickle, Anna, 199, 203
Fifteenth Kansas Cavalry, 126
Fifth Missouri Cavalry, 102
Fire Prairie, 102
First Iowa Cavalry, 72, 74, 98
First Missouri Cavalry, 73, 74
Fisk, Clinton, 154, 161, 197, 209-210
Flannery, Ike, 244
Fletcher, Thomas C., 145, 179, 233,
241

Florida, Mo., 83
Ford, J. H., 182, 193-94, 196, 209
Fort Baxter, Kan., 128-29
Fort Davidson, Mo., 221
Fort Gibson, Kan., 106, 128, 186
Fort Leavenworth, Kan., 37, 66, 98, 101-102
Fort Lincoln, Kan., 38
Fort Scott, Kan., 97, 98, 106, 115, 128, 235
Fort Smith, Ark., 15
Fort Wayne, Ind., 54
Foster, Emory, 66, 67, 98, 99
Fourth Kansas Cavalry, 100-102
Franklin, Mo., 213
Fredericksburg, Mo., 210
Frémont, John C., 12, 17, 18, 36, 37, 38, 44, 145-46, 153

Gallatin, Mo., 244
Gamble, Hamilton, 20, 32, 37, 48, 50, 83, 125, 157, 167-68, 177-79
Gardiner, Kan., 122
George, Gabriel, 63
Gilchrist, Joseph, 58
Gilvey, Armena, 118
Glasgow, Mo., 87, 154, 210, 225, 230, 239
Goodman, Thomas, 217-18
Gower, James O., 72, 73, 74, 75
Grand Pass, Mo., 172
Grand River, Mo., 90, 210
Grant, U. S., 14
Gratiot Street Prison, 161-62, 208
Gray, Barbary Jane, 182
Gray, Judge, 182
Gray, Lou, 118
Greeley, Horace, 7
Green, Martin E., 16, 17, 81
Gregg, Frank, 243
Gregg, William H., 53, 58, 63, 74, 99, 101, 110, 121-23, 127, 140
Grimes, John, 227-28
Grimshaw, Owen, 64

Grindstaff, Mollie, 118
"Guerrilla Shirts," 104
Guitar, Odon, 86, 87, 90

Hall, William A., 44
Halleck, Henry W., 20, 21, 25, 26, 27, 32, 47, 48, 49, 50, 64, 65, 79, 81, 97, 146, 149-50, 153-54, 160, 167, 169-70, 173, 176; assumes command in Missouri, 18
Haller, William, 58, 99
Hambleton, Charles, 9
Hannibal, Mo., 16, 90
Hannibal and St. Joseph Railroad, 16, 24, 33, 35, 188, 209, 220-21, 223, 226
Harding, Chester, 233, 235-38
Harney, W. S., 13, 14
Harris, Nannie, 118
Harris, Thomas A., 16, 17
Harris, W. P., 77
Harrisonville, Mo., 43, 70, 72, 100, 105, 147
Hartville, Mo., 110
Hayes, J. E., 109
Hays, Upton, 4, 79, 92, 93, 94, 95, 98, 100-101, 108, 157, 165
Hayward, J. T. K., 35
Helena, Ark., 77
Hendricks, James A., 58
Henry County, Mo., 23, 72, 98, 126, 147
Hickman Mills, Mo., 193
High Hill, Mo., 225
Hindman, Thomas C., 76, 77, 78, 79, 99, 107, 133
Holden, Mo., 189, 234
Holmes, Theophilus, 107-108, 111, 133
Holt, John D., 121, 124
Holtzclaw, Clifton, 198, 210-11
Howard County, Mo., 24, 87, 165, 193, 198, 210, 213-14, 220, 225, 238-39

Hoy, Perry, 58, 101
Hubbard, Captain, 64
Hughes, John T., 79, 93, 94, 95
Hughes and Wasson Bank, Richmond, Mo., 244
Hunnewell, Mo., 220
Hunt, Charles L., 208
Hunter, David, 18, 21
Huntsville, Mo., 137, 204, 211, 215

Illinois River, 15
Illinois Union troops, 16, 33, 35, 36, 51
Independence, Mo., 46, 47, 63, 68, 70, 93, 94, 95, 97, 99, 100-103, 140, 189, 196, 226, 245-46
Iowa Union troops, 16, 33, 51
Iron County, Mo., 221

Jackson, Claiborne F., 12, 13, 18, 29, 132; governor of Missouri, 11; secessionist, 11
Jackson, Thomas J., 33
Jackson County, Mo., 40, 46, 47, 48, 50, 56, 58, 59, 61, 64, 66, 67, 68, 69, 92, 93, 97, 98, 100-103, 109, 115, 126-27, 140, 147, 159-60, 166, 182, 193, 196, 230, 241, 245
James, Frank, 5, 30, 62, 111, 164, 215, 219-20, 239-40, 244-45
James, Jesse, 5, 62, 164, 219, 239, 244-46
James White, steamboat, 190
Jasper County, Mo., 106, 127, 186
Jefferson City, Mo., 11, 13, 15, 19, 166, 178, 190, 196, 212, 222, 234
Jennison, Charles R., 9, 37, 40, 45, 46, 47, 48, 49, 58, 59, 63, 126, 222, 226, 246; Jayhawkers, 42
Johnson, A. V. E., 216, 218-19
Johnson County, Kan., 63, 103, 122, 162, 166
Johnson County, Mo., 23, 63, 66, 72,

73, 101, 121, 127, 138, 147, 189, 193, 198, 201, 234
Johnston, Joseph, 232
John Warner, steamboat, 16, 97
Jones, Payne, 244
Joplin, Mo., 193

Kansas, 6, 7; border war, 1854-55, pp. 7, 8; elections in, 8; "bleeding Kansas," 9
Kansas City, Mo., 16, 22, 45, 46, 95, 97, 103, 115-16, 118, 126, 188, 190, 192
Kansas-Nebraska Act, 6
Kansas Union troops, 33, 35, 36, 51
Kaw River, 123
Kehoe, Martin, 73, 74
Kelsey, T. C., 209
Kenney, Richard, 219
Kerr, Christie, 118
Kerr, Nathan, 121
Keytesville, Mo., 212-13
Kice, Doctor, 229
King, Austin, 213
King, Kate, 193
King, Walter, 113
Kingsville, Mo., 138, 189, 201, 234
Kirksville, Mo., battle of, 87, 88
Knights of the Golden Circle, 207
Knob Noster, Mo., 24
Knox County, Mo., 82, 87, 165
Koger, John W., 58, 129, 219
Koger, Lee, 56

Lafayette County, Mo., 14, 48, 71, 98, 99, 101, 109, 113, 115, 126, 159, 163, 182, 190, 199, 201, 203, 209, 212, 241
Lakenan, Mo., 205
Lamar, Mo., 106, 186-87
Lamine River, 24
Lane, James H., 9, 37, 39, 42, 48, 58, 63, 115, 121, 123, 125, 246; Lane's Brigade, 38, 47, 48, 49

Lawrence, Kan., 9, 39, 55, 121-25, 131, 133, 140, 164, 177, 188, 192, 197
Lazear, Bazel, 126-27
Leavenworth, Kan., 115, 190, 192
Lee, Robert E., 33, 233
Lee's Summit, Mo., 93
Leonard, Reeves, 214
Lewis, Benjamin, 225
Lewis, Warner, 79, 106
Lewis County, Mo., 81, 82, 87, 166
Lexington, Mo., 38, 57, 71, 81, 97, 98, 113, 137, 147, 175, 189, 199-200, 203, 235-37, 239, 241-43; battle of, 17
Liberty, Mo., 30, 64, 233, 239, 243
Liberty Landing Arsenal, 9, 12
Liddel, A. J., 245
Lincoln, Abraham, 12, 29, 37, 121, 125, 144, 146, 152, 154, 164, 167-69, 174-75, 178
Lincoln County, Mo., 166
Linn County, Mo., 90, 166
Lipsey, Chalkey T., 56
Little, James, 58
Little, John, 58
Little, Tom, 244
Little Blue, steamboat, 71
Little Blue River, 71, 100, 188, 226
"Little George," Frank James's horse, 220
Little Rock, Ark., 78, 108
Little Santa Fe, 65
Livingston County, Mo., 166
Loan, Benjamin, 61, 81, 97, 147, 159-60, 163, 166, 174-75
Lone Jack, Mo., 98, 99, 101, 108, 193
Louisville, Ky., 54, 231
Loyalty oaths, 157-59
Lykins County, Kan., 56
Lynch's slave pen, 161
Lyon, Nathaniel P., 12, 13, 15, 16, 50; strategy in Missouri, 1861, pp. 14, 15

McClellan, George B., 18, 47, 48, 49, 146
McCorkle, John, 62, 118, 121
McCulloch, Ben, 15, 17, 57
McCulloch, Henry E., 111, 134-36, 139-41
McDowell, Joseph, 161
McFadden, James W., 213
McFerran, James, 199-201
McGuire, Andy, 244
McKee, William, 178
Mackey, T. J., 223
Maclean, Lauchlan, 132, 224
McNeil, John, 82, 83, 87, 88, 89, 90, 153, 165-66, 170-71
Macon County, Mo., 24, 90, 166
Macon, Mo., 16, 88, 221
McPheeters, Samuel B., 164
McReynolds, Allen, 171-72
Magruder, John B., 111, 134, 139
Malvern Hill, 107
Marcella, steamboat, 127
Marias des Cygnes River, 9
Marion County, Mo., 82, 88, 166
Marmaduke, John S., 15, 106-107
Mars, steamboat, 127, 212
Marshall, Mo., 172
Marshall, Tex., 132
Marshfield, Mo., 88
Martial law, 144-49
Martin, William H., 73
Matthews, James L., 164
Mayes, Joel, 57
Memphis, Mo., 82
Mendota, Ill., 54
Merrill, Lewis, 82, 90, 164
Mexico, 25
Mexico, Mo., 24, 221
Miami, Mo., 172
Miami County Kan., 54
Middletown Township, Mo., 166
Military commissions, 149-51
Miller, Clell, 244
Mineral Creek, Tex., 131, 136, 138

Missouri, slavery in, 5; settlement of, 6; in settlement of Kansas, 7; "Border Ruffians," 7, 8; border war, 1854-55, pp. 7, 8, 9; elections of 1860, pp. 10, 11; State Guard, 11, 12, 13, 14, 15; relationship to Union, 1860, p. 11; General Assembly, 1860, p. 11; state convention, 1860, pp. 11, 12, 19, 30; secessionists in, 11; admitted to Confederacy, 18; provisional government of, 29
Mitchell, Robert B., 65
Mitchell Bank, Lexington, Mo., 243
Moniteau Creek, 211
Monroe City, Mo., 33
Monroe County, Mo., 83, 86, 88, 166, 205
Montgomery, Bacon, 242
Montgomery, James, 9, 37, 39, 40, 42, 49, 57, 58, 59, 63
Montgomery County, Mo., 86, 166, 225
Moonlight, Thomas, 192-94, 226
Moore's Mill, 86, 87
Morrison, Edwin, 56
Morrow, Ben, 245
Mound City, Kan., 40, 235
Mount Oread, 124
Mount Zion Church, 24
Munday, Martha, 118
Munday, Susan, 118
Murphy, Doctor, 199

Napoleon, Mo., 71
Neosho, Mo., 18
Nevada, Mo., 106
Newark, Mo., 87
Newby, Lieutenant, 105
New Florence, Mo., 225
Newspaper censorship, 176-78
Newton County, Mo., 106
Ninth Missouri Cavalry, 86, 87, 90, 214
Northfield, Minn., 244-45

North Missouri Railroad, 16, 24, 33, 204, 209, 212, 216-17, 223-25

Ohio River, 15
Olathe, Kan., 101-102
Oliver, W. S., 59-60
Omaha, steamboat, 210
Order Number Eleven, 125-26, 164, 181
Order Number Ten, 120-21
Order of American Knights, 208
Orr, Semple, 178
Orrick, Mo., 227
Osage Nation, 106
Osage River, 18, 99
Osawatomie, Kan., 55
Osceola, Mo., 18, 39
Otterville, Mo., 59, 226, 244

Pacific Railroad, 15, 16, 24, 105, 226, 234, 244
Palmyra, Mo., 34, 35, 88, 89
Palmyra Massacre, 90
Paris, Mo., 83
Parke, Joseph, 211
Parman, J. V., 189
Parmer, Allen, 245
Peabody, Albert, 67
Pea Ridge, Ark., 27, 28, 77, 81
Pence, Bud, 243
Pence, Donnie, 243
Perche Creek, 204, 210
Perdee, Captain, 121, 127
Perkins, Caleb, 198
Phillips, John F., 171
Phillips, William A., 186
Pike, A. J., 122
Pike County, Mo., 40, 82, 166
Pilot Knob, Mo., 221
Pink Hill, Mo., 67, 103
Platte County, Mo., 166
Platte River, 24
Pleasant Hill, Mo., 69, 73, 75, 101, 188, 192

Pleasonton, Alfred, 222, 226
Pleyer, Anthony, 213
Poindexter, J. A., 79, 90, 91, 97, 108, 157, 165
Pomeroy, James M., 65
Pool, David, 53, 127, 194, 199, 220, 227, 235-38, 241-43
Pope, John, 20, 23, 33, 34, 35, 36, 48, 59, 145, 149-50, 233
Porter, Joseph C., 4, 79, 81, 83, 86, 90, 97, 108, 157, 165, 171; at Moore's Mill, 86, 87; death of, 88
Portland, Mo., 88
Post Boy, steamboat, 196
Potts, Levi, 245
Prairie Grove, Ark., 110
Prairie Rose, steamboat, 190
Price, Edwin, 198
Price, Robert Beverly, 211
Price, Sterling, 13, 14, 18, 19, 20, 21, 23, 24, 25, 26, 28, 38, 77, 113, 131-32, 181, 197-98, 208-209, 212, 216, 221-23, 225-26, 229, 232; commands Missouri State Guard, 14; correspondence with Jefferson Davis, 16; Major General, C.S.A., 29
Prince, W. E., 39, 43
Providence, Mo., 88
Provost marshals, 151-55
Putnam County, Mo., 166

Quantrill, Caroline Clarke, 54
Quantrill, Thomas H., 54
Quantrill, William C., 74, 75, 92, 93, 94, 95, 96, 97, 98, 99, 100-105, 108, 110, 116, 118-20, 133-41, 157, 165, 182-83, 186-89, 192-205, 209-14, 223-26; origin of, 53, 54; hero to Missourians, 57, 58, 59, 60, 61, 62, 63, 64, 65, 66, 67, 68, 69, 70, 71, 72; at Lamar, 106; Lawrence massacre, 121-25; at Baxter Springs, 128-32; death of, 230-31

Ralls County, Mo., 166
Randolph County, Mo., 90, 137, 166, 204, 215
Ray County, Mo., 190, 205, 210, 227
Red River, 131
Regan, Doctor, 199
Renick, Mo., 90, 204-205, 213, 215
Republican party, 11
Reynolds, R. M., 72
Reynolds, Thomas C., 12, 132-34, 141
Rex, George, 162
Richmond, Mo., 229, 243-44
Richmond, Va., 18, 107, 110-11, 197
Roanoke, Mo., 215
Roberts, James, 213
Robinson, Charles, 39, 44
Robinson, John M., 164
Rocheport, Mo., 204, 211-14
Roher, Philip, 186
Rolla, Mo., 15, 16, 17, 22, 27
Rollins, James S., 44, 48, 49, 164, 217
Rosecrans, William S., 181, 186, 192, 196-98, 203, 206, 208-209, 220, 230
Rose Hill, Mo., 73, 105
Rulo, Neb., 240
Russellville, Ky., 244

St. Charles, Mo., 16, 217, 221
St. Charles County, Mo., 166, 224
St. Clair County, Mo., 39
St. Joseph, Mo., 16, 192
St. Louis, Mo., 24, 69, 112, 118, 167, 169, 174, 186, 193, 208, 209, 212, 216, 224; newspapers of, 11; U. S. Arsenal at, 12, 13; Camp Jackson, 13
Saline County, Mo., 24, 160, 166, 171, 199
Salt Lake City, 55
Salt River, 24, 205
Samuel's Depot, Ky., 240
Sanderson, John, 208
Schofield, John M., 51, 77, 79, 81,

83, 84, 85, 87, 97, 108, 113, 115-16, 120-21, 125, 154, 163, 165, 167, 169-70, 177-78, 181; commands Department of Missouri, 50
Schuyler County, Mo., 166
Scotland County, Mo., 82, 166
Second Colorado Cavalry, 182, 188, 193, 196, 199
Second Missouri Cavalry, 66
Sedalia, Mo., 16, 22, 45, 93, 105, 172
Seventeenth Illinois Cavalry, 204
Seventh Kansas Cavalry, 41, 43, 44, 45, 47
Seventh Missouri Cavalry, 73, 93, 186-87, 189
Shank's Regiment, C.S.A., 140
Shawneetown, Kan., 103
Shelbina, Mo., 205
Shelby, Joseph O., 14, 79, 88, 93, 99, 100, 106-107, 110-11, 113, 140 209, 225-26
Shelby County, Mo., 82, 166, 205, 220
Shepherd, Frank, 219
Shepherd, George, 244
Shepherd, Oliver, 239, 243
Sherman, Tex., 131, 139, 141
Sherman, W. T., 14, 20, 21, 115, 138
Shreveport, La., 133
Sibley, Mo., 71, 102
Sigel, Franz, 15
Sixth Missouri Cavalry, 93
Sixth Missouri Infantry, 93
Skaggs, Larkin, 125
Smith, A. J., 222
Smith, Miss Bush, 138
Smith, Edmund Kirby, 133, 135-36, 140-41, 232
Smith, Thomas H., 215
Sneed's Hotel, Centralia, Mo., 217
Sni River, 102, 193
Snyder, S. S., 123
Sons of Liberty, 207
Southwick, Albert, 56

Spencer County, Ky., 231
Springfield, Mo., 17, 18, 26, 110, 163, 186
Spring Hill, Kan., 122
Stanton, Edwin M., 35, 48, 152-54, 168, 188, 197
Steele, William, 134
Stephens, James L., 164
Stone, Joseph, murdered by Todd, 122
Stone, Strawder, 58
Stoney Point, Mo., 67
Strachan, W. R., 89, 90, 158
Street, Joseph M., 215
Sturgeon, Isaac H., 24, 220
Sturgeon, Mo., 218, 220-21
Sugar Creek, Mo., 72
Sullivan County, Mo., 166
Sumter, Fort, 12
Sunshine, steamboat, 190
Switzler, T. A., 147

Tate, David, 65
Tatum, John, 56
Taylor, Fletcher, 193-94, 199
Terrill, Edward, 231
Theis, Adam, 218, 220
Third Indiana Artillery, 86
Third Iowa Cavalry, 83
Thomas, Mrs. Chester, 129
Thomas, Lorenzo, 47
Thompson, Gideon W., 79, 93, 94, 95, 97, 98, 99
Thorne, Joshua, 119
Thrailkill, John, 4, 198, 209, 212-13, 215-16, 220
Todd, George, 4, 53, 58, 60, 99, 121-22; origin of, 140-41, 183, 193-96, 198, 209, 212-16, 219-20, 223, 225-26; death of, 226, 246
Todd, Thomas, 210
Topeka, Kan., 192
Totten, James, 68, 84
Trans-Mississippi Department of the

Confederacy, 3, 53, 76, 107, 111, 133, 181, 197-98, 206, 232
Turner, Edmund P., 135
Twelfth Kansas Cavalry, 109

Union Hotel, Kansas City, 119
University of Missouri, 211

Vandiver, Susan, 118
Van Dorn, Earl, 28, 76
Van Horn, Robert T., 43-44, 183
Vassar Hill, Mo., 82
Vaughan, Joseph, 58
Vaughan, Richard C., 49, 109, 166, 180
Vernon County, Mo., 106, 125, 147

Wadesburg, Mo., 72
Wakefield, James H., 231
Wakenda, Mo., 203
Walker, Andrew, 56, 58
Walker, Morgan, 56, 99
Walley, Captain, 61, 147
War Eagle, steamboat, 204
Warren, Fitz Henry, 98, 99
Warren County, Mo., 166
Warrensburg, Mo., 66, 72, 172, 187-89, 199, 234-35, 237, 244

Washington, D. C., 9
Washington University, 50
Watkins, Judge, 133
Waverly, Mo., 172, 190
Weer, William, 39, 65
Welch, Warren, 245
Wellington, Mo., 71, 190, 199
Wellsville, Mo., 221
Westport, Mo., 227
West Wind, steamboat, 190
Wilkenson, James W., 182-83
William Jewell College, 243
Williams, D. C., 56
Williams, "Hank," 219
Williams, Joseph, 47
Wilson's Creek, 17, 30, 57
Wood, Hop, 63
Wright, Phineas C., 208
Wright County, Mo., 88

Yeager, Richard, 194
Yellowstone, steamboat, 212
Young, William, 213
Younger, Coleman, 5, 43, 61, 100, 118, 147, 244-46
Younger, Henry, 43, 61, 147
Younger, James, 5, 43, 61, 118, 244-46